Voting the Gender Gap

Voting the Gender Gap

Edited by
LOIS DUKE WHITAKER

UNIVERSITY OF ILLINOIS PRESS
Urbana and Chicago

© 2008 by the Board of Trustees
of the University of Illinois
All rights reserved
Manufactured in the United States of America
1 2 3 4 5 C P 5 4 3 2 1
♾ This book is printed on acid-free paper.

Library of Congress Cataloging-in-Publication Data
Voting the gender gap / edited by Lois Duke Whitaker.
p.   cm.
Includes bibliographical references and index.
ISBN-13 978-0-252-03320-9 (cloth : alk. paper)
ISBN-10 0-252-03320-5 (cloth : alk. paper)
ISBN-13 978-0-252-07525-4 (pbk. : alk. paper)
ISBN-10 0-252-07525-0 (pbk. : alk. paper)
1. Women in politics—United States—History—21st century.
2. Voting—United States—History—21st century.
3. Political participation—United States—History—21st century.
4. Women political candidates—United States.
5. Sex role—Political aspects—United States.
6. United States—Politics and government—21st century.
I. Whitaker, Lois Duke.
HQ1236.5.U6V67   2008
324.9730082—dc22   2007048037

Contents

Preface

This book grew out of a panel, "The Past, Present, and Future of the Gender Gap," held at the 2005 American Political Science Association meeting in Washington, D.C. Several of the contributors to this book were participants on this panel. As a result of the panel and further research, we found that there had basically been nothing about the gender gap in book form since Carol M. Mueller's edited book, *The Politics of the Gender Gap: The Social Construction of Political Influence* (Sage Publications, 1988). Yet, since that time, there have been numerous scholarly articles in professional journals about this topic. Thus, the idea for this book evolved.

This book features original articles by both academics and practitioners who have studied the gender gap and its implications for American politics. The practitioners' viewpoints seem especially appropriate because the gender gap has been described as a polling phenomenon. Articles feature the history of the gender gap, what polling tells us about the gender gap, the gender gap and national elections, the gender gap in voting for female candidates in congressional and statewide races, the impact of parental status on the gender gap, complexities of the gender gap, interpreting the gender gap, and the gender gap and minority populations.

The volume is designed to provide a supplemental reader on the topic of women, politics, and voting to accompany texts for courses on gender and politics, American politics, voting behavior, American political parties, interest groups, campaigns and elections, and public opinion and propaganda, to name a few potential courses for which the book might be used. The book is also suitable as a supplement for graduate-level courses as well as a resource for scholars, journalists, practitioners, and others interested in American political elections.

Acknowledgments

The editor would like to thank the contributors to this volume: Susan Carroll, Erin Cassese, Cal Clark, Janet Clark, Margaret Conway, Kathleen Dolan, Laurel Elder, Kathleen Frankovic, Steven Greene, Leonie Huddy, Mary-Kate Lizotte, Barbara Norrander, and Margie Omero. I would like to single out Susan Carroll, Cal Clark, and Janet Clark for their support in the early framing of this book. They were all three excellent sounding boards as the project grew from an idea to an actuality. Additionally, Karen O'Connor and Sarah Brewer were invaluable sources of information. I would also like to thank the members of the Women's Caucus for Political Science for their encouragement and advice—even though you are too numerous to name here, you know who you are, and I value and appreciate your help. A special word of thanks to the four reviewers commissioned by the University of Illinois Press for their comments and suggestions. Their ideas certainly helped to make the book better.

I would especially like to thank Joan Catapano, associate director and editor in chief of the University of Illinois Press, for her belief in the book from the beginning. Thanks also to the other staff members at the Press who assisted with this project.

A word of appreciation goes to my colleagues in the Department of Political Science at Georgia Southern University. A special thanks is extended to Kevin Cook, George Cox, Bob Dick, Steve Engel, Jo Hoch, Chris Ludowise, Patrick Novotny, and Debra Sabia.

And, finally, thanks to my jogging/walking buddy, Dr. Barbara Price, professor in the Finance and Quantitative Analysis Department at Georgia Southern. I am sure she has heard more about this book than she really wanted to!

The volume is dedicated to my dean, Dr. Jane Rhoades Hudak, of the College of Liberal Arts and Social Sciences (CLASS) at Georgia Southern. She has always encouraged me to seek higher goals.

Voting the Gender Gap

Introduction

LOIS DUKE WHITAKER

The importance of voting in free and fair elections to maintain successful representative democracies is stressed in the classic texts of democratic theory.[1] Social scientists, using survey research data, have established a solid body of literature examining voting behavior and the results/consequences of American elections. Beginning with the 1980 presidential election, scholars and journalists first noticed a gender gap in American voting behavior. For the purposes of this book, the "gender gap" is defined as the difference in the proportion of women and the proportion of men voting for any given candidate.

Why is the gender gap important to American politics and can it be useful in analyzing and explaining the political empowerment of women? As Kaufmann and Petrocik point out, the gender gap has become sufficiently large to be accorded the status of a party coalition–defining social cleavage.[2] Race and social class differences are more prominent, but after these two factors, only religion and religiosity rival the ability of gender to predict party preference and voting. All other social differences, such as region, union membership, age, size and place of residence, are measurably less significant predictors of party preference and voting.[3] Thus, gender can be and has been an important variable in voting behavior studies.

The gender gap is also important for the underlying causes of this gap in men's and women's political attitudes and concerns. As Dolan, Deckman, and Swers, among others, emphasize, beginning in the 1970s, survey research has demonstrated that women's greater support for social welfare spending and a more activist government role in assisting the poor, guaranteeing jobs, and guaranteeing a standard of living represent an important component of the gender gap.[4] Also, as Manza and Brooks point out, more women are dependent on an activist public sector for access to jobs, public social provision for help with child care, and other parental responsibilities and income-maintenance programs.[5]

The gender gap is important, as Carroll and Fox report, because candidates now must pay attention to women voters to win elections. In recent elections, women have voted at slightly higher rates than men. Women are also a larger proportion of the population.[6] In considering the female vote, one cannot ignore the work of such groups as Women's Voices, Women Vote. This project's goal is to increase the numbers of female voters from demographic groups of women who have never married or who are divorced, widowed, or separated. This number is estimated to be about twenty million women who are eligible to vote in upcoming elections, thus illustrating the importance that the gender gap has given the potential of this large segment of the American nonvoting population (see the group's Web site, www.wvwv.org).

This book explores the gender gap in voting and the differences found in men and women in issue preferences and partisan association. The articles explore some of the reasons for these gender gaps in elections versus the gender gaps over issues. One contributor analyzes the role of the media in setting an agenda for the gender gap. Several authors research the importance of polling and survey research in exploring the gender gap. Two articles concentrate on women candidates and the gender gap, one analyzes some of the political differences among women as a group, and one article examines the political gender gap across ethnic and racial groups in the United States.

The gender gap in voting has been evident in every presidential election since 1980. This gender gap has ranged in exit polls from a low of four percentage points in 1992 to a high of eleven percentage points in 1996. The 1980 election made history in voting behavior because a gender gap had been unprecedented in a national election. This came in the same election year when, for the first time since winning suffrage in 1920, a higher proportion of women voted than did men.[7]

In the aftermath of the 1980 presidential election, when Eleanor Smeal, then-director of the National Organization for Women (NOW), first coined the term "gender gap" to draw the media's attention to the differences in voting behavior among women and men, it was believed that a feminist agenda was driving the women's vote. Many assumed that the Republican Party's failure to endorse the Equal Rights Amendment contributed to Reagan's "woman problem." Awareness of the gap prompted both political parties to respond to women as a voting constituency in the 1984 presidential election. Democrats falsely assumed that nominating a woman, Geraldine Ferraro, as the vice presidential candidate was enough to mobilize the women's vote. The Democratic Party chose not to use Ferraro as a vehicle to champion women's issues, in fear of alienating male voters. In contrast, Ronald Reagan's pollster Richard Wirthlin conducted a detailed analysis of the issues important to women. The data collected allowed Republicans to target specific subgroups of women on the basis of economic interests. Elizabeth Dole convinced Reagan that he simply needed to communicate his record on women's issues. The strategy worked, and Reagan won by a landslide with majorities of both women and men.[8]

It is worth emphasizing that the gender gap in voting for presidential candidates did not, however, begin in 1980. It preceded the Reagan era by at least sixteen years and, if the smaller values before 1964 are to be credited, it extends back to the origins of the National Election Studies series. There was a relative Republican preference among women until 1960; they preferred Dewey, Eisenhower, and Nixon slightly more than did the men in each of these elections. In 1964, however, men were decidedly more positive than women toward the Goldwater candidacy, and the gender gap assumed its contemporary configuration of a Democratic tilt among women and a GOP tilt among men. The gender gap in voting behavior continued to grow in 1968 and 1972, virtually vanished in 1976 in the wake of Watergate and the Nixon pardon, only to reappear in 1980 at a slightly higher level than it was in 1972.[9]

However, during this period in which the gender gap surfaced, scholars have found that conventional wisdom treated gender as a distinction without political importance and scholarship confirmed this conventional wisdom.[10] For example, the 1973 and 1980 editions of a standard text in mass attitudes and behavior ended their discussion on the social basis of public opinion with a brief (twenty-seven lines in length) section on gender.[11] The section began with the statement (well rooted in the evidence) that "differences in the political attitudes of men and women are so slight as to deserve only brief mention" and included one table of data. The conclusion of the chapter noted that some of the group differences they reported might change and some group differences might increase—"perhaps even (the differences between) men and women."[12] The gender section in the 1988 edition was equally brief and began with the same statement.[13] That sentence was gone by 1991[14] and the gender section was three times as long. It was 122 lines in length in the 1995 edition.[15]

We begin this book with a history of the gender gaps. Barbara Norrander's article reviews the existence of gender gaps in partisanship, votes for candidates, and in positions on various political issues. In most cases, historical trends in these areas are covered. For example, the movement in partisanship that produced the gender gap in the 1980s has its roots in changing partisan patterns in the 1960s. The gender gap is also produced by changes in the opinions of men as well as women. Once again, this is evident in the gender gap in partisanship, where the movement of men out of the Democratic Party in the 1960s and 1970s produced a gender pattern of party preferences in the 1980s.

Norrander goes on to explain that the gender gaps in a variety of areas have distinctive histories. The gender gaps in votes for candidates are more volatile than the gender gap in partisanship. Thus, the shrinking of the gender gap in the presidential vote in 2004 is not unique, but one of a series of elections in which the size of the gender gap has increased or decreased. In issues areas, some long-term gender gaps have been identified in the areas of use of force (e.g., military intervention, handling of crime, capital punishment) and compassion issues (e.g., support for the poor, government benefits). In contrast, on issues often associated with women, such as abortion and the role of women in politics, very few gender differences exist. In the area of environmental politics, some question wordings produce gender gaps while others do not. Thus, in some areas the gender gap has been long and steady, in other areas the gender gap fluctuates, and in still other areas, an expected gender gap does not exist.

The next article focuses on the role of polling in the gender gap. Kathleen Frankovic describes how polling questions and their answers reflect what the elite regard as important parts of public opinion about women. She points out that even though the polling suggests that the idea of a female president is becoming more realistic, the polling still reflects a traditional role for women of wife and mother.

We next move to an article that explores the gender gap in the 2004 presidential election. Cal Clark and Janet Clark, in their piece "The Reemergence of the Gender Gap in 2004: The Normal Dynamics of Gender Politics Trump the Cross Pressures of 2002," find that, in 2004, the gender gap in voting, although about only half the size of the gaps in the 1996 and 2000 elections, was reestablished after vanishing in the 2002 congressional elections. Their analysis indicates that cross pressures on women over security issues formed the major factor explaining the precipitous drop in the gender gap in 2002. However, the normal differences between the voting and political attitudes of women and men reemerged in 2004. Thus, the dynamics of gendered voting seemingly reasserted themselves within a fairly short time after the shock of the tragedy of September 11.

Susan Carroll focuses on the role of the media in framing the gender gap issue in her article "Security Moms and Presidential Politics: Women Voters in the 2004 Election." She examines the phenomenon of the "security mom" and the role she played in the 2004 presidential election. Through content analysis of print media coverage and analysis of exit poll data, the author finds little support for the characterization of "security moms" as portrayed in media accounts. Instead, the attention paid to "security moms" in the presidential race very much worked to the benefit of the Bush campaign, fitting into the campaign's overall strategy and detracting interest away from women voters whose concerns could be represented by existing interest groups, thus weakening any accountability that the victorious candidate might have to women voters. The concept of the "security mom" seems largely to have worked against the Democrats and to have helped the Republicans by drawing public attention to an issue—terrorism—about which the Republican candidate was perceived as being more capable than his opponent.

The next two articles examine the gender gap and the entrance of women into public office. In her article "Women Voters, Women Candidates: Is There a Gender Gap in Support for Women Candidates?" Kathleen Dolan points out that much conventional wisdom assumes that women voters are an automatic base of support for women candidates. However, the evidence in support of this notion is limited. Her article explores sex differences in support for women candidates by examining voting for candidates for U.S. Congress from 1990 to 2000.

Margie Omero, in her article "Using Exit Polls to Explore the Gender Gap in Campaigns for Senate and Governor," maintains that, although there is much discussion of the gender gap in presidential elections, the phenomenon also occurs in statewide races. By using exit poll data from senatorial and gubernatorial races, she examines the gender gap across different campaign environmental factors, such as the party leanings of a state, the region of the country, the competitiveness of a race, the presence of an incumbent, and whether that incumbent was voted out of office. She also explores the role of candidate gender in the gender gap and tests the assumption—common among political commentators and practitioners—that women are not as well-suited to run for executive offices such as governor as they are for collaborative legislative offices. Using exit poll data and multivariate analysis, Omero shows that Democratic-dominated environments yield a larger gender gap, and that Democratic women candidates, regardless of the office for which they are running, also evoke a larger gender gap.

Some scholars maintain that the gender gap has become an important dimension of American politics in the postindustrial era. This is related to the big growth that has occurred in single-parent families, disproportionately female-headed households, and the consequent feminization of poverty. But if gender is now an important discriminating variable—which it was not in the New Deal system—the divide it locates is by no means among the most prominent. Differences separating whites and blacks are, obviously, far larger; so are many others, including those stemming from religiosity and regional subcultures.[16]

The last three articles in this volume focus on some of these differences in explaining the gender gap. Laurel Elder and Steven Greene, in "Parenthood and the Gender Gap," explore an area that, for the most part, has not been studied by political scientists. They research the role that parenthood has on political attitudes and its implications for the gender gap. The authors use original data from a national survey conducted in June 2005 of 516 respondents, half of whom were custodial parents of children under eighteen. They conclude that, although being a parent does not show significant effects across the board on all issue attitudes, parenthood and parental involvement have a significant impact on several policy issues and priorities, including education, government spending and services, health care, and gay marriage. How about the influence of this parent gap on the gender gap? They conclude that mothers are much more affected than fathers on several issues, including government spending, health care, child care, and other social welfare programs. Their research indicates that having children leads to a widening of the gender gap by more strongly pushing women in a liberal direction.

In their article, "Sources of Political Unity and Disunity among Women," Leonie Huddy, Erin Cassese, and Mary-Kate Lizotte place the gender gap in needed perspective by examining sources of political unity and disunity among women. They draw on the cumulative National Election Studies (from 1980 to 2004) to compare the size of the gender gap in presidential vote choice with the magnitude of enduring political differences among women. They focus on basic demographic characteristics such as religiosity, evangelical Christianity, work status, occupation, education, and parental and marital status to ask whether the differences among women of differing backgrounds and outlooks swamp gender differences between men and women of the same background. They test a series of logistic regression models in successive presidential elections in which gender interacts with a number of demographic factors to predict vote choice. The models were used to identify key sources of unity and disunity among women, and central differences and similarities among women are depicted in graphic form. They conclude that women are more divided than united politically, but they also evidence some limited political commonality. And although their political differences are large and suggest substantial caveats on the notion of the "women's vote," their commonalities (and those of men) are sufficient to determine electoral outcomes.

Are there racial and ethnic differences in the gender gap? What are the gender gap patterns within white, African American, Hispanic, Asian American, and Native American racial and ethnic groups? M. Margaret Conway, in "The Gender Gap: A Comparison across Racial and Ethnic Groups," uses several data sets to examine gender differences in political attitudes, beliefs, and policy preferences within these ethnic and racial groups. She finds that the political gender gap varies across ethnic and racial groups, across time, and across political objects (i.e., voter turnout and other forms of political participation, partisan identification, political attitudes, and policy preferences) as the conditions stimulating the gender gap change.

Notes

1. Niemi and Weisberg, eds., *Controversies in Voting Behavior*, 139; Flanigan and Zingale, *Political Behavior of the American Electorate*, 7.
2. Kaufmann and Petrocik, "Changing Politics of American Men."
3. Ibid.
4. Dolan, Deckman, and Swers, *Women and Politics*, 79.
5. Manza and Brooks, "Gender Gap in U.S. Presidential Elections," 1259.
6. Carroll and Fox, *Gender and Elections*, 94.
7. Carroll, "Women Voters and the Gender Gap"; Mueller, *Politics of the Gender Gap*, 16–18; Norrander, "Evolution of the Gender Gap."
8. Witt, Paget, and Matthews, *Running as a Woman*, 153–80, as cited in McGlen et al., *Women, Politics, and American Society*, 81–82.
9. Kaufmann and Petrocik, "Changing Politics of American Men"; Cook, "Democratic Clout Is Growing."
10. Kaufmann and Petrocik, "Changing Politics of American Men," 864.
11. See, for example, Erikson and Luttbeg's 1973 edition of *American Public Opinion* and Erikson, Luttbeg, and Tedin's 1980 edition of *American Public Opinion*, both cited in Kaufmann and Petrocik, "Changing Politics of American Men," 864.
12. Ibid.
13. Erikson, Luttbeg, and Tedin's 1988 edition of *American Public Opinion*, as cited in Kaufmann and Petrocik, "Changing Politics of American Men," 864.
14. Kaufmann and Petrocik, "Changing Politics of American Men," 864.
15. Ibid.
16. Ladd, "1996 Vote"; Ladd, "Media Framing of the Gender Gap," in Norris, *Women, Media and Politics*.

1

The History of the Gender Gaps

BARBARA NORRANDER

Recent election outcomes have often been couched in gender terms. The "security moms" of the 2004 election replaced the "soccer moms" of the 1996 contest. The 1992 election, after which the number of women in the U.S. House of Representatives grew from twenty-eight to forty-seven, was dubbed the "Year of the Woman." Men have not been left out of these interpretations, and the Republican victory in the 1994 congressional election was linked to the "angry white male." The notion that men and women would react differently to electoral politics is not something that always existed. Most of the early research on public opinion and voting behavior ignored gender differences, looking instead to social class, religion, region, and racial and age distinctions.[1]

Today, women and men differ in their positions on some but not all political issues. Thus, a number of gender gaps appear when examining American public opinion and voting patterns. Most of these gender gaps are relatively small, with women differing from men by five to ten percentage points. Additionally, on most issues where a gender gap appears, a majority of both women and men fall on the same side of the issue. The gender gap occurs because some women fall slightly more toward the liberal side while some men hold opinions slightly more toward the conservative side. Men's and women's opinions also have the same overall trends. The opinions of both sexes tend to move in the same direction over time.[2]

Gender Gaps Identified in Prior Research

The earliest works on public opinion, from the 1940s through the 1960s, either failed to look for gender differences or found women to be more moralistic or more conservative than men.[3] American women in the 1950s were more likely than men to support Republican candidates, and European women often provided more support for right-wing parties. Women's greater religiosity often was ascribed as a reason for these more conservative opinions. Differences in age distributions, education levels, and employment status across the two sexes also contributed to these differences.[4] The 1950s gender gap in American partisanship was due in part to the greater longevity of women. As a result, there were a greater number of older women than older men in the electorate with lingering Republican preferences from before the New Deal era. In addition, women were less likely than men to belong to unions, and union membership was associated with left-wing parties in Europe and the Democratic Party in America. Yet, in the majority of cases, women were assumed to hold the same opinion as men.

Women during this early time period also were viewed as more apolitical than men. In the 1950s, American women were about ten percentage points less likely than men to vote. These differences in turnout were based on historical circumstances, with women winning the right to vote in 1920. However, some women socialized prior to 1920 did not change their habits and become politically active. This was especially true for Southern women and women with less education.[5] Segments of this older generation of women affected women's participation rates until the 1970s. Women's involvement in social movements and civic groups was ignored by scholars focusing on voting patterns and national politics.[6]

Since the 1980 election, women vote at a higher rate than men.[7] Yet, women's overall participation in, interest in, and knowledge about politics continue to lag behind men.[8] However, when the number of female officeholders and credible female candidates increases, women's interest in politics increases.[9] The greater number of female politicians makes politics seem less exclusively a man's game.

DISCOVERING THE NEW GENDER GAP

In the 1980s, scholars and journalists begin to note a different kind of gender gap on issues as well. In this new gender gap, women held more liberal positions than men. This new viewpoint was spawned by results from polls taken during the 1980 presidential election that showed women less likely than men to have voted for Ronald Reagan. The women's movement of the 1970s also highlighted women as a political group. At first, explanations for the new gender gap were focused on women's issues, such as abortion and support for the Equal Rights Amendment (ERA). In the 1980 election, Ronald Reagan opposed abortion, and the Republican platform took a pro-life position. However, further research proved that men and women held the same positions on these issues, such that opinions on abortion and the ERA could not underlie the new gender gap in presidential votes.[10] In fact, on many issues that might be labeled as "women's issues," gender differences do not emerge. Women were more supportive than men of an expanded role for women in economic and political life in some polls conducted prior to the 1960s, but these differences disappeared as men adopted opinions favoring more equal roles for both sexes.[11] By the 1970s, opinions on women's role, the ERA, and abortion were so similar they were unable to explain gender differences in voting.

Men and women, however, were found to hold different positions on other types of issues. One of these areas is in domestic and international issues that involve use of force. In fact, gender differences on use-of-force issues often can be traced back to the earliest public-opinion polls from the 1940s through the 1960s.[12] On domestic issues, use-of-force issues find women, in comparison to men, to be less supportive of capital punishment, more in favor of gun control, and more in favor of solving underlying social problems rather than relying on force to curb urban unrest. In international issues, women's greater opposition to use of force reveals itself in less support for military intervention or military tactics that could harm civilian populations.[13]

A second major area in which gender differences are often observed is on compassion issues. Women are more likely than men to favor government actions to assist individuals suffering economic difficulties or inequalities.[14] Gender differences on compassion issues first appeared in polls from the 1970s. Reasons for these issue differences are traced either to women's greater tendency to feel empathy for others or for women being more likely to find themselves in need of government assistance in these areas.[15] In addition, men often advocate self-reliance in economic areas.

On many issues involving moral values and religion, women remain more conservative than men. Thus, women are more likely to favor restrictions on pornography and drug use. Women also are more likely than men to favor school prayer.[16] Women's greater religiosity underlies these more conservative attitudes, and these gender patterns harken back to the earlier form of the gender gap where women were viewed as more conservative than men.

In many other issue areas, evidence on gender gaps shows no patterns or inconsistent patterns. Civil rights issues produce few significant gender differences. One exception is women's greater acceptance of gays in the military.[17] In the realm of civil liberties, women sometimes show lower levels of support than men.[18] Environmental issues provide quite a mixed pattern, with a gender gap on some but not all survey questions addressing this topic.[19]

Finding underlying reasons for women's and men's differences on political issues has been complicated. A variety of reasons have been offered, but no agreement exists on which provides the best explanation.[20] Motherhood and the associated pattern of caring for other individuals provide a biological explanation for women's rejection of use of force and support for compassion programs. Meanwhile, men are seen as innately aggressive.[21] Feminist attitudes that developed from the women's movement of the 1970s are a second explanation given for the gender gap, although other scholars argue that feminist attitudes can be held by men as well as women.[22] A third explanation focuses on socialization and cultural roles leading to gender differences in acceptance of use of force and empathy for others.[23] Thus, the first of these explanations provides an answer rooted in biological differences, whereas the latter two focus on culture and socialization.

In one area of gender differences, changes in men's attitudes have the most direct link to the underlying gender gap. These gender differences are found in partisanship. Over the past few decades, men have moved out of the Democratic Party and into the Republican Party at a rate faster than women.[24] This movement is most noticeable in the South, where Southern white men who were strongly Democratic in the 1950s began to change their partisanship in the early 1960s as the Democratic Party adopted a strong stance on civil rights issues. Southern women also have become more Republican, but at a rate that is less than that of men. By the 1980s, Northern men also began moving out of the Democratic Party into the Republican Party, while Northern women tended to remain in the Democratic Party. Not until the 1990s did it appear that women began to move into the Democratic Party and away from the Republican Party.[25] An independence gap also exists in partisanship, with more men self-categorizing as independents leaning toward one of the two parties and more women opting for an identity as a weak partisan. The independence gap averages five percentage points.[26]

Continuing Trends in Gender Gaps

Prior research has identified consistent gender differences in a number of issue areas: use of force, compassion, and partisanship. In other issue areas—women's issues, civil rights and liberties, and environmentalism—the findings are more mixed. The remainder of this chapter reexamines and updates trends in eight areas (women's issues, compassion issues, use of force in domestic politics, use of force in international politics, environmental issues, moral issues, partisanship, and presidential votes). In examining these trends, surveys conducted as part of the National Election Studies (NES) and the General Social Survey (GSS) are examined. These surveys have the advantage of asking identically worded questions over an extended period of time. For example, the GSS asked the same question on gun control twenty-one times between 1972 and 2002, and the NES has asked about party identification in a consistent format since 1952. However, most of the contemporary-issue questions asked in the NES date back only to the 1970s or 1980s, and the GSS began its surveys in 1972. Thus, the historical trend lines focus mostly on public opinion since the early 1970s.

WOMEN'S ISSUES

Women's issues such as abortion, support for the Equal Rights Amendment and women's role in public life were the first to be analyzed as a cause of the gender gaps discovered in the 1980s. Yet few gender differences were found on these attitudes. These trends appear to be continuing. Public perceptions of the proper role of women in society were measured fifteen times by NES between 1972 and 2004. A seven-point question contrasts the option that "women and men should have an equal role" with "a women's place is in the home." Collapsing the first three categories to indicate support for an equal role finds increasingly large numbers of Americans favoring an equal role for women. In 1972, 49 percent held this position; in 2004, 82 percent did. Both men and women have become more liberal on this issue. A gender gap occurs in half of the surveys.[27] However, in six cases men scored as slightly more liberal, usually by six percentage points, and in one year, 2000, women were six percentage points more liberal than men. In general, men's and women's opinions on the proper role for women in society do not contain sufficient differences to underlie gender differences in policy preferences.

Abortion is a complicated political issue. Although the political debate is often framed as pro-choice versus pro-life, most Americans fall somewhere in between.[28] A plurality of Americans can be labeled as situationalists—they would allow abortions under some but not all circumstances. Past research reveals few instances of gender differences on abortion opinions. When differences were found, men approved of abortion in more cases than did women or women were more likely than men to fall in the extreme categories on abortion questions—never allowing abortions or allowing abortions in all cases.[29]

The NES asks a single question to elicit abortion attitudes with four options given: "By law, abortion should never be permitted"; "The law should permit abortion only in case of rape, incest, or when the woman's life is in danger"; "The law should permit abortion for reasons other than rape, incest, or danger to the woman's life, but only after the need for the abortion has been clearly established"; and "By law, a woman should always be able to obtain an abortion as a matter of personal choice."[30]

With this NES question, used from 1980 to 2004, on average, 39 percent of Americans favor abortion in all cases and 13 percent oppose abortion in all cases, leaving 48 percent in the two categories allowing abortion under some but not all circumstances. A gender gap occurred in four of the twelve years. In those four years, women were four percentage points more likely than men to fall in the never category, while men were more likely to fall in the situationalist categories.[31] In the NES series, however, no consistent gender gap existed for the pro-choice category. Generally, men and women do not differ significantly in their responses to the NES abortion question.

In 1972, Congress passed the Equal Rights Amendment, which would have altered the U.S. Constitution to include the statement that "equality of rights under the law shall not be denied or abridged by the United States or any state on account of sex." The proposed amendment ultimately failed to win endorsement from three-quarters of the states as required by the Constitution. NES asked the public in 1976, 1978, and 1980 whether they approved or disapproved of this amendment. Public support for the ERA fell from 70 percent in 1976 to 51–53 percent in 1978 and 1980. A gender gap occurred in two of the three years, with men being six percentage points more likely than women to favor the amendment.

When Americans are asked whether they would vote for a woman candidate for president, overwhelming majorities of men and women say they would. GSS asked such a question seventeen times between 1972 and 1998. At the beginning of the series, three-quarters (74 percent) of Americans said they would vote for a female presidential candidate. At the end of the time series, nearly all (94 percent) indicated they would do so. A gender gap in responses occurred in only four of the seventeen series. In three years, men indicated greater likelihood than women of voting for a female candidate, and in one year (1996), women indicated a greater likelihood. Nevertheless, the general pattern is once again little evidence of a consistent gender gap. Women's issues continue to show a lack of a gender gap in most cases.

COMPASSION ISSUES: GOVERNMENT SIZE
AND SAFETY-NET PROGRAMS

Gender gaps have been more often identified on compassion issues. Shapiro and Mahajan, in their analysis of trends from 1960 to 1980, typically found gender gaps averaged only three percentage points on these issues.[32] One area to look for continuation or change in the gender gap on compassion issues is the NES question intended to draw out respondents' core preferences for individual responsibility versus government assistance in providing jobs and a good standard of living. NES uses a seven-point scale, with "the government in Washington should see to it that every person has a job and a good standard of living" at one end and "the government should just let each person get ahead on his own" on the other. The first three categories are collapsed to represent a preference for a government role and the last three combined to indicate support for individual responsibility.

Given the strong sense of individualism in American political culture, a plurality (48 percent) of Americans over the years feel that it is up to individuals to provide for their own standard of living, and a third (30 percent) favor a government guarantee. NES posed this question sixteen times between 1972 and 2004. A statistically significant gender gap appeared in every survey. On average, men were more likely than women (53 versus 43 percent) to ascribe a preference for individual responsibility. Thus, the gender gap averages ten percentage points on this core definition of the proper role for the government.

Another survey question often posed in the NES asks whether the government should be providing more or fewer services. This question was asked eleven times between 1982 and 2004. Americans' responses to this item were more divided. On average, 40 percent of Americans preferred more services, while 31 percent favored fewer services. As Figure 1.1 shows, Americans' preferences for a higher level of government services have varied over the years. The percentage of Americans favoring more services was the lowest in 1982 (31 percent) and highest in 2004 (50 percent), but the pattern is more aptly described as curvilinear. Preferences for increased services rose in the 1980s, dropped in the early 1990s, and then rose again in the late 1990s. Stimson writes of a public mood and a process by which the public reacts to policy with changes in this mood.[33] Although overall public preferences for government services have varied over time, the gender gap on this issue is quite consistent. As was the case for government guarantee of jobs, the gender gap in preferences for increased government services averaged ten percentage points and was statistically significant in every survey. Across the time series, on average, 34 percent of men and 45 percent of women favored more government services.

The role of the government in assisting with health care has always been controversial. Medicare, providing health insurance to the elderly, became law in the early 1960s only when a large group of northern Democrats were

Figure 1.1. Percentage favoring more government services.

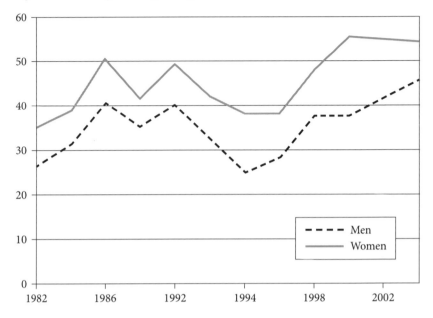

elected to Congress on the coattails of President Lyndon Johnson's 1964 land-slide victory. In the early 1990s, President Bill Clinton attempted but failed to extend health insurance to uninsured Americans. The American public is evenly split in preferences for government assistance with health insurance. In eleven of the NES surveys conducted between 1970 and 2004, a question was asked pitting preferences for a government program on one end of a seven-point scale and private insurance on the other end. On average, 44 percent preferred a government program (combining three categories of the scale), while 38 percent advocated private insurance. Public preferences were generally stable across the time period, except for an upswing in early 1990 followed by a return to more normal levels after the failure of Clinton's initiative. A gender gap in preferences for government assistance with health insurance did not become statistically significant until 1988, and the size of the gap is half as much (averaging five percentage points) as those that oc-curred for general level of government services and government guarantee of jobs. Nevertheless, continuing evidence exists of a gender gap on a variety of compassion issues, and these gender gaps may be larger than those Sapiro and Mahajan reported for the earlier era.[34]

USE OF FORCE: DOMESTIC POLICY

Women are more reluctant than men to use force in a number of domestic-issue areas. This includes policies toward quelling riots, use of the death penalty, and regulation of gun ownership. NES polled respondents about how to best handle urban unrest five times between 1968 and 1976 and then again in 1992. The question asked whether the respondent favored using "all available force to maintain law and order—no matter what results" versus "it is more important to correct the problems of poverty and unemployment that give rise to the disturbances." Respondents could place themselves on a seven-point scale from using force to correcting underlying societal problems. Combining results from three response categories reveals that a majority of Americans (51 percent) favor solving societal problems versus 26 percent favoring using force. On average, 45 percent of men and 56 percent of women favor solving societal problems. A gender gap was statistically significant in each of the surveys and averaged eleven percentage points.

Gun control legislation also is an area with consistent findings of a gender gap. GSS, in twenty-one surveys between 1972 and 2002, inquired, "Would you favor or oppose a law which would require a person to obtain a police permit before he or she could buy a gun?" On average, 69 percent of men and 83 percent of women favored police permits. During those three decades, support for police permits increased among both men and women. In the first five surveys (1972–76), 66 percent of men and 82 percent of women favored police permits; in the last five surveys (1994–2002), 74 percent of men and 87 percent of women favored permits. Because men have shown a greater increase in support for gun control laws by moving closer to the opinion of women, the gender gap has diminished somewhat. In the first five surveys, the gender gap averaged sixteen percentage points; in the last five surveys, the gap averaged thirteen percentage points.

The gender gap on the death penalty averages nine percentage points across twenty-two GSS surveys conducted between 1974 and 2002. When asked, "Do you favor or oppose the death penalty for persons convicted of murder?" 79 percent of men and 70 percent of women favor the death penalty. Public opinion on the death penalty has varied slightly over the time series. Figure 1.2 shows that public support for the death penalty increased in the 1980s before declining to 1970s levels in the 1990s. Decline in support since 1990 may be linked to changes in media coverage, which in recent years has focused more on the wrongful convictions of innocent defendants.[35]

The gender gap in support of the death penalty also has a slight curvilinear

Figure 1.2. Percentage favoring the death penalty.

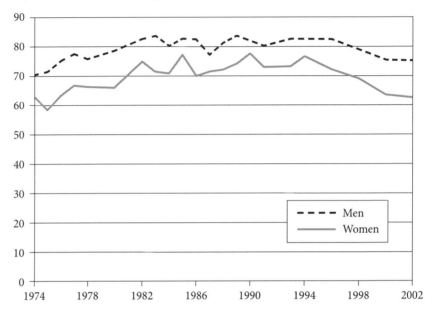

pattern. The gender gap was the largest in 1975, with a thirteen-percentage-point difference between men's and women's support. As support for the death penalty increased in the 1990s, the size of the gender gap shrunk as women's support moved closer to men's preferences. The gender gap in 1990 was only four percentage points, and its level of statistical significance was at .06. The diminishing of the gender gap may have resulted in part from a ceiling effect for men's opinion, whose support for the gender gap reached more than 80 percent. As support for the death penalty lessened in the late 1990s, the gender gap again widened, reaching thirteen percentage points in 2002.

USE OF FORCE IN INTERNATIONAL RELATIONS

One of the most consistent areas of differences between men's and women's opinions has been in the area of using military force. When NES asked its respondents in 1952 if being involved in the Korean War was the right thing to do, 57 percent of men versus 42 percent of women agreed. In the 1960s and 1970s, when NES used the same question wording to elicit public support for the Vietnam War, a similar gender gap occurred. Support for the Vietnam War fell from 61 percent in 1964 to 34 percent in 1972, but a gender gap occurred in each of these years and averaged nine percentage points. In the 1990s, NES asked in three surveys whether respondents would be very willing, somewhat willing, or never willing to use military force to solve international problems. A gender gap occurred on this question in 1992 and 1996, but not 1998. On average, women were five percentage points less likely than men to be very willing to use force to solve international problems.

When NES asked about defense spending in surveys from 1980 to 2004, men on average were eight percentage points more likely than women to favor increased spending. As Figure 1.3 shows, public preferences for defense spending was at its highest in 1980, then fell during the Reagan administration, in part because military spending had been increased. Public preferences for defense spending were the lowest in the 1990s, and the gender gap disappeared in 1990 and 1992. Preferences for military spending increased in the later 1990s and into 2000, and the gender gap reemerged.

A more general question about the role of the United States in international politics has a less direct connection to use of force, but nevertheless, a gender gap occurred in a majority of cases. The NES, in eighteen surveys between 1956 and 2004, asked respondents whether they agreed or disagreed with the following statement: "This country would be better off if we just stayed home and did not concern ourselves with problems in other parts of

Figure 1.3. Percentage favoring increased defense spending.

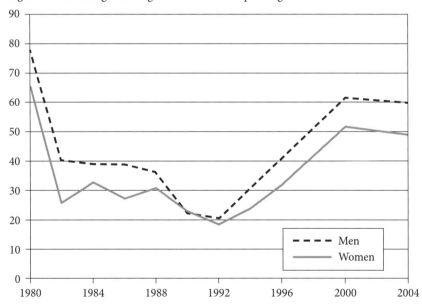

the world." Disagreeing with this statement represents an internationalist's viewpoint, an opinion that most Americans hold. On average, 77 percent of men and 72 percent of women feel that the United States should play a role in international politics. A gender gap occurred in ten of the eighteen years and averaged six percentage points. It is possible that gender differences on this question are disappearing. In the five surveys asked since 1996, a statistically significant gender gap occurred only once, in 2002.

In the three public-opinion areas where gender gaps have been consistently identified in prior research, the trends continue to show similar gender gaps. Women continue to show less support than men on use-of-force issues, whether in the domestic or international arena. A gender gap also continues on basic economic issues that fall within the realm of compassion issues. On this latter set of issues, the gender gap may have grown slightly in recent years, such that the gender gap on compassion issues is now as large as that found for use-of-force issues.

Mixed Patterns for Gender Gaps

Although gender gaps are consistently found on use of force and compassion issues, in other issue domains, the gender gap has been less consistent. Prior research disagrees about whether gender differences exist on civil rights issues or environmental questions. In many policy areas, the question is whether women are more liberal than men. In one area of public opinion, however, the gender gap is often one of women being more conservative than men. This policy area is moral issues.

MORAL ISSUES

Moral issues are a topic in which gender differences often harken back to an earlier era when women were described as more conservative than men. This conservatism was rooted in women's greater religiosity. Women today continue to be more religious than men. For instance, in the 2004 NES, 40 percent of women versus 30 percent of men indicated that they attended a religious service on a weekly basis.

The American public continues to disagree with the 1962 ruling by the U.S. Supreme Court banning prayer in school. Seventeen times between 1974 and 2002, GSS asked, "The United States Supreme Court has ruled that no state or local government may require the reading of the Lord's Prayer or Bible verses in public schools. What are your views on this—do you approve or disapprove of the court ruling?" On average, 57 percent of men and 63 percent of women oppose the Supreme Court ruling. A statistically significant gender gap occurs in half the surveys (eight of seventeen), with the average gender gap equalling five percentage points. The small size of the gender gap most likely explains its erratic pattern of statistical significance. The gender gap averages four percentage points in those years when the gap is not statistically significant and seven percentage points in years when it is significant.[36]

A more consistent gender gap is found on legalization of marijuana. Most Americans oppose legalization of marijuana, but, as Figure 1.4 shows, the numbers have fallen in recent years. This may be a reaction to the debate about medical uses for marijuana. Nevertheless, the gender gap on the legalization question has remained constant over the years. On average, women are eight percentage points more likely to oppose legalization, and this gender gap was statistically significant in all years except 1990, when the significance level was at .06.

On one other moral issue, however, the public espouses the liberal position and no gender gap occurs. Overwhelming majorities of both men and women favor sex education in schools. Asked by the GSS seventeen times between 1974 and 2002, 86 percent of men and 85 percent of women favor sex education in schools. A statistically significant gender gap occurred in

Figure 1.4. Percentage opposing legalizing marijuana.

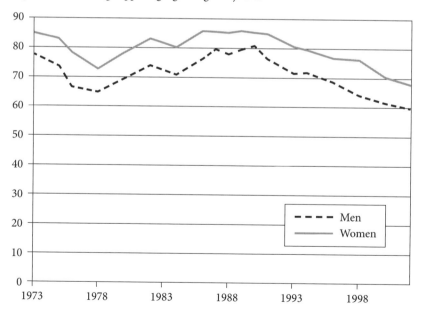

only two of these surveys: in 1975, when 5 percent more women than men favored sex education classes, and in 1986, when 4 percent more men than women favored these courses. In general, no gender differences exist on the topic of sex education in schools.

Moral issues present a mixed picture for gender differences. A constant gender gap occurred on easing marijuana laws, the gender gap on school prayer is small and significant only half the time, and no gender gap occurs on support for sex education classes. Gender differences on moral issues may be diminishing. This is not because religion has lost its influence on political attitudes. Religion is an important element to most Americans and religious beliefs influence attitudes on specific issues, such as abortion, and more generalized beliefs, such as ideology. However, religion often has similar influences for both men and women.[37]

CIVIL RIGHTS

Prior research found few consistent patterns on civil rights issues. The one exception was support for gay rights.[38] Beginning with questions on civil rights for African Americans, only rarely did a gender gap appear on the NES question involving school integration. Asked thirteen times between 1962 and 2000, a gender gap appeared in four cases. However, three of these four cases came from the most recent surveys—1992, 1994, and 2000. In these three years, nine percentage points more women than men supported the government in Washington enforcing school desegregation.

Public attitudes on civil rights issues are highly complex. Questions about affirmative action programs, for example, bring forth competing values on equality and individual responsibility. As a result, most Americans oppose affirmative action programs. In response to a NES question posed eight times between 1986 and 2004, an average of 62 percent of men and 56 percent of women were strongly opposed to affirmative action. In only three of the eight years did a gender gap appear. A more consistent gender gap occurred on the NES question asking whether the government should help blacks to improve their social and economic position or whether blacks should get ahead on their own. Asked seventeen times between 1970 and 2004, a statistically significant gender gap appeared ten times. On average, 51 percent of men feel that blacks should get ahead on their own compared to 45 percent of women. The gender gap averaged six percentage points.

Survey questions about gay rights continue to show consistent gender differences. Public opinion toward gay rights in the public sphere has shown increasing support for protection of job opportunities and service in the military. Figure 1.5 shows that both men and women have increased their preferences for protecting gays from discrimination on the job and for gays serving in the military. By 2004, 54 percent of women strongly favored protection against discrimination on the job, while 59 percent favored allowing gays to serve in the military. The figures for men were eight percentage points lower for protection against job discrimination and twelve percentage points lower for service in the military.

Public support for gay rights is much lower for issues that involve the private sphere, such as gay marriage or adoption of children by gay couples.[39] Public opinion on gay adoptions has changed in recent years, but in 2004, 57 percent of men and 47 percent of women opposed gay adoption. This does, however, represent a decline from the 75 percent of men and 70 percent of women who opposed gay adoption in 1992. A gender gap occurred in all three NES surveys that posed this question and averaged nine percentage points. In general, civil rights issues continue to provide a mixed pattern of gender differences. In the realm of gay rights, women are generally more supportive than men. However, in response to questions about civil rights for African Americans, a gender gap is less frequently observed.

Figure 1.5. Support for gay employment rights and gays in military.

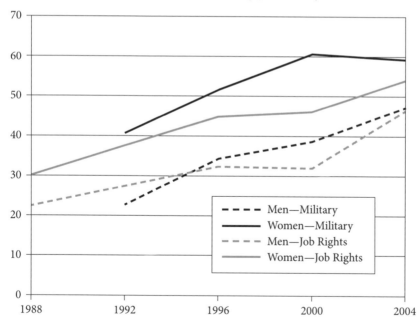

ENVIRONMENTAL ISSUES

A mixed pattern of results often occurs when searching for gender differences in opinions on environmental issues. Although some authors have found significant gender gaps, others have not.[40] GSS asked a large number of questions on environmental issues in its 1990s and 2000 surveys. The answers to twenty of these questions were examined. Some of the survey questions were repeated in up to three surveys, resulting in forty-eight opportunities for a gender gap to emerge. A statistically significant gender gap occurred in twenty-three of these cases, or about half of the time. Some repeated questions never produced a statistically significant gender gap. One such question was, "And how willing would you be to pay much higher taxes in order to protect the environment?" Other questions produced consistent and fairly large gender gaps, such as the question, "In general, do you think that nuclear power stations are: (1) Extremely dangerous for the environment; (2) Very dangerous; (3) Somewhat dangerous; (4) Not very dangerous; (5) Not dangerous at all for the environment." On this issue, the gender gap (collapsing the extremely and very dangerous categories) averaged seventeen percentage points across the two years in which the question was asked.

Environmental questions that typically evoked a gender gap included questions about whether economic growth harms the environment, how dangerous air pollution caused by industry is, how dangerous pesticides and chemicals used in farming are, concern over global warming, whether government or businesses should decide how to protect the environment, genetically altered crops, and the effect of environmental issues on economic growth, and two questions on the dangers of nuclear power. Questions that typically did not produce gender gaps included government responsibility to impose strict laws on industry, whether science will provide an answer for environmental problems, contrasting environmental concerns with prices or economic growth, paying more taxes or cutting standard of living to protect the environment, concern over pollution caused by automobiles, and the role of ordinary citizens in protecting the environment.

In trying to make sense of which environmental issues evoked gender gaps, Bord and O'Connor posit that the amount of potential risk is the key factor.[41] When an environmental issue involves questions of risk, such as nuclear power safety, a gender gap emerges, with women being more concerned than men about these potential risks. When an environmental question does not involve an aspect of risk, such as pitting higher taxes or job growth against environmental concerns, a gender gap does not emerge.

This article reviewed the trends in the gender gaps for specific types of issues. It confirms a continuing gender difference on use-of-force and compassion issues. The size of the gender gap on compassion issues, however, may now be similar to that found for use-of-force issues. As was the case in prior research, gender patterns on moral issues, civil rights, and environmental issues show mixed results. The piece next turns to partisanship, a core attitude that influences opinions about candidates and issues.

Partisanship

Partisanship remains a central attitude for the American public. In fact, in recent years, partisanship has had a resurgence as the public more often matches their partisanship to key political issues and ideological positions.[42] Partisanship influences whether someone votes (with partisans being more likely than independents to vote) and how one votes. In both the 2000 and 2004 presidential elections, more than 90 percent of the Republicans voted for George W. Bush, while more than 90 percent of the Democrats voted for Al Gore and John Kerry.

Partisan preferences have changed since 1952 when NES began asking its seven-point question aligning individuals on a scale with categories for strong Democrats, weak Democrats, independents leaning toward the Democratic Party, pure independents, independents leaning toward the Republican Party, weak Republicans, and strong Republicans. Figure 1.6 traces changes in overall partisan preferences by combining responses that indicate Democratic preferences: strong Democrats, weak Democrats, and independents leaning toward the Democratic Party. Support for the Democratic Party fell among men, from a high of 61 percent in 1954 and 1964 to a low of 41 percent in 1994. Women's support for the Democratic Party varied from 62 percent in 1964 to 51 percent in 1984, 1988, and 2002. As Figure 1.6 illustrates, men have had a more consistent decline in preferences for the Democratic Party. With each presidential-election cycle, men's support for the Democratic Party falls a little over one percentage point. No such trend exists for women, who have remained in the Democratic camp.[43]

The bottom portion of Figure 1.6 illustrates how these changes for men and women have produced a gender gap that varies over time. In the 1950s, women were more Republican than men, and this gender gap was statistically significant in 1956. The trend lines for men and women crossed in 1964, after which point women were more Democratic than men. This Democratic gender gap first reached statistical significance in 1972 and has been statisti-

Figure 1.6. Democratic identification and the gender gap.

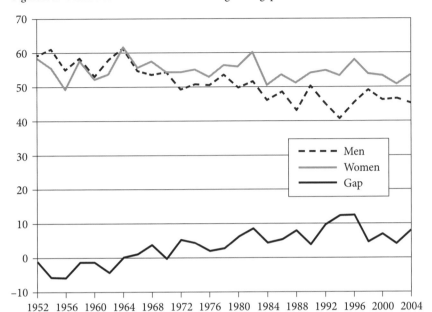

cally significant in thirteen of the last seventeen NES surveys. The size of the gender gap, however, is neither constant over time, nor has it continued to grow over time. The gender gap averaged seven percentage points in the 1980s, peaked at thirteen percentage points in 1994 and 1996, and averaged six percentage points since 1998. Presidents and their policies appear to influence the size of the gender gap, with the largest gender gaps in partisanship coinciding with Clinton's term in office.

Presidential Votes

Results from presidential elections also show that the gender gap in vote choice varies over time. Table 1.1 recaps these figures. In 1952 and 1956, a statistically significant gender gap occurred, with women being more likely than men to support the Republican candidate, Dwight Eisenhower. The next significant gender gap occurred in 1968, when men were six percentage points more likely than women to support George Wallace's third-party candidacy. Since 1972, a statistically significant gender gap has occurred in support of the Democratic candidate seven out of nine elections and in sup-

Table 1.1. Gender Gap in Votes for Presidential Candidates

Year	Democratic Candidate Gap	Republican Candidate Gap	Other Candidate Gap
1948	-2.9	2.9	
1952	-2.1	2.1	
1956	-6.2*	6.2*	
1960	-5.4*	5.4*	
1964	3.7	-3.7	
1968	4.7	1.8	-6.4*
1972	6.6**	-6.6**	
1976	0.3	-0.3	
1980	6.9*	-7.1*	.1
1984	7.6**	-7.6**	
1988	6.5*	-6.5*	
1992	10.1**	-1.5	-8.5**
1996	14.7**	-12.7**	-2.1
2000	9.1**	-9.1**	
2004	6.8#	-6.7#	

The gender gap is measured by the percentage of women minus the percentage of men voting for a candidate. Thus, a positive gap number indicates more women than men supported a candidate. The other party candidate in 1968 was George Wallace; in 1980, John Anderson; and in 1992 and 1996, Ross Perot.

$\# = p \leq .10; * = p \leq .05; ** = p \leq .01$

port of the Republican candidates in six of the nine elections. The difference in the number of significant gender gaps for the Democratic versus the Republican Party is traced to 1992, when Ross Perot's third-party candidacy drew more support from male voters and Clinton's candidacy drew more support from women, but no gender gap occurred in support for President George H. W. Bush.

The current gender gap in presidential votes preceded the election of Ronald Reagan. The first occurrence was in 1972, when Richard Nixon's landslide victory over George McGovern received greater support from men than from women. In the late 1960s and early 1970s, Southerners began to pull away from their traditional support of the Democratic Party. In 1964, five Southern states joined with Arizona in supporting Arizona's senator Barry Goldwater against the reelection of Lyndon Johnson. Much of the civil rights legislation of the 1960s passed during Johnson's presidency, whereas Barry Goldwater opposed the legislation on federalism grounds—he favored state rather than federal action on these issues. In 1968, Southerners once again deserted the Democratic Party for George Wallace's third-party candidacy.

A statistically significant gender gap occurred in support of George Wallace, with more men than women supporting his candidacy. By 1972, Southerners had become accustomed to voting for Republican candidates for presidents. Southern males in particular were deserting the Democratic Party. As a result, a gender gap occurred in the 1972 presidential vote. In 1976, Southern governor Jimmy Carter was able to pull Southern states back into the Democratic column, but this reoccurrence did not persist. Carter pursued liberal policies and faltered during the Iranian hostage crisis. Thus, in the 1980 election, Southerners and men voted to oust Carter in favor of Ronald Reagan.

Between 1980 and 2000, the gender gap as measured in support of Democratic candidates averaged nine percentage points. The gender gap, however, was not constant in size. It was the largest for the contests that elected and reelected Bill Clinton, and then fell to nine percentage points in the 2000 contest. In 2004, the gender gap fell to seven percentage points and had a statistical significance only at the .10 level. A persistent gender gap exists in presidential elections since 1980, but the size of that gap varies with each new set of presidential contenders. Some combinations of candidates evoke larger gaps, while other combinations diminish the pattern.

Conclusions

A number of gender gaps exist in diverse areas of public opinion and voting behavior. Men and women in the 1950s and 1960s were assumed to be the same in their political preferences, or women were depicted as more conservative because of stronger religious beliefs. In the 1970s and 1980s, a number of differences between men and women were recognized. Some of these gender differences actually existed in an earlier era but were not investigated by public-opinion researchers. Gender differences in use of force, for example, have shown up in even the earliest public-opinion polls. Women are more opposed than men to military intervention, and the size of the gender gap in these areas today is the same—ten percentage points—as in the earlier era. The 1970s and 1980s found a newer gender gap emerging on compassion issues—basic questions about what the government's role is in helping out citizens with economic difficulties. This gender gap was small when it first appeared, but trends investigated in this article suggest that the gender gap in these areas now equals those found in use-of-force questions.

In policy areas beyond the use-of-force and compassion issues, the appearance of gender differences in public opinion varies more by circumstance

and the nature of the survey question. For example, in environmental issues, a gender gap is likely to emerge on questions that deal with potential
risks, such as nuclear power safety, than on other aspects of environmental
policy, such as paying more taxes or imposing more regulations to improve
environmental quality. On civil rights issues, women tend to be more supportive than men of extending rights to homosexuals, but consistent gender
differences do not emerge on issues relating to other minority groups. Gender
differences on moral issues may be diminishing.

The gender gaps in partisanship and in presidential voting began to appear in the 1960s as men moved away from the Democratic Party and its
candidates. Some women, particularly Southern women, also moved away
from the Democratic camp. However, other women retained loyalties to the
Democratic Party, perhaps because of the party's positions on compassion
issues. As we move into the twenty-first century, women and men continue to
have slightly different partisan identities, which produce similar distinctions
in support for presidential candidates. However, the sizes of these differences
vary. Some electoral cycles, because of candidates or issues, provoke slightly
larger gender gaps, while in other electoral cycles, the size of the gender gap
is reduced. In addition, underlying reasons for the gender gap in presidential
voting can vary across elections.[44] Gender gaps in partisanship and presidential elections are reoccurring phenomena of contemporary American
politics, but the extent and reasons for these patterns reflect the changing
conditions of each new election cycle.

Notes

1. Andersen, "Gender and Public Opinion," in Norrander and Wilcox, *Understanding Public Opinion.*

2. Page and Shapiro, *Rational Public.*

3. Andersen, "Gender and Public Opinion," in Norrander and Wilcox, *Understanding Public Opinion*; Campbell et al., *American Voter*; Maurice Duverger, *The Political Role of Women* (Paris: UNESCO, 1955); Hastings, "Hows and Howevers of the Woman Voter"; Lane, *Political Life.*

4. Andersen, "Gender and Public Opinion," in Norrander and Wilcox, *Understanding Public Opinion.*

5. Campbell et al., *American Voter*; Wolfinger and Rosenstone, *Who Votes?.*

6. Andersen, "Gender and Public Opinion," in Norrander and Wilcox, *Understanding Public Opinion.*

7. Kenski, "Gender Factor in a Changing Electorate," in Mueller, *Politics of the Gender Gap.*

8. Delli Carpini and Keeter, "Measuring Political Knowledge"; Delli Carpini and Keeter, *What Americans Know About Politics*; Frazer and Macdonald, "Sex Differences in Political Knowledge"; Kenski and Hall Jamieson, " Gender Gap in Political Knowledge," in Hall Jamieson, *Everything You Think You Know About Politics*; Mondak and Anderson, "Knowledge Gap"; Verba, Burns, and Lehman Schlozman, "Knowing and Caring About Politics."

9. Atkeson, "Not All Cues Are Created Equal"; Burns, Lehman Schlozman, and Verba, *Private Roots of Public Action*; Schwindt-Bayer and Mishler, "Nexus of Representation"; Verba, Burns and Lehman Schlozman, "Knowing and Caring About Politics."

10. Adell Cook, Jelen, and Wilcox, *Between Two Absolutes*; Fiorina, Abrams, and Pope, *Culture War?*; Mansbridge, "Myth and Reality."

11. Andersen, "Gender and Public Opinion," in Norrander and Wilcox, *Understanding Public Opinion*; Erskine, "The Polls"; Simon and Landis, "The Polls—A Report."

12. Andersen, "Gender and Public Opinion," in Norrander and Wilcox, *Understanding Public Opinion*; Norrander, "Is the Gender Gap Growing?" in Weisberg and Box-Steffensmeier, *Reelection 1996*; Shapiro and Mahajan, "Gender Differences in Policy Preferences"; Smith, "Polls"; "Women and Men: Is Realignment Under Way?" (n.a.)

13. Conover and Sapiro, "Gender, Feminist Consciousness, and War"; Fiorina, Abrams, and Pope, *Culture War?*; Fite, Genest, and Wilcox, "Gender Differences in Foreign Policy Attitudes"; Mueller, *War, Presidents and Public Opinion*; Mueller, *Policy and Opinion in the Gulf War*; Nincic and Nincic, "Race, Gender, and War"; Page and Shapiro, *Rational Public*; Shapiro and Mahajan "Gender Differences in Policy Preferences."

14. Beutal and Marini, "Gender and Values"; Hutchings et al., "Compassion Strategy"; Kaufmann, "Partisan Paradox"; Page and Shapiro, *Rational Public;* Shapiro and Mahajan, "Gender Differences in Policy Preferences"; "Women and Men: Is Realignment Under Way?"

15. Erie and Rein, "Women and the Welfare State," in Mueller, *Politics of the Gender Gap.*

16. Norrander, "Is the Gender Gap Growing?" in Weisberg and Box-Steffensmeier, *Reelection 1996*; Shapiro and Mahajan "Gender Differences in Policy Preferences."

17. Erikson and Tedin, *American Public Opinion.*

18. Erikson and Tedin, *American Public Opinion;* Norris, "Gender Gap" in Mueller, *Politics of the Gender Gap*; Shapiro and Mahajan, "Gender Differences in Policy Preferences"; Tedin, "Mass Support for Competitive Elections."

19. Davidson and Freudenburg, "Gender and Environmental Risk Concerns."

20. Andersen, "Gender and Public Opinion," in Norrander and Wilcox, *Understanding Public Opinion.*

21. Caldicott, *Missile Envy*; Fukuyama, "Women and the Evolution of World Politics"; Ruddick, "Maternal Thinking"; Ruddick, *Maternal Thinking.*

22. Conover and Sapiro, "Gender, Feminist Consciousness, and War"; Adell Cook and Wilcox, "Feminism and the Gender Gap."

23. Conover and Sapiro, "Gender, Feminist Consciousness, and War"; Gilligan, *In a Different Voice*; Miedaian, *Boys Will Be Boys*; Peterson, *Gendered States*.

24. Kaufmann and Petrocik, "Changing Politics of American Men"; Norrander, "Evolution of the Gender Gap"; Wirls, "Reinterpreting the Gender Gap."

25. Kaufmann, "Culture Wars, Secular Realignment, and the Gender Gap."

26. Norrander, "Independence Gap."

27. This includes 1994, when the level of statistical significance was .055, and 2000, when it stood at .054.

28. Adell Cook, Jelen, and Wilcox, *Between Two Absolutes*; Fiorina, Abrams, and Pope, *Culture War?*.

29. Andersen, "Gender and Public Opinion," in Norrander and Wilcox, *Understanding Public Opinion*; Adell Cook, Jelen, and Wilcox, *Between Two Absolutes*; Shapiro and Mahajan, "Gender Differences in Policy Preferences."

30. NES used a different question wording for the abortion issue surveys conducted from 1972 to 1980. The analysis listed here is for the current format of the abortion question, which was asked from 1980 to 2004.

31. Similar findings are reported by Andersen, "Gender and Public Opinion," in Norrander and Wilcox, *Understanding Public Opinion*.

32. Shapiro and Mahajan, "Gender Differences in Policy Preferences."

33. Stimson, *Public Opinion in America*.

34. Sapiro and Mahajan, "Gender Differences in Policy Preferences."

35. Fan, Keltner, and Wyatt, "Matter of Guilt or Innocence."

36. An NES question on school prayer allowing four options (none, silent prayer, general prayer, or Christian prayer) that was asked seven times between 1986 and 1998 showed a statistically significant gender gap in four of the surveys. An earlier NES question with a favor/oppose format found a statistically significant gender gap in four of the five surveys taken between 1964 and 1984.

37. Norrander and Wilcox, "Gender Gap in Ideology."

38. Erikson and Tedin, *American Public Opinion*.

39. Wilcox and Norrander, "Of Moods and Morals," in Norrander and Wilcox, *Understanding Public Opinion*.

40. Those reporting gender gaps on environmental issues include: Mohai and Bryant, "Is There a 'Race' Effect?"; and Whittaker, Segura, and Bowler, "Racial/Ethnic Group Attitudes Toward Environmental Protection." Those finding no gender differences on environmental issues include: Jones and Dunlap, "Social Bases of Environmental Concern"; Uyeki and Holland, "Diffusion of Pro-Environment Attitudes?"; and Van Liere and Dunlap, "Social Bases of Environmental Concern."

41. Bord and O'Connor, "Gender Gap in Environmental Attitudes."

42. Abramowitz and Saunders, "Ideological Realignment in the U.S. Electorate"; Adams, "Abortion"; and Fiorina, Abrams, and Pope, *Culture War?*.

43. Regressing the percentage of Democratic affiliation against a year-count variable produces a coefficient for men of –.30, which is statistically significant at the .01 level. Multiplying this coefficient by the four years in the presidential-election cycle produces a drop of 1.2 percentage points with each new election. In a model for women, the coefficient for the year-count variable is –.05 and is not statistically significant.

44. Chaney, Alvarez, and Nagler, "Explaining the Gender Gap in U.S. Presidential Elections."

2

Women and the Polls

Questions, Answers, Images

KATHLEEN A. FRANKOVIC

America's public opinion polls serve as cultural indicators of what kinds of questions are important and acceptable in journalistic discourse. They tell us about what the journalistic elite cares, what is acceptable language to use when engaging the public, and what the elite expectations are about what the public knows and cares. In these ways, "the polls" define the image we have of women. They state which women matter, they create an image of women by deciding what should be asked about them, and they provide the data that allow news organizations to categorize women. Reports of poll-based data put into words the image of women the polls create.

The topic of women became important to pollsters in 1980, when the "gender gap" emerged and underscored the political consequences of gender.[1] Women were less likely than men in that election to vote for Ronald Reagan, and that fact was responsible for many theories about why—from abortion rights,[2] to fear of war,[3] to women's propensity to make situational ethical decisions.[4]

Before 1980, gender had not necessarily been part of the public opinion discussion. Theoretically, that was perfectly understandable. Attitudinal differences are thought to stem from differences in culture, reinforced by physical as well as emotional segregation. But women and men are *not* physically isolated from each other by neighborhood or work situations (although their statuses in the workplace, and sometimes in the home, could be quite different). In theory, differences should be muted when there is communication and contact. In fact, early standard political science literature reports little gender difference in policy attitudes or candidate preference, only differences in turnout, involvement, and efficacy.[5] As late as 1975, Gerald Pomper claimed, "There are few issues that are primarily related to a person's gender. . . . Nor is social segregation between the sexes likely as long as hormones do their pleasant work."[6]

Even as an analytic variable, gender is sometimes missing from early survey research. An early 1950s study about public reaction to the testing of the hydrogen bomb has no report of the role of gender on attitudes about using and testing the bomb, although the differences between men and women in their knowledge of hydrogen weaponry are highlighted.[7] Because nearly every poll that reports results by gender has shown large gender differences in opinions about guns, war, and weaponry, this seems amazing.

When reports of the gender gap in public opinion and voting in the 1980s were written, they reflected the perceived newness of the phenomenon. So did the words of many feminist observers. There were high expectations that, in fact, the women's vote would be decisive and progressive.[8] That dream disappeared with the reelection of Ronald Reagan in 1984 and the 1988 election of his vice president, George H. W. Bush. However, it returned with the election and reelection of Democrat Bill Clinton and the invention of a "year of the woman" in 1992 and the "year of the gender gap" (as well as the "soccer mom") in 1996. In 2000, the "marriage gap" replaced the gender gap in news discussions (although the actual election day gender gap was sizable), and in 2004, a relatively small gap was attributed to the importance of social issues and fear of terrorism.

Gender gap media coverage rises and falls. It rose during the 1984 campaign, when women's groups lobbied for a representative on the Democratic national ticket (resulting in then-Congresswoman Geraldine Ferraro's nomination to run for vice president on a ticket headed by Walter Mondale).[9] And 1992, the year after Supreme Court Justice Clarence Thomas was confirmed by the Senate despite charges of sexual harassment made by Professor Anita Hill, was expected to be the "year of the woman." That year, six Democratic women won their party's nominations for U.S. Senate; five were elected.

But gender gap coverage was most intense four years after 1992's "year of the woman." National press coverage of the "gender gap" rose dramatically in 1996 from 1992 levels.[10] Eighty-two stories about the election and the gender gap appeared in the *New York Times* throughout 1996, compared with only ten in 1992. The *Washington Post* tripled its number of stories, from fifteen to forty-five. *USA Today* stories discussing the gender gap grew from twenty-five in 1992 to forty-six in 1996. Gender gap stories, like all political stories, were most frequent in the latter part of the campaign season.

The coverage of the gender gap as gender gap declined in the next two presidential-election cycles. In the election of 2000, coverage declined to forty-four stories in the *New York Times,* thirty in the *Washington Post,* and twenty-four in *USA Today.* In 2004, references were even fewer about the gender gap and the election—only thirteen stories in the *Times,* twelve in the *Post,* and seven in *USA Today.*

Whatever the national political and media implications, the gender gap is first of all a polling phenomenon, and public opinion polling has affected our views of what women are and what their roles should be. That can be examined by taking note of the questions asked of women and about women, the answers received, and their impact on the *images* of the proper roles for women. Those polling questions and answers inform the media and help frame media coverage of women's roles and women's issues. They also affect the type of coverage given to the importance of gender in political campaigns.

Questioning Women

News interest in learning the political opinions of women predates their right to vote. In 1896, many media conducted large-scale straw polls to learn about voting preferences and rejected opinion filtered through party leaders.[11] Women's political opinions also were sought, although they were linked to their position as consumers.

In October 1896, newspapers throughout the country reported an attempt to see "what effect the women's vote will have on national affairs." It was organized, not by the government, but by the Postum Cereal Food Coffee Company. The article read as follows:

> For the first time in the history of this country an opportunity for women to publicly express their choice for president is offered. The method is unique. . . . A manufacturer who has business relations with most of the prominent newspapers in the United States proposes the plan as follows: All women over 18 are entitled to one vote. The votes by states will be shown in the papers on every Wednesday and Saturday until November 4th. Women are requested to read more than one side of the question and act upon their own judgement. Write the name of the candidate on a postal card and write your own name and address clearly, also city and state.[12]

The next sentence added a surprising instruction to the would-be women voters. "On the lower left hand corner, give the name of a banker or grocer who knows you." This rather crass requirement, which suggests that the woman "voter" might be solicited for a commercial purpose, was justified in the paper with reference to ballot integrity. "This precaution is to prevent flooding the mail with fictitious votes. Names unknown to grocer or banker will be thrown out." Not only that, but the company "pledge[s] their integrity and honor to report the vote exactly as received, without fear or favor."[13]

The "fair voter" would receive an acknowledgment of her ballot, the instructions continued, asking each woman to "read more than one side of the question and act upon their own judgement. Every honest woman" was urged "not to hesitate to expend a penny to register her preference at this most interesting time in history."

In the final tabulation, as reported in the *New York Daily Tribune*,[14] there were 13,000 votes reported. Most votes came from Indiana, Michigan, Ohio, and New York. Well over 10,000 were cast for William McKinley, the Republican nominee and the election winner. As would be true when women finally did receive the vote, women in this straw poll supported the Prohibition Party much more than did the actual (male) voters.

One grateful woman voter expressed her feelings on simply being asked. She told the Postum Company that "through this one act, you prove that you think your Mothers, wives, sisters and sweethearts are Citizens of these United States. I never was a foreigner, and yet this is the first time I have ever been a citizen."[15]

Although that "voter" praised the motives of the Postum Company as elevating women, the Postum Company clearly had other reasons for its women's vote project, most especially the promotion of its product. The final report in the participating papers includes an argument for why people should be drinking Postum in place of their coffee!

Women in the Survey Process

George Gallup claimed he became interested in opinion polling because of a woman. His mother-in-law, Ola Babcock Miller, was nominated in 1932 as the Democratic candidate for secretary of state in Iowa. That year, the Iowa Democratic Party did what both political parties do when they are competing in a state where they are the underdog party—they nominated a "sacrificial lamb" to hold the party's place on the ballot. Iowa was then a heavily Republican state. Mrs. Miller was the widow of a weekly newspaper editor who had been the Democratic Party's candidate for governor in 1926. In 1932, however, her electoral fortunes were improved by the Depression and the national candidacy of Franklin Delano Roosevelt. Gallup said: "She had never had any political experience or any business experience, and much to the consternation of her family she was elected."[16] It's not clear whether Gallup used his newspaper research experience to conduct an actual poll for her, but he admitted that this experience made him think that in fact national polls could be done.

Even though a woman may have been modern polling's muse, for many years women in polling labored hard in the field, but not in management. For years, U.S. survey textbooks referred to "he" when speaking of researchers and "she" when speaking of interviewers. That was still the case in many places around the world, including Great Britain, in the 1990s. There were economic reasons for women's role as interviewers in the early days of survey research. Most interviewing jobs are only part-time assignments. One early study asked interviewers (who mostly were engaged in door-to-door interviewing) what they looked for in a job. Interviewers wanted flexible hours, a job that fitted in with their life, the freedom to accept or reject assignments, and extra income—in short, a part-time job.[17] Interviewing provided that. However, because interviewers could do their work only in a limited geographical area, work was limited. But once telephone interviewing supplanted door-to-door interviewing, it became more like a full-time job and the proportion of male interviewers increased.

The dominance of women as data collectors from the 1930s to the 1970s is quite different from the dominance of men as ballot counters in the days of the *Literary Digest* and newspaper straw polls, which flourished from 1896 to the 1930s. Those thousands and sometimes millions of ballots were nearly always counted by men. These jobs would have been full-time assignments, at least during the election season, and the economic impact of the Depression would also have encouraged men to take these jobs.[18]

Women's link with the field operation meant that their presence at major industry events in the mid-twentieth century would be limited. The first national meetings of survey research organizations in the 1940s were dominated by men. In the eleven sessions of the 1946 meeting in Central City, Colorado, that led to the formation of the American Association for Public Opinion Research (AAPOR), there were only four women among the forty speakers and chairs, and one of the four women discussed interviewing.[19] Soon after its founding in 1946, AAPOR had an organizational membership almost evenly divided between men and women. But it did not elect a woman president until 1977. It did not give its most important award (the AAPOR Award) to a woman until 1980. In fact, in AAPOR's first sixty years of existence, there were only eight women presidents and four AAPOR Award winners. The first of those award winners was honored posthumously; the next two jointly with their spouses.

The only prominent woman in the early days of the European Society for Opinion and Marketing Research was Helene Riffault. The Market Research Council, a limited-member association founded in New York in 1927, did not even permit women to become members until more than thirty-five years later, in 1963. It did not elect a woman president until 1979, more than fifty years after its founding.

The link between women and interviewing in the field is clear in the story of Ruth Clark, a well-known newspaper researcher, who began her research career as an interviewer and "inadvertently" invented exit polling. In the 1950s, Clark was a door-to-door interviewer, mainly working on market research projects. In 1964, she worked for Lou Harris, and was sent to conduct interviews in Maryland on its primary election day. Tired of door-to-door interviewing to look for voters, she decided to talk with them as they left the polling place. As she put it, "I told Lou what I had done, and by the [Republican] California primary in June, the exit poll was put to full use," with Barry Goldwater voters dropping blue beans into a jar and Nelson Rockefeller voters dropping red beans.[20]

Gender and How It Affects the Interview

Whether the person asking the question affects the answer given is a major issue in survey research,[21] as there is serious discussion of how to train interviewers (including questions of the amount of "rapport" that should be established between interviewer and respondent) and how to understand the meaning of answers. Survey researchers have investigated race of interviewer effects,[22] as well as the impact of which gender is asking a question.

Two characteristics—race and sex—are at least partly identifiable over the telephone. This raises practical and current questions for understanding survey results because respondents may worry about offending those asking the questions. Are respondents more likely to give accurate answers when speaking to someone of their own sex or race or when speaking to someone of a different sex or race?

The sex-of-interviewer effects were not explored in any depth until the 1980s—after the job of interviewer ceased being defined as a "female" one and the proportion of male interviewers increased.[23] Not surprisingly, the pattern of gender differences in answers has been especially pronounced on matters involving women. For example, support for the failed Equal Rights

Amendment in the 1980s was greater among both men and women when the question was posed by a woman than when it was posed by a male interviewer. There are also differences in responses about abortion.

There are also differences when women are asked about their health, especially about women's health issues and what steps they have taken to protect their own health. In a CBS News poll conducted in February 1997, women were more likely to report both the desirability of taking healthful actions and personally taking such actions to women interviewers than they were to men interviewers. Sixty-four percent of women interviewed by men said women should get mammograms once a year between the ages of forty and forty-nine, whereas 74 percent of women interviewed by women said that. There was also a slight increase in women reporting to women that they give themselves monthly breast examinations.

Both sexes are more attuned to the language of gender discrimination when they are interviewed by someone of the potentially discriminated-against gender. In that same CBS News poll, when asked whether the government favors men, women, or treats both equally when it comes to health issues, 25 percent of male respondents interviewed by a woman said the government favors women over men, but 42 percent of men said that when they were interviewed by a man. As for women, 47 percent told the male interviewers that the government gives "too little attention" to women's health issues, but 68 percent said that to a woman interviewer.

In April 2006, a CBS News poll also found a similar impact of the gender of the interviewer on some questions about women—but only for male respondents. Do most working women do so because they want to or because they need to? When interviewed by a male interviewer, 57 percent of male respondents said most working women do so because they need to; when interviewed by a female interviewer, 69 percent said so. And when men were asked to evaluate whether the women's movement had ever done anything to improve their own lives, 41 percent told a male interviewer it had, but 49 percent told a woman interviewer it did. Women respondents were much more likely to give credit to the women's movement, and to say women worked out of necessity, and to say so uniformly to both men and women interviewers.

The differences in answers given to interviewers of different genders, while potentially troublesome, don't necessarily make the survey process hopelessly flawed. For better or worse, an interview is an interaction between individuals. And although on the surface the same-gender interviewer–respondent interaction should give more accurate responses, it can just as likely be subject to false gender consciousness. As the gender composition of the interviewing staff became more balanced, it became just as likely that men and women would be interviewed by someone of their own sex as by the opposite sex. Women's perceptions that they had personally experienced discrimination actually rose during the period (1970–84) when men entered the interviewing force, suggesting that the change in the composition of the interviewing force produced increased gender awareness.

How "the Polls" Define Women: Images of Women

Perhaps the longest time series on women's roles are the following poll questions, first asked more than fifty years ago, and frequently repeated by the Gallup Organization and the National Opinion Research Center:[24]

> Should a woman work outside the home if she has a husband capable of supporting her?

> If your party nominated a qualified woman for president, would you vote for her?

Obviously, support for the notion of women working—even if they had a husband and even if he was capable of supporting her—has increased over time: 81 percent supported women working in the 1998 National Opinion Research Center (NORC) General Social Survey, compared with just 22 percent when Gallup first asked it sixty years before. The percentage stating that they would vote for a "qualified" woman of their own party is now 92 percent[25]—far above the 33 percent who said they'd be willing to do that in 1945.

Although women had been working long before 1938, when Gallup first asked whether that was appropriate, women in politics were relatively new. Women in the United States had received the right to vote only in 1920. The concept of women as potential presidential candidates would seem unlikely for a long time; in fact, when the public was asked if it would accept a woman as a presidential candidate, that question usually was embedded in questions about other unlikely outsider candidates: a black (then "Negro"), a Jew, an atheist, and, later, a homosexual candidate. Defining women here meant defining them as something odd (and perhaps even unqualified, despite the question wording) in the political world.

One other long-term time series that illustrates the pollsters' views of women is the Gallup record of the "most admired woman." Since 1947, respondents have been asked, "What woman that you have heard or read about, living today in any part of the world, do you admire most? And who is your second choice?" This was always separate from the "most admired man," a list that almost without exception was headed by the country's current chief executive. The most admired women list usually included women related by birth or marriage to that top executive. As seen in Table 2.1, there are now more women with their own careers on the list, but political wives remain.

The 1947 list of America's most admired women was led by the nation's previous first lady—Eleanor Roosevelt. It contained five other women who, whatever their own skills and talents, had "family ties"—Madame Chiang of China (wife of that country's president, Chiang Kai-shek), Claire Boothe Luce (a writer whose husband edited *Time* magazine), Princess Elizabeth (not yet Queen Elizabeth), and both Bess and Margaret Truman, the wife and daughter, respectively, of President Harry Truman. The other principal names included one entertainer, Kate Smith; a nun who cared for polio victims, Sister Kenny; and Helen Keller, who overcame both blindness and deafness—woman as entertainer, woman as nurturer, and woman as victim to be admired. The last name on the list, Dorothy Thompson, was a crusading journalist.

The 1996 list also contained a nun who nursed the sick, Mother Teresa, who led the list. There were three first ladies (plus one would-be first lady): Hillary Clinton, Barbara Bush, Nancy Reagan, and Elizabeth Dole. Princess Elizabeth had become Queen Elizabeth, and was joined on the list by her then–daughter-in-law Princess Diana. This more modern list included two entertainers—Oprah Winfrey (among the very few black women ever on the list) and Barbra Streisand—but there was also one former head of government, Margaret Thatcher of Great Britain, and one current secretary of state, Madeleine Albright. Although in many ways the 1996 list looked like the 1947 list, the women politicians added a new dimension.

That political dimension has continued through the most recent asking of the question in 2005. That year, a former first lady still led the list, but Hillary Rodham Clinton was also a U.S. senator and potential presidential candidate. It should also be pointed out that the poll used her maiden name in 2005 but only her married name in 1996. Women in politics dominated at the top; after Clinton, current Secretary of State Condoleezza Rice and Margaret Thatcher were third and fifth. Oprah Winfrey was second and First Lady Laura Bush fourth.

A relatively new set of polling questions about women are those that deal with women in the military. Here too, changing times are obvious in the types of questions asked. In the 1940s, the Gallup questions were few and simple. Should single women be drafted for war jobs? In 1942, 69 percent said

Table 2.1. Most Admired Women

1947	1996	2005
Eleanor Roosevelt	Mother Teresa	Hillary Rodham Clinton
Madame Chiang Kai-Shek	Hillary Clinton	Oprah Winfrey
Sister Kenny	Oprah Winfrey	Condoleezza Rice
Kate Smith	Madeleine Albright	Laura Bush
Clare Boothe Luce	Margaret Thatcher	Margaret Thatcher
Princess Elizabeth	Barbara Bush	Angelina Jolie
Mrs. Truman	Princess Diana	Maya Angelou
The Queen of England	Elizabeth Dole	Martha Stewart
Helen Keller	Queen Elizabeth	Elizabeth Dole
Margaret Truman	Nancy Reagan	Barbara Walters
Dorothy Thompson	Barbra Streisand	Sandra Day O'Connor
		Nancy Reagan
		Barbara Boxer

Source: Gallup Polls

yes when asked about those between the ages of 21 and 35. Which women's branch of service had the best uniforms? In January 1944, Americans liked the U.S. Navy Wave uniforms the best.

By the 1990s, the changes in the perceived role of women as well as changes in the military illustrated by the Persian Gulf War and the fighting in Kosovo have affected the kinds of questions deemed appropriate. Now, during the war in Iraq, the public is asked to assess its feeling about women serving in combat roles and requiring women to register for the draft. In June 2005 CNN/*USA Today*/Gallup poll, 67 percent favored allowing women in the military into combat jobs, and 42 percent would favor including women if a military draft were reinstated.

Which Women Matter?

The polls define which women are worth asking about. There are more polls today, and therefore more questions, so women currently prominent have the most questions asked about them. Two women have dominated those polls: more than a thousand questions each have been asked about Monica Lewinsky and Hillary Rodham Clinton. They are by far the two most frequently named women in news polls. Between 1998 and 2005, Monica Lewinsky was in first place; only in 2006 did questions about Senator Clinton outnumber questions about Lewinsky.

The results are shown in Table 2.2. Geraldine Ferraro, the first woman nominated for vice president, is in the second tier, along with Elizabeth

Table 2.2. Selected Women Mentioned in Poll
Questions, 1935–36 and 2006

Name	Number of Questions
Hillary (Rodham) Clinton	1,783
Monica Lewinsky	1,725
Geraldine Ferraro	295
Elizabeth Dole	292
Paula (Corbin) Jones	244
Nicole (Brown) Simpson	178
Anita Hill	126
Janet Reno	117
Condoleezza Rice	97
Terri Schiavo	93
Laura Bush	86
Nancy Reagan	85
Sandra Day O'Connor	67
Princess Diana	64
Barbara Bush	57
Martha Stewart	55
Tonya Harding	53
Nancy Kerrigan	47
Madeleine Albright	26
Jacqueline Kennedy	25
Margaret Thatcher	20
Eleanor Roosevelt	16
Cindy Sheehan	14
Queen Elizabeth (Princess Elizabeth)	13
Mother Theresa	12
Dianne Feinstein	12
Nancy Pelosi	11

Source: Roper Center Poll Database

Dole, wife of a former presidential candidate and later a potential candidate herself. To date, there have been fewer questions about women like Secretary of State Condoleezza Rice, former Attorney General Janet Reno and former Supreme Court Justice Sandra Day O'Connor. Former first ladies are the subjects of multiple poll questions, although other women often mentioned in the polls are as likely to be victims and accusers (Nicole Brown Simpson, Terri Schiavo, and Paula Jones) as to be decision makers.

1946–96: Fifty Years

The Roper Poll archive contains twenty-three items from 1946 with the word "woman" in their text. Fifty years later, there were more polls asking more questions overall, so there were almost three times as many questions (sixty-two) with the word "woman" in their texts. The differences in fifty years in poll sensibility are striking, as shown in Table 2.3, although there are also some surprising consistencies.

More than half of the twenty-three 1946 items (fourteen) were explicit comparisons between the sexes. Examples of those were "Would you rather be a man or a woman?"; "Who has more common sense, a man or a woman?"; and "Who's more to blame when a marriage fails—the man or the woman?" In 1946, two of those questions were attempts to define the "perfect" woman: asking respondents the best height for a woman and the right age for her to marry.

Nine questions in 1946 were about the job market, an appropriate area given the time—shortly after the end of World War II and the return of men to a workplace that had been taken over by women during the war. "Should a woman work outside the home if she has a husband capable of supporting her?"; "Who has a more interesting life—a woman with a job or a woman who stays at home?" There were also two versions of a question that said a lot about the sense of the limited role of women in the postwar workplace; both were from the *Fortune* magazine poll conducted by the Roper Organization.

First version: "Suppose a company is faced with the necessity of laying off some of its employees. If they have to make a choice between a married woman who is very efficient at her job and whose husband could support her, and a married man with a family who does the same kind of work but is not as efficient, which do you think they should keep?"

Twenty-one percent said that the company should retain the more efficient

Table 2.3. Sixty Years' Difference in Poll Questions about Women

	1946	1999	2005
Gender comparisons	14	2	4
Women in the workplace	9	—	—
Defining women	2	11	—
Women and family	—	—	—
Abortion	—	35	34
Sex	1	8	—
Woman as president			9
Woman on the Court			22
Total	26	56	69

Source: Roper Center Poll Archive. Questions may be counted in several categories.

married woman, while 74 percent, more than three times as many, would choose the less efficient married man.

Second version: "Suppose a company is faced with the necessity of laying off some of its employees. If they have to make a choice between a single woman who is very efficient at her job and whose brother could support her, and a married man with a family who does the same kind of work but is not as efficient, which do you think they should keep?"

Perhaps a brother was viewed as less responsible for a sister than a husband for a wife—34 percent said they would retain the more efficient single woman. Still, nearly twice as many, 59 percent, would keep the less efficient married man. Fifty years later, there were no questions specifically about the workplace.

There was at least one major change indicating woman's advance. In 1946, pollsters asked, "Would you rather have a man or woman as your Representative in Congress?" In 1996, they asked "Is your Representative in Congress a man or woman?" (The 1946 pollster also felt it was necessary to ask whether a man or a woman would make a better head of the PTA, of the local Red Cross, and of the local school board. In 1996, the head of the national Red Cross was a woman.)

Some of the uses of the word "woman" in 1996 had to do with defining a specific individual and underscoring her gender. Among the 199 poll questions is one about a "woman named Paula Jones" who was suing President Bill Clinton for sexual harassment (similarly, in 1999, several polling organizations asked questions about "a woman named Juanita Broaddrick" who accused the president of rape). Shannon Lucid was described as a "woman astronaut." Twice the word was used as a comparison between the standard definition of marriage and a different kind—whether the public thought same-sex marriage should be treated the same as a marriage "between a man and a woman." Five times it defined a subject to be asked about, from a "woman vice president" to a "woman on welfare."

Only twice in 1996 were Americans asked to compare men and women directly. Once was in a question about custody and divorce, asking whether children after divorce are better off if a man or a woman is given custody. But one comparison from the Gallup Organization had a fifty-year trend: "Would you rather ride in a car driven by a man or a woman?" While amusing, the question's results (like those of the most admired woman time series) suggest that some stereotypes continue. In 1946, 66 percent of respondents said they would rather ride in a car driven by a man and only 12 percent would choose to ride in a car driven by a woman. Fifty years later, although the margin was narrower, men were still viewed as better drivers; 51 percent said they would choose to ride in a car driven by a man, while 22 percent would choose a car driven by a woman.

Eight questions in 1996 had something to do with sex (including one asking whether it was wrong for a woman to have sex outside of marriage). There were even several questions from ABC News about breast size. In 1946, only one question was even tangentially related to sex: whether it was worse when a woman was "unfaithful" than when a man was.

More than half—thirty-five—of the 1996 questions were about an issue that directly affected women, an issue concerning a woman's body—the issue of abortion. That emphasis continued in 2005. Abortion questions were the single most dominant set of poll questions about women.

There were questions about new topics, too—a Supreme Court seat and a possible presidential candidacy. And in the first three months of 2006, the only questions asked about women were about the possibility of a woman president and abortion. These poll questions themselves raise concerns about the relative importance of a woman's desires and a woman's choices. What happens inside a woman's body is now a dominant public issue and a dominant poll topic, along with the speculation about a woman's role in the political system.

WOMEN POLITICIANS IN THE POLLS

As candidates, women combat long-held stereotypes about themselves. Americans generally view women who run for political office as more honest than their male counterparts, more likely to care about people, and sometimes as better managers, but they do not see women as either stronger leaders or as more skilled at foreign policy. And despite the poll finding that 92 percent of Americans say they would vote for a qualified woman of their own party for president, many people aren't sure a woman can be qualified. In a poll conducted in 1987 by Hickman-Maslin Research for the National Woman's Political Caucus, 31 percent said that a woman would not do as good a job as a man would in carrying out the responsibilities of the presidency (just 8 percent said a woman would do a better job).

The image of political women in polls today may be set by the varying images of one woman acknowledged to be running for president—Hillary Rodham Clinton. Her overall image—despite a temporary rise in favorable ratings based on sympathy after the first revelations about her husband's relationship with Monica Lewinsky—has been barely positive, with nearly as many Americans expressing negative as positive views of her. However, Clinton scores well on a number of characteristics, including several that are decidedly female. For example, a CBS News poll in June 2003 found 62 percent of Americans saying that Clinton had done a good or excellent job raising her daughter Chelsea and 52 percent describing her as a good role model for wives. An ABC News poll in May 2006 echoed those findings: 65 percent of its respondents said Hillary Clinton had strong family values, and 58 percent said she was an "open and friendly person."

Clinton also did well in some areas in which male politicians have historically had an edge; in both polls, more than two out of three described her as a strong leader. Eighty-three percent told CBS News that she worked hard, which suggests that her apparent success at women's work has not taken time from her job as a politician. However, she did not fare quite as well on a question related to foreign policy matters: whether Americans would have confidence in her ability to handle a crisis—46 percent said they would; 44 percent said they would not.

Clinton does well on one of the characteristics that help women politicians—caring—but does less well on another "female" characteristic—honesty. By 55 percent to 34 percent, Americans say that she cares about the needs and problems of "people like yourself." But when asked whether she says what she believes or what she believes people want to hear, by 47 percent to 41 percent, Americans said she was more likely to pander.

What was most striking (and perhaps most suggestive of women's problems as they run for high office) was the response Americans gave when asked what they would ask Hillary Clinton if they had the opportunity. Nearly one in four Americans said they would ask her not about policies or politics, but about her marriage.

Conclusion: Women and the Polls

Polling is of course about what is visible and not necessarily about what is real. But questions and their answers reflect what the elite (which has itself become more gender-balanced) regard as important parts of public opinion about women, as well as the image of women that the elite want to present to the public. What has happened over time is a change in focus. As interviewers and researchers became more balanced in gender, the nature of the questions also changed. Survey questions now ask about women who are more likely to be part of the political world. And the notion of a woman running for president has become a reality instead of a speculation. But despite the increased visibility of women in power and the changing role of women in America, the polling image of women continues to include women in the traditional gender role of wife and mother.

Notes

1. Jo Freeman's work, however, indicates that there were gender differences in voting throughout the century, although the direction varied from those measured in the past twenty years; see Freeman, *Room at a Time.*

2. Klein, *Gender Politics.*

3. Frankovic, "Sex and Politics."

4. Gilligan, *In a Different Voice.*

5. Berenson, Lazarsfeld, and McPhee, *Voting;* Campbell et al., *American Voter.*

6. Pomper, *Voter's Choice,* 84.

7. Withey, *4th Survey of Public Knowledge.*

8. See Smeal, *Why and How Women Will Elect the Next President;* and Abzug with Kelber, *Gender Gap.*

9. Frankovic, "The Ferraro Factor," in Mueller, *Politics of the Gender Gap.*

10. Much of the following discussion is adapted from Frankovic, "Why the Gender Gap Became News."

11. Frankovic, "Public Opinion Polls," in Graber, Norris, and McQuail, *Politics of News.*

12. Ibid.

13. See the *New York Daily Tribune,* October 28, 1896, for one of the presentations of the results.

14. *New York Daily Tribune,* November 17, 1896.

15. Ibid.

16. Interview by Mrs. Miller with George Gallup, June 9, 1983.

17. *Proceedings, 1946 Central City Conference,* American Association for Public Opinion Research: Central City, Colorado, 1946.

18. See the *Literary Digest* photograph and contrast it with the cover story on George Gallup, "The Black and White Beans," *Time Magazine,* May 8, 1948, 21–23, which features a photograph of Mrs. Irene Kadlec interviewing in New York City.

19. Sheatsley and Mitofsky, *A Meeting Place.*

20. Cited in Rosenthal, "Ruth Clark." Clark had an even more interesting history. A Communist, she and her family immigrated to the Soviet Union after World War II, returning to the United States only in 1953. Her daughter Judith was a member of the radical Weather Underground and was sentenced to prison as the result of an armored-car robbery that resulted in the deaths of two policemen and a guard.

21. For an early example, see Katz, "Do Interviewers Bias Poll Results?"; and Hyman et al., *Interviewing in Survey Research.*

22. Shuman, Steeh, and Bobo, *Racial Attitudes in America;* Shuman and Converse, "Effect of Black and White Interviewers."

23. See Ballou, "Respondent/Interviewer Gender Interaction Effects"; Kane and Macauley, "Interviewer Gender and Gender Attitudes."

24. Much of the data in this section comes from the iPoll database of the Roper

Center at the University of Connecticut, which has archived more than 500,000 poll questions asked by nearly all the public pollsters, with results that date back to the 1930s *Fortune* poll and the Gallup Poll; www.ropercenter.uconn.edu.

25. CBS News/*New York Times* poll, January 2006. Question: If your party nominated a woman for President, would you vote for her if she were qualified for the job?

3

The Reemergence of the
Gender Gap in 2004

CAL CLARK AND JANET M. CLARK

The "gender gap," in which women vote for Democratic candidates to a significantly greater extent than men do, seemingly became a permanent feature of the political landscape in the United States during the last two decades of the twentieth century. As indicated in Table 3.1, this difference in voting of approximately eight to ten percentage points first appeared in the 1980 presidential election, although the underlying gap in partisan identification had grown more slowly and gradually starting in the 1960s.[1] Subsequently, it marked all presidential contests during the last two decades of the twentieth century, with the largest gaps of eleven to twelve percentage points occurring in the 1996 and 2000 presidential elections. The gender gap in congressional voting was somewhat slower to develop, but by the late 1990s, it had reached the level of presidential returns. Before 1980, in sharp contrast, there had been little systematic difference in how women and men voted; the few significant gender gaps that did occur (e.g., for Dwight Eisenhower) were based on women's greater support for Republicans.[2] This gender gap, though "not a chasm,"[3] clearly represented an important new element in American politics. In fact, by the late 1990s, the size of the gender gap approached the differences in voting produced by such central factors as income, education, region, and religion.[4]

In 2002, in sharp contrast, Table 3.2 shows that the gender gap in voting for Congress and in the presidential approval ratings of George W. Bush almost disappeared.[5] Clearly, these midterm elections reflected a very significant change in voting behavior compared to the patterns of the previous two decades. However, a gender gap of seven percentage points reemerged in the 2004 presidential race as John Kerry was supported by 51 percent of the women but only 44 percent of the men.[6] Even this level, though, is significantly less than the gender gap in the 1996 and 2000 presidential elections, although it is consistent with the differences between the voting patterns of women and men during the 1980s and early 1990s.

Two factors, in particular, might be adduced to explain this decline in gendered voting in the United States at the opening of the twenty-first century. First, the tragedy of September 11, 2001, raised unprecedented security issues that were widely seen as increasing the appeal of the Republican Party

Table 3.1. Gender Gap in Voting for Democrats

	Measured by Exit Polls			Measured by NES Survey		
	President					
	Men	Women	Gap	Men	Women	Gap
1980	36%	45%	9%	36%	42%	6%
1984	37%	44%	7%	37%	45%	8%
1988	41%	49%	8%	43%	50%	7%
1992	41%	45%	4%	42%	52%	10%
1996	43%	54%	11%	47%	60%	13%
2000	—	—	—	45%	56%	11%
2004	44%	51%	7%	45%	51%	6%
	House of Representatives					
	Men	Women	Gap	Men	Women	Gap
1980	49%	55%	6%	56%	53%	−3%
1982	55%	58%	3%	54%	60%	6%
1984	48%	54%	6%	53%	57%	4%
1986	51%	54%	3%	59%	62%	3%
1988	52%	57%	5%	59%	59%	0%
1990	52%	55%	3%	59%	69%	10%
1992	52%	55%	3%	57%	62%	5%
1994	42%	53%	11%	45%	49%	4%
1996	45%	54%	9%	44%	52%	8%
1998	29%	40%	11%	44%	48%	4%
2000	—	—	—	44%	53%	9%
2002	—	—	—	46%	45%	−1%
2004	—	—	—	50%	55%	5%

Sources: Susan Carroll and Debbie Walsh. "Gender Gap Persists in the 2004 Election." *CAWP Advisory.* New Brunswick, N.J.: Center for American Women and Politics, 2004. www.cawp.rutgers.edu.

Cal Clark and Janet Clark. "The Gender Gap in the Early 21st Century: Volatility from Security Concerns" in Lois Duke Whitaker, ed., *Women in American Politics: Outsiders or Insiders?* 4th Ed. Englewood Cliffs, N.J.: Prentice-Hall, 2005. pp. 47 & 55.

Table 3.2. Gender Gap in 2002 Congressional Elections and Bush Approval

House Vote	House of Representatives		
	Gender		
	Men	Women	Gender Gap
Democrat	46%	45%	−1%
Republican	50%	48%	−2%
Other	4%	7%	3%

Senate Vote	Senate		
	Gender		
	Men	Women	Gender Gap
Democrat	45%	48%	3%
Republican	49%	48%	−1%
Other	6%	3%	−3%

Bush Approval	Approval of George W. Bush as President		
	Gender		
	Men	Women	Gender Gap
Disapprove strongly	19%	19%	0%
Disapprove	10%	12%	2%
Approve	22%	22%	0%
Approve strongly	49%	47%	−2%

to women; indeed, security issues appear to account for the disappearance of the gender gap in the 2002 Congressional elections.[7] Second, the election of George W. Bush as president in 2000 led to an intensification of "culture wars" about religious issues because of his responsiveness to religious groups and social conservatives who played a leading role in his election and reelection.[8] Because women tend to be more strongly religious than men, the growing salience of political conflict over religious issues could have made them more supportive of the Republican Party. Indeed, Karen Kaufmann has shown that women's greater religiosity has limited the width of the gender gap in partisan identification to a significant extent.[9] In short, fundamental shifts in the nature of security and culture war issues could well have created cross pressures on a considerable number of women who had previously supported Democrats, resulting in an attenuation of the gender gap in voting.

This article, hence, explores the gender gap in the 2004 presidential election using data from the National Election Studies (NES) conducted by the Survey Research Center (SRC) of the University of Michigan, supplemented by data on a few select variables from the 2000 and 2002 NES surveys. In particular, we test the hypothesis that changed issue perspectives in the early twenty-first century have created cross pressures on significant groups of women that act to weaken the gender gap in voting, at least in the short run. The first section presents the theoretical model that is applied. Two empirical sections then test various aspects of the model. Section 2 examines the simple differences between the voting of women and men to test the hypotheses developed in the theoretical model; and Section 3 supplements these results by deriving specific estimates for how much individual issues actually contributed in the gender gap in voting for John Kerry in 2004. Both approaches find that, although women voters were evidently subjected to considerable cross pressures in 2002, the normal dynamics of gendered voting reasserted themselves in 2004, albeit in somewhat altered forms from 2000.

Explanations of the Gender Gap in Voting

The gender gap in voting is presumed to reflect similar differences or gaps on a fairly broad array of issues, such as those regarding women's rights and status, support for an activist government to ameliorate social ills and to help the disadvantaged in our society, opposition to violence and threats to the safety of communities and individuals, and empathy and support for those who have been marginalized by America's traditional and patriarchal society.[10] More fundamentally, as discussed in more detail by Barbara Norrander in her article, these issues reflect several distinct yet somewhat intertwined dimensions on which women and men have different political perspectives: (1) "consciousness" about the role and status of women in American society; (2) "culture wars" over the challenge to traditional values that modernization brings; (3) "compassion" about the needy in society; (4) "cost bearing" that has been created by the growing feminization of poverty during the past several decades; and (5) "conflict aversion" resulting from women's greater opposition to violence.

Many scholars view the feminist movement, which began in the late 1960s, as the principal agent of the changes in women's gender consciousness, which ultimately gave rise to the gender gap in political attitudes and voting. The feminist movement, according to this theory, politicized women's issues in the sense that it generated the consciousness that women should act in a politically concerted manner to promote their own autonomy and interests. Thus, the rise of this feminist consciousness creates a political agenda that is disproportionately supported by women. From this perspective, the gender gap resulted from the growing gender consciousness among women as the feminist movement became increasingly successful in articulating new social and political norms to which, over time, more and more women subscribed.[11] Consequently, a substantial gender gap on views concerning women's role in society would be expected, which, in turn, should explain much of the gender gap in voting.

Feminism is just one in a set of social and cultural issues that became increasingly important in American politics during the last quarter of the twentieth century. These include civil rights, the role of religion, patriotism, gay rights, and crime. These issues have been termed the "culture wars" division in U.S. politics because they evoke fundamental differences over basic values.[12] Women are generally assumed to be more liberal than men on these issues (with the exception of religiosity) for several interrelated reasons. First, women are assumed to be more willing than men to transcend the traditional patriarchal culture in the United States; second, they are more sympathetic to other groups (e.g., minorities and gays and lesbians) who have been marginalized and repressed by the traditional culture; and, third, they are more supportive than men of disadvantaged groups in our society.[13]

A third issue dimension of women's compassion has also been seen as an important factor promoting the gender gap. This theoretical strand is rooted in the assumption that women have significantly different values than men's. In Carol Gilligan's view, women react psychologically to the world.[14] According to this theory, women, as compared to men, place more emphasis on "connectiveness" in personal and community relations rather than abstract rights and power considerations and on personal collaboration and issue resolution rather than competition and confrontation. This emphasis on interpersonal relationships, in turn, makes women relatively liberal on issues affecting the less fortunate in society and less likely than men to vote strictly in terms of their own economic self-interest.[15]

Because of this "compassion," consequently, women are viewed as supporting a more activist government and more generous welfare policies than men. More recently, the growing "feminization of poverty" has also pushed women in a liberal direction on these issues from self-interest arising from gender-specific cost bearing.[16] Finally, women have long been viewed as more strongly opposed to violence than men, both in terms of avoiding wars in foreign policy and reducing violence in domestic affairs, creating a fifth dimension of what might be termed conflict aversion.[17]

Table 3.3 summarizes how the differences between the positions of women and men on these five issue dimensions were hypothesized to generate the gender gap in voting during the 1980s and 1990s. The first column indicates

Table 3.3. Summary of Hypotheses about How Individual Issues Dimensions Should Affect the Gender Gap in Voting

Issue Dimension	Women Assumed To Be More Liberal than Men	Issue Should Affect Women More than Men	Changed Dynamics in Early 21st Century
Consciousness	Yes	Yes	None
Culture wars	Yes (except religion)	???	Greater salience of religious issues makes women more conservative
Compassion	Yes	???	None
Cost bearing	Yes	Yes	None
Conflict aversion	Yes	???	After Sept 11th, women, especially those with families, became much more conservative on security issues

that, with the partial exception of women being more religious than men,[18] women are assumed to be more liberal than men on each of these dimensions, predisposing them to be more supportive of Democratic candidates. This implies the following five hypotheses:

H1—Women will be more liberal than men on consciousness issues; therefore, they should be more likely to support Democratic presidential candidates.

H2—Women will be more liberal than men on culture war issues, with the exception of being more religious; therefore, they should be more likely to support Democratic presidential candidates.

H3—Women will be more liberal than men on compassion issues; therefore, they should be more likely to support Democratic presidential candidates.

H4—Women will be more liberal than men on cost-bearing issues; therefore, they should be more likely to support Democratic presidential candidates.

H5—Women will be more liberal than men on conflict aversion issues; therefore, they should be more likely to support Democratic presidential candidates.

Furthermore, these differences in position were assumed to be intensified for consciousness and cost bearing because these issues were more salient to women than to men. This suggests the two following hypotheses:

H6—Because of the central importance of consciousness issues to their lives, these issues will have a bigger impact on women's votes than on men's, thereby increasing the effect of consciousness issues on the gender gap in voting.

H7—Because cost bearing should be considerably more of a problem for women than for men as a result of their much broader responsibility for caring for children and the elderly as well as for themselves, these issues will have a bigger impact on women's votes than on men's, thereby increasing the effect of cost-bearing issues on the gender gap in voting.

Thus, these seven hypotheses provide an explanatory model for the gender gap in voting during the 1980s and 1990s. As noted in the introduction, however, the first few years of the twenty-first century witnessed major changes in American politics that certainly had the potential to reverse the dynamics that had produced the gender gap in voting in the late twentieth century. Most spectacularly, the tragedy of September 11 created a huge jump in popular support for national security. Security concerns appeared to have changed the political allegiance of women with families (who were dubbed "Security Moms") to a significant extent, undercutting the normal dynamics of the gender gap. Indeed, the new effects of security issues provided the major explanation for why the gender gap vanished in the 2002 elections for the House of Representatives.[19] This certainly suggests that the fifth hypothesis about the impact of women's presumed "conflict aversion" on the gender gap in voting needs reformulation:

H5a—September 11 greatly increased the security concerns of important groups of women (i.e., those with families), subjecting them to cross pressures on their voting decisions; therefore, the positive effect of conflict aversion issues on the gender gap in voting should decline drastically, if not vanish.

Second, albeit somewhat more indirectly, the growing salience and intensity of "culture war" issues during the presidency of George W. Bush would also have been expected to create cross pressures on a substantial number of women. Women have traditionally been more religious than men, and their greater religiosity has affected their political perspectives.[20] The growing stress on such issues as school prayer, display of the Ten Commandments, abortion, stem cell research, the teaching of evolution, and church-state relations in general, therefore, should create greater cross pressures on religious women both in their voting and in their support for culture war issues, thus indicating a need to reformulate the second hypothesis:

H2a—Growing conflict over religious issues will affect women more than men because of their greater religiosity; therefore, the positive effect of culture war issues on the gender gap in voting should decline drastically, if not vanish.

The next two sections test these hypotheses in several different ways. Section 2 examines evidence that the predicted cross pressures actually had emerged in the attitudes of women at the time of the 2004 election; and Section 3 applies a sophisticated methodology to estimate how much specific indicators of the five dimensions in our model contributed to the gender gap in presidential voting for John Kerry. All these analyses indicate that the hypothesized cross pressures were significant for the gender gap but that their dynamics differ markedly between the conflict aversion and culture war areas.

Evidence of Cross Pressures on Women Voters in the Early Twenty-First Century

During the 1990s and up through the 2000 elections, as shown by Barbara Norrander's historical data in her article, women were significantly more liberal than men on a wide array of political issues that covered the consciousness, culture wars, compassion, cost bearing, and conflict aversion dimensions, although there were important exceptions to this tendency as well, such as abortion, about which women and men have had very similar attitudes.[21] Consequently, the "issue basis" for the gender gap in voting existed in all the areas, consistent with our original five hypotheses. In contrast, events at the beginning of the twenty-first century suggested that marked attitudinal changes might well have occurred in significant groups of women that would have created cross pressures in terms of their voting behavior. In particular, these dynamics would predict that women would become more conservative on conflict aversion and religious issues but not on consciousness, compassion, cost bearing, or nonreligious culture war issues.

This section examines data on the different issue positions and voting patterns of women and men to test the five initial hypotheses about the issue basis of the gender gap in voting for the 2004 presidential election, as well as the two hypotheses about cross pressures on women's voting reducing or eliminating the gender gap in 2002 and 2004. The first part shows that, as expected, little change occurred in how women and men differed on consciousness, compassion, cost bearing, and nonreligious culture war issues in 2004 compared to the 1990s. The second reports fairly dramatic change on the conflict avoidance dimension, as women changed their beliefs significantly in this area in 2002, explaining much of the drop in the gender gap in voting, but this effect had generally faded by 2004. Finally, the third part finds little evidence that similar additional cross pressures emerged concerning religious issues.

CONTINUING GENDER DIFFERENCES ON CONSCIOUSNESS, NONRELIGIOUS CULTURE WARS, COMPASSION, AND COST BEARING

There is little reason to believe that the conventional differences between women and men on consciousness, compassion, cost bearing, or the nonreligious dimensions of the culture war issues would change in the early twenty-first century; Table 3.4 on gender differences in political attitudes in 2004 provides strong support for this supposition. The top part of the table clearly demonstrates that, as expected, women continued to be significantly more feminist than men. For example, 55 percent of the women but only 41 percent of the men in the NES sample expressed a positive view of feminists, creating a fairly pronounced gender gap of fourteen percentage points. On the other hand, there was almost no difference between women and men in support for abortion; 38 percent of the women and 36 percent of the men took the unambiguously pro-choice position that abortion should always be allowed. This might seem quite significant given the centrality of abortion to the agenda of the feminist movement. However, this does not really represent an attitudinal shift that can be attributed to the intensification of culture wars over the past few years because there has been little difference in the attitudes of women and men about abortion since the issue became prominent in the 1970s.[22] Similarly, as the second part of the table shows, women were also more liberal than men on nonreligious culture war issues, such as attitudes toward gays and lesbians.

Similar results also hold for the compassion and cost-bearing dimensions. Regarding compassion, the third part of Table 3.4 demonstrates that women were indeed considerably more liberal than men concerning a wide array of government programs. They were more likely than men to want government to do more (61 percent to 52 percent) and to support an expansion of government services in general (54 percent to 47 percent). They also were more likely to favor increased spending for many specific programs: helping the poor (60 percent to 54 percent), public schools (78 percent to 74 percent),

Table 3.4. Differences between Women and Men on Compassion
and Cost Bearing, 2004

Issue	Men	Women	Difference
Consciousness			
Like feminists	41%	55%	14%*
Pro-choice on abortion	36%	38%	2%
Nonreligious culture wars			
Favor gay marriage	33%	35%	2%
Favor gays in military	76%	86%	10%*
Like gays and lesbians	29%	38%	9%*
Compassion			
Government should do more	52%	61%	9%*
More government services	47%	54%	7%*
More spending for poor	54%	60%	6%*
More school spending	74%	78%	4%
More child care spending	58%	63%	5%*
More social security spending	58%	68%	10%*
More welfare spending	19%	27%	8%*
Favor tax cuts	62%	56%	–6%*
Cost-bearing			
Family income under $35,000	32%	41%	9%*
Own finances improving	47%	40%	–7%*

* Statistically significant at .05 level.

child care (63 percent to 58 percent), social security (68 percent to 58 percent), and welfare (27 percent to 19 percent). In addition, women were less
supportive of tax cuts than men (56 percent to 62 percent), in contrast to the
late 1990s when they were more conservative on this issue.[23] Cost bearing is
even less likely to change in the short term because it reflects fairly permanent
socioeconomic conditions; unfortunately, the data in Table 3.4 confirm that
women continue to be at a substantial financial disadvantage in American
society. For example, 41 percent of women but only 32 percent of men had
family incomes of under $35,000; women were also significantly less likely
than men to believe that their own finances had improved over the past year
(40 percent to 47 percent).

RAPID CHANGE IN THE ATTITUDES ON CONFLICT
AVERSION AND THE GENDER GAP

Unlike compassion and cost bearing, the early twenty-first century was
marked by fairly dramatic change in the area of conflict aversion. Throughout
the 1980s and 1990s, women had clearly expressed higher levels of pacifism

and antimilitarism than men. Furthermore, these differences were found to be a major cause of the gender gaps in voting and partisanship[24] in line with H5 in our theoretical model. In 2000, for example, Table 3.5 shows that women were significantly less likely to favor increased defense spending than men (36 percent to 41 percent). The tragedy of September 11 produced a very substantial change in Americans' attitudes about national security, leading to major jumps in both men's and women's support for a robust defense budget. Not only did the proportion of women wanting increased defense spending almost double between 2000 and 2002, from just over a third to just under two-thirds, but women's antimilitarism compared to men's was actually slightly reversed. In the 2002 NES study, women were more supportive of increasing defense spending than men by the narrow and not statistically significant margin of 61 percent to 57 percent. Similarly, slightly more women than men wanted increased spending on the war on terrorism (66 percent to 63 percent) and had a positive view of the military (89 percent to 83 percent). Certainly, therefore, women's new greater conservatism vis-à-vis men in this important issue area created strong cross pressures in terms of their normally more liberal voting patterns, as predicted by H5a.

Yet this eruption of cross pressures concerning conflict avoidance proved to be only temporary. The bottom segment of Table 3.5 shows that the normal relationship between gender and views about national security had reasserted itself by the time of the 2004 election. In 2004, women's enthusiasm for more spending for defense and the war on terrorism had dropped precipitously, although men's changed far less. Consequently, the traditional difference between the genders reemerged, with women compared to men being less supportive of more defense spending by ten percentage points (49 percent

Table 3.5. Differences between Women and Men on Conflict Avoidance, 2000, 2002, and 2004

Response	Men	Women	Difference
2000			
Want more defense spending	41%	36%	−5%*
2002			
Want more defense spending	57%	61%	4%
Want more war on terrorism spending	63%	66%	3%
2004			
Want more defense spending	59%	49%	−10%*
Want more war on terrorism spending	50%	37%	−13%*

* Statistically significant at .05 level.

to 59 percent) and of more spending for the war on terrorism by thirteen percentage points (37 percent to 50 percent). Indeed, the difference between women and men in this area was substantially larger in 2004 than at the time of the last pre–September 11 election in 2000. Clearly, therefore, the potential cross pressures on women concerning security issues in 2002 dissipated quite quickly.

Examining whether women were more liberal than men on the conflict aversion issues at various times can only suggest the potential impact of this issue on the gender gap in voting because there is no direct measure of how the issue positions of women and men affected their behavior on election day. One method to see how an issue actually affected the gender gap in voting is to use it as a control variable in a multivariate table analysis, as is done in Table 3.6. There are three parts to this table: one for Al Gore voters in 2000, one for Democratic House voters in 2002, and one for John Kerry voters in 2004. For each Democratic candidate, in turn, the gender gap for all voters is given first. Then the sample was divided into those who wanted more defense spending and those who did not, and the gender gap in voting was computed separately for each of the subsamples. Thus, in essence, attitudes about defense spending were used as the control variable for the relationship between gender and Democratic vote.

Introducing a control variable in such a multivariate table can produce a wide variety of effects on the initial relationship.[25] Four are relevant to our

Table 3.6. Gender Gap in Voting for Democrats, Controlling for Attitudes on Defense Spending, 2000, 2002, and 2004

Results	Men	Women	Gender Gap
2000 Voters for Al Gore			
All Voters	47%	57%	10%*
Those Wanting More Defense Spending	32%	37%	5%*
Those Not Wanting More Def Spending	58%	66%	8%*
2002 Voters for Dem House Candidate			
All Voters	46%	45%	−1%
Those Wanting More Defense Spending	38%	34%	−4%
Those Not Wanting More Def Spending	57%	63%	6%*
2004 Voter for John Kerry			
All Voters	46%	52%	6%*
Those Wanting More Defense Spending	27%	29%	2%
Those Not Wanting More Def Spending	70%	73%	3%

* Statistically significant at .05 level.

analysis here. First, the gender gap in voting could be entirely the result of attitudinal differences between women and men about defense spending. In that case, there would be a significant gender gap for all voters, but there would be no difference in the voting of women and men who shared a position on defense spending. Second, attitudes about defense spending could have no impact on the gender gap, in which case the gender gaps for the two categories of defense spending would be approximately the same as the one for all voters. Third, support for defense spending could explain some, but not all, of the gender gap in voting. In this intermediate case, the gender gaps in the subsamples would be lower than the one for all voters but still above zero. Finally, support for more defense spending might have a different effect than opposition, creating different gender gaps in the two subsamples.

In 2000, the pattern of the gender gaps is most consistent with women's greater liberalism on defense spending, explaining some but not all of the gender gap in voting of ten percentage points, again providing support for H5. The gender gaps for both those who wanted more defense spending (five percentage points) and those who did not (eight percentage points) are lower than the gap for all voters, but still well above zero. The pattern in 2002 was quite different, however. A normal gender gap of six percentage points existed among those who did not want defense spending increased, as 63 percent of the women and 57 percent of the men in this category voted for Democratic House candidates. For those who wanted more defense spending, in contrast, women were actually less likely than men to vote Democratic (34 percent to 38 percent). This suggests that women with a special concern about national security were pushed in a Republican direction more strongly than similar men, consistent with H5— that September 11 had created new cross pressures for many women. However, this effect was short-lived because the original pattern of attitudes about defense spending, explaining some but not all of the gender gap in voting, reestablished itself in 2004. This is consistent, furthermore, with Susan Carroll's finding in her article that there was very little evidence that stereotypical "security moms" played a major role in the 2004 election.

WOMEN'S GREATER RELIGIOSITY

Our second hypothesis about new political dynamics after 2000 (H2a) was that the intensification of "culture wars" after George W. Bush's election would create growing cross pressures on religious women. In direct contrast to attitudes about security issues, there is little evidence of the hypothesized cross pressures on women in this area of the culture wars. Table 3.7 does show that women are more religious than men. For example, in 2000, 2002, and 2004, women were more likely than men to say that religion was important in their lives by eleven to fourteen percentage points, as slightly over 80 percent of women and about 70 percent of men held this belief. Thus, women's degree of religiosity compared to men's evidently did not change during the first half of the first decade of the 2000s, but the hypothesis about growing cross pressures on religious women did not necessarily predict that it would.

There is one facet of Table 3.7 that is consistent with the premise of growing cross pressures on religious women: the difference between women and men concerning their views about Christian fundamentalists that emerged in 2002. Because fundamentalists had taken a leading role in the culture wars, they were more politicized and controversial than general religious institutions. In 2000, despite their greater religiosity, women were no more likely than men (36 percent each) to express a positive view of Christian fundamentalists. Two years later, however, 40 percent of women, as compared to 35 percent of men, viewed fundamentalists positively, creating a statistically significant gender gap of five percentage points that continued in 2004 when 53 percent of women and 48 percent of men had favorable feelings toward fundamentalists. This change is fairly marginal in size, but it is consistent with H2a—that the growing salience of culture wars during the Bush administration has increased the appeal of at least some parts of conservatism to religious women.

The real test of a cross-pressure hypothesis, such as H2a or H5a, requires the direct examination of how opinions on specific issues affect (or do not

Table 3.7. Differences between Women and Men on Religiosity, 2000, 2002, and 2004

	Men	Women	Difference
2000			
Religion important in life	70%	81%	11%*
Like Christian fundamentalists	36%	36%	0%
2002			
Religion important in life	69%	83%	14%*
Like Christian fundamentalists	35%	40%	5%*
2004			
Religion important in life	71%	82%	11%*
Like Christian fundamentalists	48%	53%	5%*

* Statistically significant at .05 level.

affect) the gender gap in voting, such as the results presented in Table 3.6. In the current case, the culture war cross-pressure hypothesis would predict that the gender gap in voting would narrow, vanish, or even be reversed among the more religious but not among the more secular. The results for our two indicators of religiosity are presented in Table 3.8. The hypothesis clearly is disconfirmed by these results. In 2000, neither indicator of religiosity had any impact on the gender gap in voting because Gore's gender gap of more than ten percentage points was almost exactly replicated both by those who did and did not believe that religion was important in their lives and by those who did and did not hold positive views of Christian fundamentalists. Two years later, the data are a little ambiguous because the overall gender gap for Democratic House candidates vanished, but controlling for the two indicators of religiosity produced the same results for all the subgroups. Finally, when a significant gender gap in voting of more than six percentage points for John Kerry reemerged in 2004, similar gender gaps existed for both the more religious and more secular groups.

This subsection has tested hypothesis H2a—that the growing importance of culture war issues during George W. Bush's administration might have

Table 3.8. Gender Gap in Voting for Democrats, Controlling for Religiosity, 2000, 2002, and 2004

2000 Voters for Al Gore	Men	Women	Gender Gap
All voters	47%	57%	10%*
Religion important in life	41%	53%	12%*
Religion not important in life	56%	70%	14%*
Like Christian fundamentalists	38%	45%	7%*
Do not like fundamentalists	50%	60%	10%*
2002 Voters for Dem House Candidate	Men	Women	Gender Gap
All voters	46%	45%	−1%
Religion important in life	37%	39%	2%
Religion not important in life	56%	54%	−2%
Like Christian fundamentalists	37%	39%	2%
Do not like fundamentalists	52%	51%	−1%
2004 Voters for John Kerry	Men	Women	Gender Gap
All voters	46%	52%	6%*
Religion important in life	42%	50%	8%*
Religion not important in life	56%	63%	7%*
Like Christian fundamentalists	33%	42%	9%*
Do not like fundamentalists	57%	63%	6%*

* Statistically significant at .05 level.

rekindled conflicts between feminists and nontraditional women.[26] This, in turn, would pull more religious and traditional women in a Republican direction at the polls, narrowing or eradicating their differences from similar men, which would reduce the overall gender gap in voting. However, the enhanced cross pressures predicted by H2a clearly did not affect the gender gap in voting in either 2002 or 2004. Neither general religiosity nor views about Christian fundamentalists affected the gender gap in voting in any of the last three national elections. That is, women's greater religiosity has evidently not created new or additional cross pressures that weaken gendered voting.

The Impact of Consciousness, Culture Wars, Compassion, Cost Bearing, and Conflict Aversion on the 2004 Gender Gap in Voting

Any complete estimation of how specific attitudes and characteristics affect the gender gap in voting must incorporate two very different types of effects.[27] The first is what has been called "positional" effects. When women and men differ in their attitudes on an issue, such as support for more social security spending or favoring laws that protect gay rights, this constitutes a difference in "position" that could well result in different voting patterns. Positional effects are positive in the sense that they widen the gender gap when women are more liberal than men. Conversely, if women are more conservative than men on an issue, the effect will be the negative one of narrowing the gender gap. For almost all the issues considered here, the positional effects, if they occurred, were positive, as women were more conservative than men only on religiosity and, in 2002, several security issues.

A second type of effect has been called "relational." An issue does not necessarily affect the votes of women and men to the same extent. For example, in our theoretical model, we predicted that consciousness (H6) and cost-bearing (H7) issues would affect women's votes more than men's. Estimating the relational effects involves using a technique such as regression to calculate whether the effects of a specific independent variable, such as having positive feelings for feminists, on voting are the same for women and men. If there are relational effects, they can be either positive or negative. Assuming that a positional effect for an issue is positive, the relational effect will be positive if the effect is greater for women than for men. Conversely, it will be negative or actually act to narrow the gender gap if the issue has a bigger impact on men's than women's votes. Unlike positional effects, which are almost always positive, relational effects are probably about as likely to be negative as positive.

This section derives a set of estimates about how much individual indicators of consciousness, culture wars, compassion, cost bearing, and conflict aversion contributed to the gender gap in voting for John Kerry. The first part summarizes the sophisticated methodology for making these estimates that was developed by Martin Gilens;[28] and the second presents the results for each independent variable's impact on the gender gap in voting.

THE GILENS MODEL FOR ESTIMATING HOW MUCH INDIVIDUAL FACTORS CONTRIBUTE TO THE GENDER GAP IN VOTING

Martin Gilens drew upon a little-used technique that had been developed by Donald Stokes in early treatments of public opinion data[29] to separate and estimate these two very different types of effects.[30] Once the variables in the analysis are suitably recoded,[31] parallel regressions must be run separately for women and for men. The positional effects are measured by the means or averages (μ's) of the independent variables, and the relational effects are measured by the slope or raw regression coefficients (b's). The effect of the variable for either men or women is estimated by the product of μ multiplied by b; and the contribution of the variable to the gender gap is calculated by subtracting this product ($\mu \times b$) for men from the similar product for women.

Obviously, with two different effects, both of which can be either positive or negative, a variable might have one of several different types of impacts on the gender gap. Table 3.9 summarizes these different types of influence. The effect is primarily positional (either positive or negative) when men and women have different means or μ's but similar b's on the independent variable. The effect can also be primarily relational when women and men have similar μ's but different b's. More complex situations exist when both positional and relational effects are present. These effects are reinforcing when they are in the same direction. Conversely, as we will see, there are a surprising number of attitudes where the effects are counterbalancing in the sense that the positional effects are positive but the relational ones are negative.

We applied the Gilens's 1988 statistical model to estimate the contribution to the gender gap in presidential voting in 2004 of a central indicator for each of the five potential explanations for women's greater support of Democratic candidates at the polls, using data from the NES survey. Defense spending was used as the indicator of "conflict aversion" issues; the importance of religion was used for the culture war issue; consciousness issues were tapped by atti-

Table 3.9. Types of Effects from Analysis of How an Issue Affects the Gender Gap in Voting

Neither Positional Nor Relational	μ and b same for both women and men
Single Effects	
Positional positive	Women have higher μ than men on item with positive association with Democratic vote; b's are same for both men & women
Positional negative	Women have lower μ than men on item with positive association with Democratic vote; b's are same for both men & women
Relational positive	Women have higher b than men on item with positive association with Democratic vote; μ's are same for both men & women
Relational negative	Women have lower b than men on item with positive association with Democratic vote; μ's are same for both men & women
Combined Effects	
Reinforcing effect	Both positional and relational effects are in the same direction of widening or narrowing the gender gap
Counterbalancing effect	Positional effect widens gender gap, while relational effect narrows it; or vice versa

tudes about feminists; cost bearing was measured by family income; and two indicators (support for expanding government services and for more spending to help the poor) were used as indicators for compassion issues because of the contrasting effects that they exercise on the gender gap in voting.

Table 3.10 shows the simple direct impact of each of these five independent variables on the gender gap in the Kerry vote of 5.6 percentage points in the NES sample. The first column contains the size of the gender gap (either positive or negative) that can be attributed to the effect of the item in question according to Gilens's statistical model; the second shows the relative importance of this figure by converting it to a percentage or share of the actual gender gap. Finally, the last column indicates what type of effect produced these figures (e.g., positional or reinforcing).

In 2004, the gender gap in voting was considerably smaller than in the 1996 and 2000 elections. For example, in the 2000 NES sample, Al Gore had a gender gap of 10.4 percentage points because he was supported by 57.3 percent of the women but only 46.9 percent of the men among the respondents to this survey. To give an idea of how the dynamics of the gender gap

Table 3.10. Estimates of Specific Issues' Direct Contribution to the Gender Gap in Voting for Kerry, 2004*

Explanatory Variable	Net Effect on Gender Gap	Share of Gender Gap of 5.6% pt	Type of Effect
Culture wars Religion important	–1.9% pt	–34%	Positional
Conflict aversion Defense spending	–1.2% pt	–21%	Counterbalancing
Consciousness Feminists	13.6% pt	243%	Reinforcing
Cost bearing Family income	5.9% pt	105%	Reinforcing
Compassion Poor spending	5.3% pt	95%	Reinforcing
Government services	–2.5% pt	–45%	Counterbalancing

* 51.8% of women but only 46.2% of men voted for Kerry, creating a gender gap of 5.6 percentage points (51.8% – 46.2%).

in voting shifted over the first four years of the new millennium, therefore, we show the net change between the gender gaps between 2000 and 2004 in Table 3.11. For example, the top line in the table shows that the overall gender gap was almost halved between the two elections as it fell from 10.4 percentage points to 5.6 percentage points for a net change of –4.8 percentage points. The rest of the table then reports the net changes in the impacts on the gender gap exercised by each of the five explanatory factors.

These results provide valuable supplements to the analysis in Section 2 in the several distinct ways described in the following subsections. First, the precise estimates that can be made with Gilens's model allow a more subtle evaluation of the cross-pressures hypotheses. Second, the specification and measurement of "relational" effects allow us to test the hypotheses that consciousness and cost bearing should affect women's votes more than men's. Finally, the complexity of the issue base of the gender gap[32] emerges in the contrasting effects that compassion issues have on the gender gap in voting.

MORE SUBTLE EVIDENCE OF CROSS PRESSURES AND THE GENDER GAP

The data analysis in Section 2 demonstrates that there was little discernible change in how women's greater religiosity affected the gender gap in voting. This disproved our original hypothesis that the intensification of the culture

Table 3.11. Change in Specific Issues' Direct Contribution to the Gender Gap in Voting for Gore (2000) and Kerry (2004)

	2004	2000	Net Change
Overall gender gap*	5.6% pt	10.4% pt	–4.8% pt
Explanatory variable	Effect on gender gap**	Effect on gender gap**	
Culture wars			
Religion important	–1.9% pt PO	–1.0% pt CB	–0.9% pt
Conflict aversion			
Defense spending	–1.2% pt CB	5.8% pt RF	–7.0% pt
Consciousness			
Feminists	13.6% pt RF	–1.3% pt CB	+14.9% pt
Cost bearing			
Family income	5.9% pt RF	2.0% pt PO	+3.9% pt
Compassion			
Poor spending	5.3% pt RF	0.9% pt CB	+4.4% pt
Government services	–2.5% pt CB	2.6% pt CB	–5.1% pt

* In 2004, 51.8% of women but only 46.2% of men voted for Kerry, creating a gender gap of 5.6 percentage points (51.8% – 46.2%); in 2000, 57.3% of women but only 46.9% of men voted for Gore, creating a gender gap of 10.4 percentage points (57.3% – 46.9%).
** Types of effects: PO positional; RL relational; RF reinforcing; CB counterbalancing.

wars in the early part of this decade would lead to a drop in the gender gap because of growing cross pressures on religious women, thereby demonstrating that views about religion cannot explain changes in the gender gap after 2000. Still, women are clearly more religious than men, and this undoubtedly undercuts the gender gap in voting at least a little because religiosity is associated with supporting Republicans at the polls. The estimates in the top segment of Table 3.10 support this supposition because women's greater religiosity resulted in a "negative" contribution of –1.9 percentage points to the gender gap in voting for 2004. That is, if women and men had been equally likely to feel that religion was important in their lives, Kerry's gender gap of 5.6 percentage points would have been 1.9 percentage points, or about one-third greater. This effect was primarily positional in that religiosity had approximately equal effects on the votes of men and women, so the net effect of –1.9 percentage points derived from women's greater conservatism. In addition, this effect was slightly larger than it had been in the 2000 presidential contest, when a similar positional difference (see Table 3.7 above) was counterbalanced by religiosity's influence on voting differing somewhat between women and men.

The analysis in Section 2 found strong evidence that attitudes on security or "conflict aversion" created cross pressures that helped reduce the gender gap in voting in 2002. In strong contrast, the normal pattern of women's being more liberal and pacifist in this area reasserted itself in 2004 (see Tables 3.5 and 3.6). Applying Gilens's model to defense spending in the second segments of Tables 3.10 and 3.11 demonstrates a more subtle but still very significant difference between how this issue affected gendered voting in 2000 and 2004. In 2000, attitudes toward defense spending had a "reinforcing" impact on the gender gap in voting. That is, women were more liberal than men for a positive positional effect, and defense spending had a significantly bigger impact on women's votes than men's for a positive relational effect. These two positive effects combined for a total contribution of 5.8 percentage points to Gore's overall gender gap of 10.4 percentage points, consistent with previous findings for the 1980s and 1990s.[33]

The situation in 2004 was strikingly different. The positional differences between women and men were even larger in 2004 than 2000 (see Table 3.5). Yet attitudes on defense spending had a much greater impact on men's votes than on women's. This resulted in a negative relational effect that was even larger than the positive positional one, creating a "counterbalancing effect" of –1.2 percentage points. Thus, adding "relational effects" to the analysis, as can only be done with Gilens's highly sophisticated methodology, demonstrates that conflict aversion did act to reduce John Kerry's gender gap slightly. Although this effect is only marginal at most, the absolute change from 2000 displayed in Table 3.11 is striking. Comparing the impacts of attitudes about defense spending on the gender gap in voting shows a net change of seven percentage points. That is, the gender gap for John Kerry would have been twice as big if the relationships among gender, support for more defense spending, and presidential vote that held in 2000 had not changed considerably in 2004.

THE GREATER IMPACT OF CONSCIOUSNESS AND COST BEARING ON WOMEN'S VOTES

Our theoretical model predicted that consciousness variables would have a larger impact on women's than men's votes because these issues directly affect women's lives (H6). In addition, it predicted that cost bearing should have a stronger impact on the votes of women than men because of women's wider responsibilities for the care of children and the elderly (H7). The data in Table 3.10 confirm both these hypotheses for the 2004 presidential election, quite dramatically so in the case of consciousness. Yet Table 3.11 shows that neither of these two hypothesized relational effects held true in 2000, again indicating subtle but very significant changes in the issue base of the gender gap in voting during the first half of this decade.

As we saw in Table 3.4, women had considerably more positive views of feminists than men did in 2004. This issue also had a much greater impact on women's votes than men, creating a "reinforcing effect." Consequently, as reported in the third segment of Table 3.10, attitudes about feminists made a huge positive contribution to Kerry's gender gap of 13.6 percentage points that was two and a half times the actual difference between women's and men's support for him among respondents to the NES survey. Similarly, family income, our indicator of cost bearing, had a very strong reinforcing effect in which women were considerably more likely than men to have low incomes (see Table 3.4), and income affected women's votes more than men. Overall, this contributed 5.9 percentage points to Kerry's gender gap, or slightly more than its actual magnitude. This huge "overdetermination" of the gender gap by these two variables indicates that the effects of consciousness and cost bearing must have been offset by the impact of other attitudes and factors that acted to narrow the gender gap in voting, such as those exercised by religiosity and support for increased defense spending that were discussed in the previous subsection.

Somewhat surprisingly, perhaps, neither of these predicted relational effects existed for the 2000 gender gap in support for Al Gore. In 2000, family income had the same effect on the voting of men and women, resulting in this variable's making a small positive positional contribution of 2.0 percentage points in the gender gap because women were significantly less affluent than men. The 2000 results for attitudes about feminism, moreover, were strikingly different than those for 2004. Just as in 2004, women were considerably more likely than men to express a positive attitude toward feminists (47 percent to 37 percent). However, this attitude affected the votes of men much more than women, creating a counterbalancing effect so large that it actually narrowed Gore's gender gap by 1.3 percentage points. The more sophisticated analysis of the gender gap in voting provided by Gilens's technique, therefore, uncovers a very significant shift in the dynamics of gendered voting during the first administration of George W. Bush. Consciousness and cost-bearing issues became much more important for women compared to men, while conflict aversion issues became much less so.

THE COMPLEXITY IN THE IMPACT OF COMPASSION ISSUES ON THE GENDER GAP IN VOTING

The data in Table 3.4 show that women were more liberal than men on a wide range of compassion issues concerning governmental activism and redistributive policies. Although these positional effects are the same, the relational effects exercised by specific compassion issues differed substantially. Some affected women's votes more than men's, creating reinforcing relationships that made strong positive contributions to the gender gap in voting for John Kerry. In contrast, others were more important to men than to women, setting off counterbalancing effects. These are illustrated in the bottom segment of Table 3.10 by attitudes about spending to help the poor and about the level of government services, respectively. Spending for the poor represents the epitome of "compassion," and its much greater impact on the votes of women than men in 2004 resulted in a reinforcing effect of 5.3 percentage points. The positional effect for support for increasing government services was almost exactly the same as it was for increasing spending to help the poor (see Table 3.4). Yet, the negative relational effect that it had was so great that it more than offset the positive positional one, creating an overall impact on Kerry's gender gap of –2.5 percentage points. These contrasting effects of compassion issues, therefore, again underline the complex dynamics of the gender gap in voting.

The Changing Dynamics of the Gender Gap

During the 1990s, the gender gap became fairly pronounced and seemingly permanent in voting in national elections in the United States. After 2000, however, the differences between the voting patterns of women and men became somewhat more volatile. The gender gap vanished in the 2002 congressional elections before bouncing back in 2004 to a level about half that in the 1996 and 2000 elections (see Table 3.1). This article tested the hypotheses that the changed security situation after September 11 and the intensification of partisan conflict over cultural issues combined to create new cross pressures on significant groups of women that led to a reduction of the gender gap in voting. Our analysis indicates that cross pressures about security issues (but not religiosity) created the precipitous drop in the gender gap in the 2002 congressional elections. However, these direct cross pressures had generally faded away by the time of the 2004 presidential contest just two years later. The normal dynamics of gendered voting, therefore, seemingly reasserted themselves within a fairly short time of the shock administered by the tragedy of September 11. Yet more sophisticated analysis of the specific factors normally assumed to cause the gender gap in voting found subtle but important differences between how voting was gendered in the 2000 and 2004 presidential elections, underlining the fact that certain groups of women now form key contested constituencies in the battle of our increasingly polarized parties to gain an advantage in the closely divided electorate.[34]

Notes

1. Norrander, "Evolution of the Gender Gap."
2. Chaney, Alvarez, and Nagler, "Explaining the Gender Gap"; Clark and Clark, "Gender Gap in 1996," in Whitaker, *Women in Politics*; Conover, "Feminists and the Gender Gap"; Dolan, "Voting for Women"; Gilens, "Gender and Support for Reagan"; Kaufman, "Culture Wars, Secular Realignment"; Kaufman, "Partisan Paradox"; Kaufmann and Petrocik, "Changing Politics of American Men"; Klein, *Gender Politics*; Mattei and Mattei, "If Men Stayed Home"; Mueller, *Politics of the Gender Gap*; Norrander, "Evolution of the Gender Gap"; Seltzer, Newman, and Voorhees Leighton, *Sex as a Political Variable*; Shapiro and Mahajan, "Gender Differences in Policy Preferences"; Stoper, "Gender Gap Concealed and Revealed."
3. Seltzer, Newman, and Leighton, *Sex as a Political Variable*.
4. Clark and Clark, "Gender Gap in 1996," in Whitaker, *Women in Politics*.
5. Clark and Clark, "Gender Gap in the Early 21st Century," in Whitaker, *Women in Politics*.
6. Carroll and Walsh, "Gender Gap Persists."
7. Clark and Clark, "Gender Gap in the Early 21st Century," in Whitaker, *Women in Politics*.
8. Micklethwait and Woolridge, *Right Nation*.
9. Kaufmann, "Partisan Paradox."
10. Chaney, Alvarez, and Nagler, "Explaining the Gender Gap"; Clark and Clark, "Gender Gap in 1996," in Whitaker, *Women in Politics*; Gilens, "Gender and Support for Reagan"; Kaufman, "Culture Wars"; Kaufman and Petrocik, "Changing Politics of American Men"; Rinehart, *Gender Consciousness and Politics*.
11. Carroll, "Women's Autonomy and the Gender Gap"; Conover, "Feminists and the Gender Gap"; Freeman, *Politics of Women's Liberation*; Huddy, Neely, and Lafay, "Trends"; Misciagno, *Rethinking Feminist Identification*; Rinehart, *Gender Consciousness and Politics*.
12. Hunter, *Culture Wars*; Leege et al., *Politics of Cultural Differences*.
13. Hutchings et al., "Compassion Strategy"; Seltzer, Newman, and Leighton, *Sex as a Political Variable*.
14. Gilligan, *In a Different Voice*.
15. Hutchings et al., "Compassion Strategy"; Kaufman and Petrocik, "Changing Politics of American Men"; Shapiro and Mahajan, "Gender Differences in Policy Preferences"; Stoper, "Gender Gap Concealed and Revealed"; Welch and Hibbing, "Financial Conditions, Gender, and Voting."
16. Goldberg and Kremen, *Feminization of Poverty*; Misciagno, *Rethinking Feminist Identification*.

17. Conover and Sapiro, "Gender, Feminist Consciousness, and War"; Gilens, "Gender and Support for Reagan"; Wilcox, Ferrara, and Allsop, "Group Differences in Early Support for Military Action."

18. Kaufmann, "Partisan Paradox"; Stoper, "Gender Gap Concealed and Revealed."

19. Clark and Clark, "Gender Gap in the Early 21st Century," in Whitaker, *Women in Politics*.

20. Kaufmann, "Culture Wars, Secular Realignment, and the Gender Gap"; Stoper, "Gender Gap Concealed and Revealed."

21. Clark and Clark, "Gender Gap in the Early 21st Century," in Whitaker, *Women in Politics*; Seltzer, Newman, and Leighton, *Sex as a Political Variable*.

22. Conway, Steuernagel, and Ahern, *Women and Political Participation*; Shapiro and Mahajan, "Gender Differences in Policy Preferences."

23. Clark and Clark, "Gender Gap in the Early 21st Century," in Whitaker, *Women in Politics*; Clark, Clark, and Patterson, "Evolving Issue Base of the Gender Gap."

24. Conover and Sapiro, "Gender, Feminist Consciousness, and War"; Gilens, "Gender and Support for Reagan"; Smith, "Polls"; Stoper, "Gender Gap Concealed and Revealed"; Wilcox, Ferrara, and Allsop, "Group Differences in Early Support for Military Action."

25. McGaw and Watson, *Political and Social Inquiry*, pp. 437–44.

26. Conover and Gray, *Feminism and the New Right*; Luker, *Abortion and the Politics of Motherhood*; Sears and Huddy, "On the Origins of Political Disunity Among Women," in Tilly and Gurin, *Women, Politics, and Change*.

27. Chaney, Alvarez, and Nagler, "Explaining the Gender Gap"; Gilens, "Gender and Support for Reagan"; Kaufmann and Petrocik, "Changing Politics of American Men."

28. Gilens, "Gender and Support for Reagan."

29. Stokes, "Some Dynamic Elements"; Stokes, Campbell, and Miller, "Components of Electoral Decision."

30. Gilens, "Gender and Support for Reagan."

31. The dependent variable of presidential vote is coded 0 for Bush and 100 for Kerry. The independent variables are coded to range from 0 (low value) to 1 (high value) with the intermediate values proportionately spaced between them. Finally, the independent variables are recoded so that they are positively correlated with a Kerry vote (i.e., opposition to more defense spending is scored high).

32. Clark, Clark, and Patterson, "Evolving Issue Base of the Gender Gap."

33. Clark, Clark, and Patterson, "Evolving Issue Base of the Gender Gap"; Gilens, "Gender and Support for Reagan."

34. Greenberg, *Two Americas*; Stonecash, Brewer, and Mariani, *Diverging Parties*.

4

Security Moms and
Presidential Politics

*Women Voters in the
2004 Election*

SUSAN J. CARROLL

A gender gap, defined as the absolute difference between the proportion of women and the proportion of men voting for the winning candidate,
was clearly evident in the 2004 presidential election. The nationwide exit poll
conducted by Edison Media Research and Mitofsky International showed
that 48 percent of women compared with 55 percent of men had voted for
George W. Bush, resulting in a gender gap of seven percentage points.

The 2004 gender gap was neither the largest (eleven percentage points in
voting for Bill Clinton in 1996) nor the smallest (four percentage points in
voting for Bill Clinton in 1992) for presidential elections since 1980. In fact,
gender differences in voting in 2004 appeared very average in magnitude;
the mean gender gap for all presidential elections from 1980 to 2000 was 7.7
percentage points.[1]

Nevertheless, Kerry's failure to do better among women was one of the
explanations commonly offered for his defeat in the 2004 presidential race.
Although Kerry won a majority, 51 percent, of women's votes, he fell short of
the 54 percent of women's votes that Al Gore won in 2000. Bush did notably
better with women in 2004, winning 48 percent of their votes, compared to
only 43 percent in 2000.[2]

In an article in the *Washington Post* on the day after the election, reporter
Dana Milbank echoed the conclusion drawn by many others throughout the
country who attributed Bush's better showing with women in 2004 to security moms, observing, "Bush narrowed his deficit among female voters to five

percentage points from 11 in 2000—evidence that 'security moms' doubted Kerry's ability to fight terrorism."[3] Similarly, refuting the idea that evangelical Christians concerned with moral values tipped the election in Bush's favor, an editorial in the *St. Louis Post-Dispatch* several days after the election identified the behavior of security moms as critical to Bush's victory: "What mattered then? A significant shift toward Mr. Bush among Hispanics and women helped Mr. Bush's margin of victory. . . . The votes of married white women—security moms, as they've been called—nearly closed the gender gap."[4]

Just as "soccer moms" were portrayed as the pivotal women voters in the 1996 elections and their support viewed as one of the reasons Clinton won reelection,[5] "security moms" became the most sought-after group of women voters during the latter stages of the 2004 election. And their supposed "swing" toward Bush was seen by many as a major reason Bush defeated Kerry.

This article examines the phenomenon of the "security mom" and the role she played in the 2004 election. Through content analysis of print media coverage and analysis of exit poll data, I show that the empirical data collected from voters offer little support for the characterization of security moms as portrayed in media accounts. Nevertheless, I argue the attention paid to "security moms" in the presidential race very much worked to the benefit of the Bush campaign, fitting into the campaign's overall strategy and detracting interest away from women voters whose concerns could be represented by existing interest groups, thus weakening any accountability that the victorious candidate might have to women voters.

Description of Data Sets

I use two different data sets in examining the role played by security moms in the 2004 election. The first data set, enabling me to analyze print media coverage of the security mom phenomenon, is composed of data coded from all articles published between July 1 and November 30, 2004,[6] in newspapers included in the "Major Papers" category within LexisNexis, in which the term "security mom(s)" and the word "election(s)" both occurred in the text of the article. A total of 130 articles,[7] published in both domestic and international newspapers, met these criteria. These 130 articles were published in thirty-nine different papers, including thirteen in the *Washington Post,* ten in the *New York Times,* ten in the *Boston Globe,* nine in the *Pittsburgh Post-Gazette,* and eight in the *Chicago Sun-Times.*

The second data set, enabling me to examine the attitudes and preferences of voters, is the National Election Pool (NEP) exit poll conducted by Edison

Media Research and Mitofsky International. This nationwide poll was conducted with 11,719 voters at a sample of 250 polling places on election day; also included were 500 absentee and early voters in thirteen states.

From Soccer Mom to Security Mom

During the 1996 presidential election, consultants involved in the presidential campaigns gave the name "soccer mom" to a group of voters that they targeted and saw as potentially critical to the outcome of the election. Newspaper coverage of that election commonly portrayed the soccer mom as a mother who lived in the suburbs, was a swing voter, was busy and stressed out, worked outside the home, and drove a minivan or sport-utility vehicle. Newspaper coverage also described the soccer mom (although somewhat less frequently) as middle-class, married, and white.[8] Both presidential campaigns in 1996 appealed to so-called soccer moms through their children, emphasizing issues such as education, V-chips, school uniforms, student financial aid, drug use among young people, smoking among children, and teen curfews.[9]

Although soccer moms were much discussed in news coverage of the 1996 and 2000 elections, the first reference to "security moms" in a major paper (as defined by LexisNexis) did not appear until March 7, 2003. In an article in the *New York Times,* Democratic Senator Joseph R. Biden, Jr., was quoted as saying, in the aftermath of September 11, 2001, "Soccer moms are security moms now."[10] The *New York Times* reporter may have lifted this quote from a piece entitled "How Soccer Moms Became Security Moms" by Joe Klein that had appeared a few weeks earlier in *Time* magazine. Klein argued that the "war on terrorism is two wars, one for men and one for women." Although men were focused on special forces and bombing runs, women, according to Klein, were concerned with "protection of hearth and home against the next terrorist attack." In support of his thesis, Klein cited Joe Biden: "When I was out campaigning last fall [2002], this [a possible terrorist attack] was all women wanted to talk about. . . . Not schools, not prescription drugs. It was 'What are you doing to protect my kids against terrorists?' Soccer moms are security moms now."[11]

This theme of soccer moms changing into security moms following September 11, 2001, was a common one in media coverage leading up to the 2004 election. *Time* followed up on the Klein piece with another, lengthier article four months later entitled, "Goodbye, Soccer Mom. Hello, Security Mom." The article opened as follows:

Swing voters have always been elusive creatures, changing shape from election to election. The profile and assumptions about them in one contest seldom apply to the next one. This axiom is proving true again with that most-talked-about slice of American political demography: the Soccer Mom. Since 9/11, polls suggest she has morphed into Security Mom. . . . She's someone, in short, like Debbie Creighton, a 34–year-old Santee, Calif., mother of two who voted for Bill Clinton twice and used to choose the candidates who were most liberal on abortion and welfare. "Since 9/11," Creighton says, "all I want in a president is a person who is strong."[12]

Business Week jumped on the security mom bandwagon with an article in December 2003 entitled "'Security Moms': An Edge for Bush?" The *Business Week* reporter observed, "Married women with children—many of them the so-called Soccer Moms who twice backed Bill Clinton—have been drifting toward the GOP in the aftermath of the horrific September 11 attacks. That has led some pollsters to dub these largely suburban, socially progressive voters 'Security Moms.'"[13] The *Business Week* story also quoted Democrat Celinda Lake, one of the first political pollsters to argue that men and women voters viewed security issues in different ways, predicting, "White, married moms are going to be the biggest swing group next year."[14]

Despite the attention security moms received in news magazines such as *Time* and *Business Week* well in advance of the 2004 election, newspapers showed very limited interest in this phenomenon until mid-September 2004. Only nine articles mentioning security moms were published in major newspapers in the period from July 1–September 15, 2004 (Table 4.1). However, coverage picked up considerably in mid- to late September. In early to mid-September 2004, Bush experienced an upswing in popular support following a very successful Republican convention, which focused on security and terrorism-related themes and the tragedy in Breslan, where hundreds of Russian schoolchildren were held hostage by terrorists and many were killed during an attempted rescue mission. In their effort to explain Bush's rise and Kerry's decline in the polls (which actually occurred among both women and men), many journalists—and pollsters—looked to "security moms." For example, a September 23 article in the *Washington Post* reported, "'It is a problem that these women do not feel the Democrats are focused on security,' said Democratic pollster Celinda Lake, whose most recent bipartisan Battleground 2004 poll shows Kerry leading Bush among women by four percentage points. The same poll showed Kerry in June with a 10–point lead among women. . . . 'The security moms,' if you will, are part of the agenda-setting here,' Lake said."[15]

Table 4.1. Publication Dates of Newspaper Articles Referring to Security Moms

Dates	Number of Articles	% of Articles
July 1–September 15	9	6.9
September 16–30	22	16.9
October 1–15	25	19.2
October 16–November 7	59	45.4
November 8–30	15	11.5
N =	130	100.0

The print media continued to focus attention on security moms through the first half of October, but interest in security moms peaked during the last two and one-half weeks before the November 2 election and in the first few days of postelection analysis (Table 4.1). Almost one-half of all stories in major papers that mentioned security moms were published between October 16 and November 7 (Table 4.1). The increase in newspaper references to security moms just before and after the election undoubtedly resulted in part from the greater number of election-related stories that were published in those weeks. However, the increase also can be partially attributed to the fact that security moms were seen as critical swing voters whose decisions could make the difference in what was clearly a very close election.

Attributes of Security Moms

The idea that security moms were swing voters who could determine the outcome of the election was a prevalent theme of newspaper coverage during the 2004 election. Table 4.2 presents the most frequently mentioned characteristics attributed to security moms in print media coverage. Being swing voters tops the list, with more than one-fifth of all stories explicitly describing or clearly implying that security moms were swing voters.

The idea that the soccer moms of 1996 and 2000 had become security moms—an idea evident in the passages from *Time* and *Business Week* magazines—also was a frequently mentioned theme in newspaper coverage. About one in every five stories suggested that security moms were the same voters as the soccer moms from previous elections (Table 4.2).

Besides being "swing voters" and former "soccer moms," the most frequently mentioned attributes of security moms were that they were "mothers" (or had children) and that they were "married" (Table 4.2). Each of these characteristics appeared as a descriptor in almost one of every five stories.

Table 4.2. Most Frequently Mentioned Attributes of
Security Moms

Attribute	Percentage of Articles*
Are swing voters	21.5
Are/were soccer moms	19.2
Are mothers/have children	19.2
Are married	17.7
Are white	10.0
Live in the suburbs	9.2
Are Republican or support Bush	9.2

* N = 130. Percentages do not add up to 100.0 percent because
more than one attribute could be mentioned in an article, and many
articles mentioned no attributes.

Three other characteristics were mentioned less frequently but often
enough to be noted. One of every ten articles described security moms as
"white." And almost that many referred to security moms as "living in the suburbs" and as being either "Republican" or "Bush supporters" (Table 4.2).

This last characterization is most interesting because it reflects a dissenting
view expressed by journalists regarding the political proclivities of security
moms. Although more than twice as many journalists repeated the dominant
characterization of security moms as swing voters whose votes were up for
grabs, some journalists portrayed security moms as women who were "reli-
ably conservative and consistently vote Republican"[16] or as "really women who
would have voted for Bush anyway."[17] In large part, this dissenting view seems
to reflect the influence of a September 29, 2004, memo written by Anna Greenberg of Greenberg Quinlan Rosner Research, Inc., in which the Democratic
pollster presented data challenging the idea that security moms were swing
voters as well as other common assertions about security moms.[18] Although
Greenberg's memo had some impact, it did not change the dominant discourse
about security moms; of the 130 stories referring to security moms in major
papers, only thirteen, or 10 percent, expressed any skepticism whatsoever
about the existence or dominant characterization of security moms.[19]

One of the interesting aspects of the newspaper coverage of security moms
in the 2004 election was how frequently no description of any kind was provided. Somewhat surprisingly for a term that came into usage only recently,
more than one-third, 37.7 percent, of all the articles made only passing reference to security moms, providing no definition or discussion of this group of
voters whatsoever. Apparently, many journalists simply assumed that their
readers were familiar with the term or that its meaning was self-evident.

Issue Concerns of Security Moms

Not surprisingly, security moms were seldom portrayed in print media coverage as interested in any issue other than security, terrorism, and the safety of their families and children. Article after article described security moms as women "who are fearful of another attack within the United States,"[20] "who are fearful for their family's future,"[21] and "who worry about terrorism and security."[22] A journalist for the *St. Louis Post-Dispatch*, somewhat tongue-in-cheek, offered one of the most colorful portrayals of the concerns of security moms: "Security moms allegedly are soccer moms who have evolved. Once fretting about momly things like education, health care, poor folks and breathing air with no detectable color or texture—girlie-man Democratic stuff—security moms have moved on to bigger frights. Really, they are more like insecurity moms. You might be a security mom if you think your child is more likely to die of smallpox or anthrax than of Alzheimer's."[23]

Seventy-six of the articles in major newspapers that referred to security moms also discussed the issues of concern to them in the election. More than three-fourths of these, 77.6 percent, mentioned terrorism, security, or safety (usually of families or children) as an issue of concern to security moms. Another 18.4 percent of newspaper stories referred to a leadership quality (e.g., proven leader, protector, strong leader), usually linked to the war on terror, as a concern of security moms. Other issues were seldom mentioned. The next most frequently mentioned issue was the economy, discussed as a concern of security moms in only 6.6 percent of newspaper articles. The impression these articles gave the reader was that security moms were concerned primarily with the security and the safety of their children and families and secondarily with electing a strong, proven leader who would protect their families. Little else seemed to matter; terrorism and security trumped all other issues.

Just as newspaper articles portrayed security moms as almost single-mindedly focused on terrorism and safety, so too did these stories present the presidential campaigns and candidates as appealing to these voters largely on the basis of security issues. Actually, the vast majority of news stories, 75.4 percent, did not discuss specific attempts by the presidential candidates to win the votes of security moms. But in stories where candidate appeals were described, 56.3 percent of the appeals focused on national security, terrorism, or safety while another 21.9 percent were based on leadership qualities (e.g., proven leader, protector, strong leader) commonly linked to the war on terror.

Exit Poll Data and Security Moms

Exit poll data from 2004 reveal several problems with the portrayal of security moms in the print media. First, the exit poll data suggest that the security moms (whether defined demographically as married mothers or white married mothers) were not more concerned with terrorism than other groups of voters with similar marital and/or parental statuses. Nor did they vote more heavily for George W. Bush than other voters who shared some, but not all, of their characteristics, thereby determining the outcome of the election. Finally, there is nothing in the exit poll data to suggest that security moms were swing voters.

CONCERN WITH TERRORISM AMONG WOMEN AND WHITE MARRIED MOTHERS

Two questions included in the exit poll are useful in assessing voters' level of concern with terrorism and national security. First, voters were asked, "Which *one* issue mattered most in deciding how you voted for president?" Second, voters were asked, "How worried are you that there will be another major terrorist attack in the U.S.?" Obviously, if security moms were as consumed with fears about terrorism as the media suggested, they should have identified terrorism as the issue most important to their voting choices and also expressed concern that there would be another terrorist attack. Table 4.3 presents gender differences in responses to both of these questions.

Most of the voters who reported that terrorism was the issue that mattered most in their choice for president voted for Bush (81.8 percent of women and 88.8 percent of men). However, contrary to what one might expect based on most media accounts, women were significantly less likely than men to identify terrorism as the issue that was most important in determining their vote (Table 4.3). Moreover, only a modest proportion of women, 16.6 percent, reported that terrorism was the issue that mattered most in their voting decisions. Larger proportions of women voters chose moral values

Table 4.3. Gender Differences among All Voters on Terrorism Measures

	Percentage Women	Percentage Men	tau_b =
Reported terrorism as issue that mattered most in vote choice	16.6 ($N = 3675$)	21.9 ($N = 3229$)	−.08*
Very worried about another	24.9 ($N = 1805$)	17.3 ($N = 1441$)	−.09*

* Significant at the .001 level.

(23.5 percent) or the economy and jobs (18.7 percent), and almost as many identified Iraq (14.5 percent) as the most important issue.

Women who fit a commonly offered description of security moms—white, married, with children[24]—were similarly less likely than men who shared their demographic characteristics to identify terrorism as the issue that was most important to their choice for president. Significantly fewer white married mothers, 18.9 percent, picked terrorism than white married fathers, 24.4 percent (tau$_b$ = −.06, p = .01). (And white married women with children were almost twice as likely to identify moral values, 34.3 percent, as terrorism as the most important issue affecting their presidential choice.) Thus, there is no evidence on this measure that terrorism trumped other issues for most women generally or for white married mothers in particular; nor is there any evidence on this measure that terrorism was more important to women's choices for president than to men's.

On the second measure, in contrast, differences are consistent with the idea that terrorism was of greater concern to women than to men. Women were significantly more likely than men to be very worried that the United States would be subject to another terrorist attack (Table 4.3).

Further examination, however, reveals that this measure offers little in the way of support for the idea that women's concern about terrorism helped swing them toward support of Bush. Although about one-fourth of all women voters were very worried about another terrorist attack, these women voted heavily, 58.3 percent, for Kerry, not Bush!

Moreover, although women who fit a commonly offered description of security moms—white, married, with children—were significantly more likely than men with the same characteristics to be very worried about another terrorist attack (tau$_b$ = .14, p < .001), they were not likely to be more worried about another terrorist attack than were other groups of women. In fact, although 20.5 percent of white married women with children (security moms) expressed great concern about another terrorist attack, white unmarried women without children were just as likely (21.8 percent) and white unmarried women with children much more likely (30.5 percent) to be very worried about a future attack. Apparently, it was the unmarried mothers, not the supposed security moms, who had the highest levels of fear about the threat of terrorism.

VOTING FOR BUSH: SECURITY MOMS COMPARED TO OTHERS

Table 4.4 provides a closer look at the candidate preferences of security moms (defined here as white married mothers concerned about terrorism as measured two different ways) compared with men and women of varying marital and parental statuses. Among security moms defined as white married mothers *who reported that terrorism was the issue that mattered most in their voting choice,* 92.9 percent voted for Bush. But white married fathers who reported terrorism as the issue most important to their voting choices—i.e., men who could be considered "security dads"—voted at an equally high rate for Bush. Thus, if the safety of their children was motivating moms to vote for Bush, it apparently was motivating the dads just as much. Moreover, married women without young children voted just as heavily for Bush as did security moms (Table 4.4), suggesting that being a "mom," or concern over the safety of one's children, was not the only, or even most critical, factor motivating voters concerned with terrorism to vote for Bush.

Findings are similar when security moms are defined as white married women *who were very concerned that there might be another major terrorist attack* (Table 4.4) although the number of cases is small and these data should be viewed more cautiously. Although 58.7 percent of them voted for Bush, "security dads" (white married fathers worried about another terrorist attack) voted for Bush at an even higher rate, 65.6 percent. Moreover, married women who had no children under the age of eighteen were slightly more likely than security moms to prefer Bush over Kerry. Unmarried women— with or without children—were much less likely than married women—with or without children—to vote for Bush (Table 4.4), suggesting that something related to marriage (perhaps economic standing) was a more important factor than being a "mom" in determining whether those women who feared a terrorist attack voted for Bush or Kerry.

Table 4.4. Votes for Bush among Security Moms and Other Groups of Varying Gender, Marital, and Parental Status

	Terrorism was issue that mattered most in vote	Very worried about another terrorist attack
	% Vote for Bush	% Vote for Bush
Security moms (white married mothers)	92.9	58.7
White married fathers	94.5	65.6
White unmarried mothers	89.2	41.7
White unmarried fathers	100.0	75.0
Married women without young children*	94.3	67.4
Married men without young children	91.1	59.5
Unmarried women without young children	78.9	38.6
Unmarried men without young children	85.6	38.5

* Young children are those under age 18, reflecting the way the question was asked on the national exit poll.

SECURITY MOMS AS SWING VOTERS?

Just as the evidence from the national exit poll fails to offer support for the idea that security moms were more concerned with terrorism than other voters and voted for Bush on this basis, so too does the exit poll fail to offer strong and convincing support for the notion that security moms were swing voters. Table 4.5 presents information about party identification, political ideology, and timing of voting decisions for security moms, defined two different ways, compared with all women voters. If security moms were swing voters whom Bush won over because of the way he dealt with terrorism in the campaign, one might expect to find that they were less Republican and less conservative than women voters generally and that they made their voting decisions later in the campaign. Table 4.5 offers little evidence that this was the case.

White married women for whom terrorism was the issue that mattered most in their voting decision were much more heavily Republican and somewhat more conservative than women voters generally (Table 4.5). Moreover, most of them—and a slightly larger proportion than for women overall—made their decision about which candidate to support more than a month in advance of the election. Certainly this does not seem a likely profile for swing voters; rather, by and large, these seem to be strong Republican supporters.

Although white married women who were very worried about another terrorist attack were slightly less likely to identify themselves as conservatives (and more likely to identify as moderates) than women overall, they nevertheless were slightly more Republican and about equally as likely as women overall to have made their voting decision more than one month before the election. Although the political ideology of these women is consistent with

Table 4.5. Party Identification, Political Ideology, and Timing of Voting Decision for Security Moms Compared with All Women Voters

	Percentage of white married moms for whom terrorism was the issue that mattered most in vote	Percentage of white married moms who were very worried about another terrorist attack	Percentage of all women women
Republican	65.7	40.5	35.3
Conservative	43.6	25.4	30.5
Made voting decision more than one month before election	82.7	76.8	77.2

the idea that they may have been swing voters, their levels of Republican identification and the timing of their voting decisions are not.

Discussion and Implications

The security mom was the hot new woman voter of 2004. Security moms made the list—along with eight other terms, including Mess O'Potamia, red state/blue state, TiVo, and wardrobe malfunction—of *Time* magazine's buzzwords of the year.[25] The *Macmillan English Dictionary* also named the "security mom" as one of its fifty-two "Most Popular New Words of 2004."[26]

The media portrayed the security mom as a former soccer mom transformed by the events of September 11, 2001. Worried about future terrorist attacks and single-mindedly focused on the safety of her family and children, she was, according to most media reports, a swing voter who would help determine the outcome of the 2004 election.

Yet, despite considerable media attention, empirical support for the common characterization of security moms was found to be sorely lacking in the 2004 national exit poll data. Certainly, white married mothers concerned with terrorism existed and voted in the 2004 election. But they were less likely than white married dads to identify terrorism as the issue that most influenced their choice of presidential candidates. And although white married moms were more likely than white married dads to be very worried about another terrorist attack, they were no more likely than white unmarried women without children, and less likely than white unmarried women with children, to be concerned about a future terrorist incident. Moreover, white married women concerned with terrorism hardly fit the profile of swing voters. They were heavily Republican, more conservative than women voters generally, and for the most part had decided upon a candidate before the final month of the campaign.

In the absence of compelling evidence to support the characterization of security moms so prevalent in media reports on the 2004 election, the pertinent question becomes, "Why did this characterization of women voters get so much play, especially in the final weeks before the election?" The answer to this question is beyond the scope of the analysis offered in this paper, but some speculative and tentative responses can be offered.

Part of the explanation may be that the security mom was an excellent fit with the Bush campaign's unwavering focus on the theme of national security. National security was the issue where Bush had the greatest advantage over Kerry in the polls, and terrorism became the focal point of both the

Republican convention and the campaign. Attention to security moms complemented the Republican campaign strategy and helped to keep the public focused on the issue where they thought Bush was strongest. Several sources attribute the first use of the term "security mom" to Republican pollster David Winston,[27] but prominent Democrats, such as Senator Joe Biden and pollster Celinda Lake, espoused support for the idea of the security mom as well. Perhaps these Democrats were motivated by a desire to get their party to take the issue of national security, and women's perspectives on it, seriously. Nevertheless, in the final analysis, the concept of the security mom seems largely to have worked against the Democrats and to have helped the Republicans by drawing public attention to an issue—terrorism—where the Republican candidate was perceived as more capable than his Democratic opponent.

The phenomenon of security moms also worked to the advantage of George W. Bush and his campaign by allowing him to appear to be responsive to women voters without making specific commitments that he might have had to follow through on once reelected. By talking about terrorism and national security, George W. Bush appeared to be responding to the concerns of security moms during his campaign. And because security moms were the most targeted and visible group of women voters in the last few weeks before the election, he thereby appeared to be responsive to the concerns of women voters more generally. Nevertheless, Bush made few or no promises to women voters as women. Instead, he promised only to continue to try to protect their children and families and to fight terrorists abroad so we would not have to fight them on U.S. soil. Once the election was over, there was no organized interest group of security moms to pressure the Bush administration, nor were there any campaign commitments to women as women (not just as moms) to which existing women's groups could hold Bush accountable.

Although the security mom phenomenon served Bush and his campaign well, the security mom also proved to be a blessing for journalists, who are always looking for a new story or new perspective on an old story. The security mom news frame provided reporters with a new "hook" or "peg" for writing about women voters and the gender gap,[28] especially when Bush's numbers increased in the polls in early to mid-September following the Republican convention and the Breslan tragedy. Security moms provided a convenient and novel explanation for Bush's bump in the polls even if the underlying evidence to link security moms to his increased public support was generally lacking.

But if the interests of Republicans and journalists were served well by the phenomenon of the security mom, the interests of women voters by and large were not. Several years ago, in an analysis of media coverage of women voters in the 1996 elections, I argued:

> Instead of empowering feminist and other women's organizations, the soccer mom news frame actually led to the disempowerment of most women through its narrow portrayal of women voters and their interests. The soccer mom frame created the illusion that Bill Clinton and Bob Dole were reaching out to and promising to address the concerns of women voters when, in fact, the candidates were actually paying little attention to large subgroups of women. The fact that soccer moms were portrayed by the media as the only women voters who really mattered made it easier for the candidates to ignore voters who might be politically unpalatable (e.g., women on welfare, women immigrants) or who might push to have their concerns addressed in the campaign or placed on the president's agenda (e.g., women of color, pro-choice activists, professional women).[29]

A similar argument can be made about the media's focus on security moms in 2004. To the extent the media focused on security moms, they diverted attention away from other women voters and permitted the candidates to overlook their concerns. And women voters did have concerns other than security. In a survey conducted on November 1–2, 2004, by Lake Snell Perry and Associates for Votes for Women 2004, a nonpartisan network of women's organizations created to monitor the gender gap in the 2004 presidential election, women identified health care, education, and the economy and jobs as the top issues they wanted the president to address over the next four years. Large proportions of women voters also indicated that they would like to see the administration give priority to violence against women, women's equality under the law, and equal pay.[30]

In addition to diverting attention away from other women voters and their concerns, the focus on security moms—as moms—also erased from public view any interests the women who fit the security moms' demographic profile (white, married, with children) may have had in roles or capacities other than as fearful protectors of their children and families. Susan Douglas and Meredith Michaels have documented and analyzed the cultural idealization of motherhood that has occurred in recent years, arguing that the "new momism . . . redefines all women, first and foremost, through their relationships to children."[31] Portrayed not as women with a range of interests, roles, and concerns, but rather as one-dimensional, single-issue voters, security moms appear to be the most recent political manifestation of this new "momism." In the context of presidential politics, the new momism has so far proven to be a development that has contributed to the disempowerment, rather than to the political empowerment, of women.

Notes

1. Center for American Women and Politics, "Gender Gap Persists in 2004 Election"; Center for American Women and Politics, "Gender Gap."
2. Center for American Women and Politics, "Gender Gap Persists in 2004 Election."
3. Milbank, "Deeply Divided Country Is United in Anxiety," A28.
4. "Beyond Simplicity," *St. Louis Post-Dispatch*, November 9, 2004, B6. This editorial and others like it seem to have drawn heavily on the analysis of Mark J. Penn, a prominent Democratic pollster involved with the 1996 Clinton reelection campaign, who wrote an editorial in which he identified Hispanics and white married women (whom he did not label "security moms") as the key groups responsible for Bush's reelection. See Penn, "It's the Moderates, Stupid."
5. Carroll, "Dis-Empowerment of the Gender Gap"; Vavrus, "From Women of the Year to 'Soccer Moms'"; Vavrus, *Postfeminist News.*
6. July 1 was chosen as the initial date to avoid the primaries but encompass both nominating conventions and the bulk of the general election campaign. November 30 was chosen as the end date to allow sufficient time after the election to catch most of the postelection analysis.
7. Letters to the editor identified through this search were excluded from the analysis. Articles that were reprinted in multiple papers were counted only once.
8. Carroll, "Dis-Empowerment of the Gender Gap."
9. Carroll, "Dis-Empowerment of the Gender Gap."
10. Purdum, "Threats and Responses," A15.
11. Klein, "How Soccer Moms Became Security Moms," 23.
12. Tumulty et al., "Goodbye, Soccer Mom," 26.
13. Starr, "'Security Moms.'"
14. Ibid., 60.
15. Romano, "Female Support for Kerry Slips," A7.
16. Morin, "Swing Voters," D1.
17. Sweet, "Did the Women's Vote Count?" 60.
18. Greenberg, "Re: The Security Mom Myth."
19. Of the 101 news stories published subsequent to the date of Greenberg's memo (i.e., on September 30 or thereafter), only ten, or 9.9 percent, in any way questioned the dominant characterization of security moms.
20. Seelye, "Kerry in a Struggle for a Democratic Base," A1.
21. Barber, "Bush Gambles the Presidency," 13.

22. Morin, "Swing Voters," D1.

23. Cuniberti, "Power of the Security Mom," E1.

24. In media coverage, as reported earlier, security moms were often described as married and mothers and somewhat less often described as white. I have chosen for this analysis to include the race variable and operationalize security moms as white, married women with children under the age of eighteen. However, I have examined all findings presented in this paper for married women with children (regardless of race) as well, and although the numbers may differ slightly, the findings and conclusions are the same for married women with children as for white married women with children.

25. "The Year in Buzzwords," *Time*, December 27, 2004, 24.

26. "Most Popular New Words of 2004," *Macmillan English Dictionary*, http://www.macmillandictionary.com/New-Words/2004–chart-2004–words.htm.

27. "Zoology of Swing Voters"; Gilson, "Wild Cards"; Tumulty et al., "Goodbye, Soccer Mom."

28. For discussions of the functions performed by media news frames, see Gitlin, *Whole World Is Watching*; Entman, "Framing U.S. Coverage"; Entman, "Framing"; and Norris, "Introduction" in Norris, *Women, Media, and Politics*.

29. Carroll, "Dis-Empowerment of the Gender Gap," 11.

30. "The Gender Gap and Women's Agenda for Moving Forward," Memo. Washington, D.C.: Lake Snell Perry and Associates, November 9, 2004.

31. Douglas and Michaels, *Mommy Myth*, 22.

5

Women Voters, Women Candidates

Is There a Gender Gap in Support for Women Candidates?

KATHLEEN A. DOLAN

Over the past twenty-five years or so, gender gaps have been visible in many different aspects of American politics—for example, party identification, vote choice for president, and public opinion on policy issues. These gaps have been present for a good period of time and, although the size of the gap between women and men on any particular political concern can ebb and flow, their direction is fairly stable. Since the 1980s, women in the United States tend to be more likely to identify themselves as Democrats than men, vote for Democratic presidential candidates in higher proportions than men, and take particular positions on social, economic, and moral issues.

There is another area, however, in which people assume a gender gap exists—support for women candidates. Conventional wisdom and intuition could cause even the most casual observer of American politics to assume that women voters would more naturally support women candidates more often than men voters would. Although there is often anecdotal evidence of the presence of this "affinity effect," and some empirical support for the claim, there is little to support a conclusion that there is a stable, permanent gender gap in support for women candidates. Instead, the degree to which women voters support women candidates is shaped by several important factors beyond a shared sex/gender identity. The goal of this article, then, is to more closely examine the evidence for a gender gap in support for women candidates to determine whether any gender gap is a long-term, stable part of our political life or a more limited short-term occurrence that is shaped by the context of a particular election.

Why Should We Expect a Gender Gap
in Support for Women Candidates?

The notion that women voters should be an automatic base of support for women candidates has been an implicit, and sometimes explicit, assumption of much of the work done on women candidates. This work suggests that there are several reasons we should expect this gender gap to emerge. First, women may vote for women candidates because they seek descriptive representation. Here we mean that women voters who are mindful of the underrepresentation of women in elected office may choose women candidates because they want to change the status quo. That women would be more likely to act on an interest in descriptive representation than would men is obvious from the current figures on women's presence in elected office in the United States. In 2006, women held 15 percent of the seats in Congress, 25 percent of statewide elected offices, and 23 percent of the seats in state legislatures.[1] Indeed, Rosenthal found that women have a stronger preference for same-sex representation than do men.[2] Other recent studies have confirmed the idea that women are more likely to desire same-sex representation than are men. Posing questions about a hypothetical election race between a woman and a man, Sanbonmatsu demonstrated that women were more likely to prefer candidates of a particular sex than were men and were more likely to prefer women, while men had less of an identifiable sense of gender affinity at work when choosing candidates.[3] This may well be because men in the United States are not in a position of feeling underrepresented in governing bodies and, as a result, do not need to seek out male representation for this reason. Women, on the other hand, have a quite different experience and may use their vote to address the situation.

Women voters may well seek to increase the presence of women in office by voting for women candidates, but it is probably a bit simplistic to assume that women voters will vote for someone simply because of her sex. Instead, other research suggests that a sense of shared gender identity may motivate women voters to select women candidates. Here these positive feelings toward women candidates "as women" are shaped, perhaps, by a sense that women's political fortunes are bound up with other women.[4] Beyond feelings of gender affinity, issues can play an important role in the relationship between women voters and women candidates. Past work demonstrates that there are "group-salient" issues that draw women voters to women candidates. Issues like sexual harassment, abortion, or child care tend to be of greater importance to women voters and they may see women candidates as uniquely suited to dealing with these issues.[5] Indeed, most of the research that finds a gender gap in support for a woman candidate points to a role for issues in the support that women voters give women candidates. For example, in examining support for women candidates for the U.S. Senate in 1992, Paolino found no evidence that women supported women simply because of their sex.[6] Instead, it was the interplay of issues such as the underrepresentation of women in office and sexual harassment that drew women voters to women candidates. Plutzer and Zipp found that all women running for governor or U.S. Senate in that year did not enjoy a boost in support from women.[7] The races in which women voters were more likely to choose women candidates were those in which the woman candidate ran "as women" on gendered issues. More recent research on the elections of 1996 and 1998 at local, state, and congressional levels found that women who campaigned on issues of importance to women and targeted their appeals to women's groups were more likely to reap an electoral benefit than other candidates.[8] Clearly then, it would seem that issues can help make the link between women voters and women candidates that a shared sex itself might not provide.

Finally, any greater likelihood that women voters will chose women candidates may be based not so much on a shared gender identity, but instead on a set of ideological or partisan sympathies. In the contemporary period, women in the United States are more likely to identify with the Democratic Party than the Republican Party, and more women candidates run for office as Democrats than as Republicans. Since 1990, 65 percent of the women who have run for Congress have done so as Democrats.[9] During that same period, 55 percent of women in the public identify themselves as Democrats.[10] It may be the case then that women voters are simply choosing candidates of their party, many of whom happen to be women. This overlap in party location of women voters and women candidates makes it difficult to really identify a gender gap in support for women candidates because there is a gender gap in almost every election in the United States between a Democrat and a Republican. Some argue that the key to identifying a gender gap in support for women candidates requires us to see if women prefer women even after considering political party.[11] The complexity of the party/sex overlap is demonstrated by some research that found women candidates receiving greater support from women voters than from men. For example, Cook examines voter support for ten women candidates for U.S. Senate in 1992, all Democrats.[12] Fox examines voter support for four women candidates for governor and U.S. Senate in California in 1992 and 1994.[13] Again, the women candidates were all Democrats. So although these women candidates may have been receiving an electoral boost from the support of women voters, it is difficult to tell how much of this support was motivated by their sex and how much was driven by a shared party or ideological orientation.

There are reasons, both empirical and intuitive, that should cause us to expect a gender gap in support for women candidates. Yet, at the same time, we know that women voters do not always vote for women candidates, and some women never do. And to assume an affinity effect in some way reduces women to naive, reflexive political actors who choose candidates based on one outward characteristic. Instead, women may be more likely to choose women candidates than men voters would be, but this dynamic is probably shaped by the same political forces that shape other vote choice decisions— incumbency, political party, race, and the level of office being sought. For example, some studies have demonstrated that certain subgroups of women— African Americans, liberals, feminists, and well-educated women—are more likely to choose women candidates than are other women.[14] Other work has shown that women voters may be more likely to choose women candidates in some circumstances—for example, when they are incumbents or running for a particular office—than others.[15] Indeed, understanding the complexity of the gender gap in voting for women candidates is the goal of this article.

Evaluations of Women in Politics

One of the first ways we can examine whether there is a gender gap in support for women candidates is to think about how people evaluate those women. Acceptance of women candidates or other women in the political world is built on a set of attitudes people have about whether politics is a suitable endeavor for women. Generally, public opinion polling tells us that peoples' attitudes toward women in the political arena have changed dramatically over time, moving toward being more accepting of women and seeing women as having the appropriate abilities to take part in governing.

Table 5.1 presents data on how the public responds to questions about whether politics is appropriate for women. These data are from the General Social Survey and the National Election Studies, two long-standing surveys of the American public. On each question there is a clear evolution in public thinking about women in a more "liberal" or accepting direction. For example, in considering whether women should have an equal role with men in social and political life, 50 percent of respondents in 1974 agreed. After steady increases through the 1980s and 1990s, by 2004, 78 percent agreed with this position. The same general pattern is evident on the question of

Table 5.1. Attitudes about Womens' Capacity for Politics, 1974–2004

	Equal Role for Women and Men (Agree)[a]		
	Women	Men	All
1974	49%	53%	50%
1984	52	56	53
1994	64	67	65
2004	79	77	78
	Men Better Suited for Politics than Women (Disagree)[b]		
	Women	Men	All
1974	54%	53%	53%
1984	61	62	61
1994	80	78	79
2004	77	72	75
	Women Take Care of Home, Not Country (Disagree)[b]		
	Women	Men	All
1974	65%	64%	64%
1984	73	75	74
1994	86	85	86

[a] National Election Study, 1972–2004.
[b] General Social Survey, 1972–2002.

whether men are better suited for politics than are women and whether women should take care of home, not country. Further, there is no obvious gender gap on any of these issues. The evolution in thinking about women in political life has followed the same general path for women and men, and this evolution seems to have taken place at about the same rate. The differences in response between women and men are generally very small, about one or two percentage points. The only real exception to that is the 5.4 percent difference in 2004 in response to the question of whether men are better suited for politics than women. Here, women are more likely to disagree than women, but, again, the difference is small.

On the question of whether women can make a positive contribution to government, we see a fairly significant gender gap. At several points since 1975, Gallup has asked people, "Do you think this country would be governed better or governed worse if more women were in political office?"[16] Table 5.2 presents the findings on this question for the period 1975–2000. Clearly, as we have seen with other attitudinal issues, the American public has become more supportive of the idea of women in government over time. Today, women actually seem to have a bit of an advantage in the minds of the public, with 57 percent of respondents saying that this country would be governed better with more women in office. This is opposed to the 17 percent who think more women would cause us to be governed less well. When we break things out by sex, we see that women are considerably more likely to believe that increasing the number of women in office would be a positive for our country, 64 percent to 50 percent of men. Clearly women and men are responding to different ideas about whether there is something about women that makes them better at governing, which is a significant turnaround from a time when being a woman was seen as a liability in the public world.

Another question about women's place in politics that pollsters have long asked gauges public reaction to the idea of a woman president. In 1936, the American Institute for Public Opinion (now the Gallup Organization) began asking the following question: "Would you vote for a woman for president if she were qualified in every other respect?" Clearly, the wording of the question reveals some sense that it was indeed a woman's sex that was the disqualifying characteristic. Not surprisingly, 65 percent of respondents in 1936 said no.[17] However, over time, the question wording and the public response changed. By the 1950s, a majority of the public supported the idea of a woman president. Since the 1970s, support for a woman president has climbed steadily, reaching the current levels of 92 to 95 percent, depending on the poll. As with the general attitudes on women in political and social life, there is not much of an obvious gender gap in support for a woman president. The data at the bottom of Table 5.2 demonstrate that women and

Table 5.2. Attitudes about Women in Political Office, 1974–2002

U.S. Governed Better with More Women in Office[a]		
	Women	Men	All
1975	36%	29%	33%
1984	32	24	28
2000	64	50	57
Vote for a Qualified Woman for President[b]		
	Women	Men	All
1974	80	81	80
1984	80	85	82
1994	92	92	92
2002	93	95	94

[a] Gallup Poll, January 4, 2001.
[b] General Social Survey, 1972–2002.

men have been equally supportive and have experienced increases in support that are very similar over the years.

One recent survey framed the question of a woman president a bit differently. A CBS poll done in February 2006 found 92 percent of the public expressing willingness to vote for a woman for president.[18] But when asked the question whether "America is ready for a woman president," only 55 percent said yes. So it would appear that many Americans see themselves as willing to support a woman president, but are not so sure that others would do the same. Interestingly, men are more likely to say that America is ready for a woman president than are women, by 60 percent to 51 percent. Although the survey does not get at the reasons why people think we are ready or not, it may be that women, who have more immediate contact with gender issues on a day-to-day basis, are less optimistic about the country's openness to women at the highest level.

There are two other points to consider when thinking about public reactions to women in politics. First, the attitudes revealed in Tables 5.1 and 5.2 are in response to questions about women and men in general or a hypothetical "woman president." It may well be the case that peoples' attitudes about specific women and men could be different. One aspect of supporting political candidates and leaders is assessing their potential for success in office. Peoples' general impressions of how the sexes are situated on any particular personality trait may or may not be relevant to their evaluation of a particular candidate or leader in the political world. For example, recent polling data demonstrated that the two women most frequently mentioned as presidential candidates in 2008, Hillary Rodham Clinton and Condoleezza Rice, were each supported by half of the survey respondents and opposed by half of the respondents.[19] Therefore, we should be open to the possibility that not every individual woman leader will be evaluated as competent and capable by the public or be supported at levels as high as those seen for hypothetical candidates. Second, we should keep in mind that questions that ask people to express opinions on sensitive social issues like sex/gender or race may cause some respondents to offer "socially desirable" answers. Whether they want to appear more enlightened to the interviewer or wish to hide their sexism, some respondents may offer a position that masks their true feelings. On the other hand, the 10 percent of the public that thinks that a woman's place is in the home and the 25 percent that thinks that men are better suited for politics than women in 2004 does tell us that women candidates and officeholders could still experience critical evaluation from some people.

Evaluations of Women Candidates

Although the information discussed above provides a rich source of understanding of how women and men think about women in the political world,
the major limitation is that all of these questions deal with hypothetical or
generic women in politics. As discussed earlier, it is probably too simplistic to think that people will react to a political candidate or leader simply
on the basis of her sex. Instead, people most likely evaluate women candidates after considering all relevant political factors—for example, political
party, issue positions, and incumbency. For this reason, it is important to
examine how voters who have actually been faced with women candidates
evaluate them. One way to do this is by using data from the National Election Studies (NES). The National Election Studies are biennial surveys of a
random sample of adults in the United States that asks about a wide range
of political opinions and actions. One thing people are asked to do is offer
evaluations of the candidates running for the U.S. House of Representatives
in their district. We can use these data to see how people evaluated women
who ran for the House from 1990 to 2000 and see if there is a gender gap in
these evaluations. The analysis presented here focuses on three aspects of
these evaluations: (1) how much information women and men have about
women candidates; (2) how women and men evaluate the ideology of women
candidates; and (3) whether women and men feel positively or negatively
toward women candidates. Because the NES asks people for their reactions
to the candidates from each major party, the findings are presented separately for Democratic and Republican candidates. This is an added benefit,
in that it allows us to determine if women and men evaluate Democratic
and Republican women in a similar or different fashion.

INFORMATION

One aspect of evaluating women candidates for whom we might expect a
gender gap is the amount of information people have about these women.
Information is an important precursor to electoral support because people
generally will not vote for a candidate about whom they know little or nothing. If there is an assumption that women voters are more likely drawn to
women candidates than are men because women candidates provide some
sort of descriptive representation, then we might assume that women voters would have more information about these women, perhaps a heightened
sense of awareness of the presence of women candidates. We can examine
this by employing a series of questions in the NES that allow us to measure

how much information people possess about their congressional candidates. If women voters are more attuned to the presence of women candidates in the political environment, then we would expect to see differences in the amounts of information about these candidates held by women and men. Contrary to what a gender affinity hypothesis would expect, there are no significant differences in the amount of information women and men have about women candidates. In evaluating Democratic women, women voters tend to have a bit more information about them than do men (women's mean = 1.47, men's mean = 1.37). For Republican women, the opposite is true, with men having just a bit more information than women (women's mean = 1.14, men's mean = 1.39). Figure 5.1a demonstrates, however, that the differences are very small and are not significant at all. We can draw from this, then, a sense that women in the public are no more or less attuned to the presence of women candidates than are men and that women candidates are successful in making themselves known to the public generally.

POLITICAL IDEOLOGY

There is a significant literature that demonstrates that the public views women candidates through a consistent lens of gender stereotypes. One of the forms that these evaluations take is the fairly common assumption that women candidates are more liberal than men candidates.[20] Recent work has demonstrated that people perceive women candidates as even more liberal than they actually are.[21] Yet there is little work that examines whether women and men in the public perceive women candidates in the same way ideologically. Figure 5.1b presents data from the NES, which asked people to rate the ideology of their district's candidates for the House on a seven-point scale, on which 1 is "extremely liberal" and 7 is "extremely conservative." Taking women Democratic candidates first, we see that there is no gender gap in ideological evaluations of these women: women and men both see Democratic women as more liberal than conservative, but the difference in their evaluations is not significant (women's mean = 3.35, men's = 3.23). However, in looking at evaluations of Republican women candidates, we see a more significant gender gap. Men tend to see Republican women candidates as more conservative than women do (women's mean = 4.37, men's = 4.76) and the difference, while not enormous, is statistically significant. Unfortunately, NES data do not allow us to determine why this difference occurs. But one possible explanation might be that women in the public, who tend to be more liberal than men, may project an expectation of greater liberalism on women candidates, regardless of party.

Figure 5.1. Evaluations of women candidates for U.S. House of Representatives, 1990–2000. *Source:* Dolan 2004.

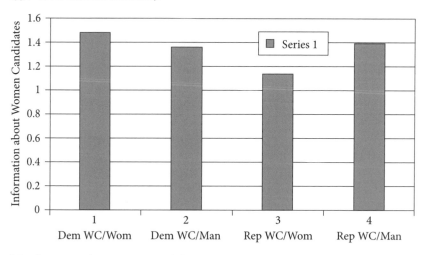

(a) Information about women candidates

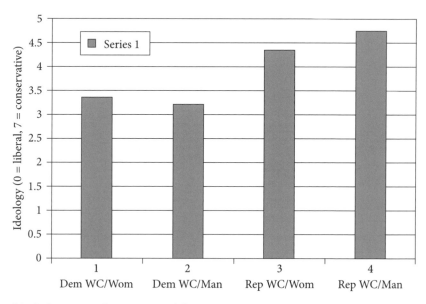

(b) ideology scores for women candidates

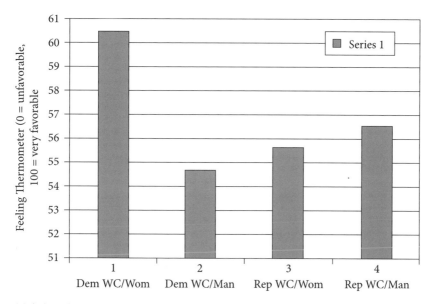

(c) feeling thermometer scores for women candidates

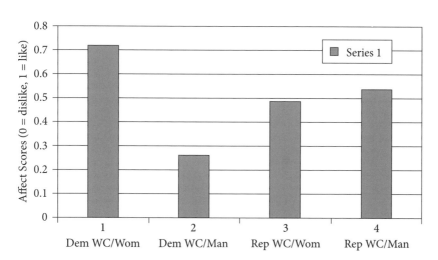

(d) affect scores for women candidates

AFFECT

Beyond evaluating candidate ideology, the NES asks respondents to offer some sense of how they feel about the candidates. This measure of candidate affect takes two forms: one is a question that asks people to rate how warmly they feel toward each candidate on a scale where 0 is "unfavorable/don't care for" and 100 is a "favorable/warm" evaluation. The second is a count of the positive and negative comments that each respondent makes about each House candidate. If the expectation of a gender gap in support for women candidates is based, in part, on the idea that women have a gender affinity with women candidates, then it should follow that they feel more warmly toward women candidates. Here again we see important differences in how people evaluate women candidates based on their political party. As the data in Figure 5.1c and 5.1d indicate, there are no significant differences in the way that women and men feel about Republican women candidates on either measure of affect. For example, women give Republican women candidates an average feeling thermometer score of 55.7 out of 100, while men give them a score of 56.6. However, we see fairly large differences between women and men in their affect toward Democratic women candidates. There is a six-point difference in the feeling thermometer scores assigned by women and men to Democratic women candidates, with women being more favorable. And there is a large and significant difference in the number of positive comments women and men made about Democratic women (women's mean = .71, men's mean = .26). Clearly, women in the NES sample feel much more positively about Democratic women candidates than do men. This could be evidence of the importance of "party overlap" between women in the public and women candidates: a greater likelihood of a shared party identity could be leading to higher support scores.

Voting for Women Candidates

Although understanding evaluations of women candidates is an important element of examining their possibilities for success, it is whether they can attract votes that really counts. Most of the recent research on this question indicates that women candidates can win votes at the same rate as similar men candidates.[22] Any traces of bias that once limited the electoral success of women candidates seems to have disappeared. However, knowing that women candidates don't suffer a disadvantage at the polls does not mean that all groups of people support them equally. As the works cited earlier suggest, there is a lingering assumption that women voters will be more likely to choose women candidates than will men. The same NES data used to determine the types of information people hold about women candidates also allows us to examine whether there is a gender gap in voting for them. The findings presented here include all U.S. House and Senate races from 1990–2000 in which a woman ran against a man in the congressional districts and states included in the NES sample.

The notion that an "affinity effect" makes women voters more likely to choose women candidates than men voters does appear to have some support from these data, but the relationship is not overwhelming. In House races, women voters are more likely to vote for the woman candidate than men voters are. Figure 5.2 compares the likelihood of a woman voting for a woman candidate in these races to that of a man voter. Although women voters are more likely than men to choose women candidates in these House races, they are not overwhelmingly more likely to. On a continuum where completely rejecting women candidates is 0 and perfect support for them is 1, women's likelihood of voting for women House candidates is .59, which is just more than fifty-fifty odds. The likelihood of men voting for women is .50. Thus, women are more likely to vote for women House candidates in this time period than are men, but the difference, while significant, is not enormous. Also, in Senate elections, women voters are no more likely than men voters to choose a woman candidate (not shown). That we only find an affinity effect for House races and not Senate elections may have more to do with the characteristics of these two types of election and less to do with how people feel about women candidates. Past research tells us that House elections are rather low-visibility affairs in which voters may not have much information about the candidates. In this situation, candidate sex may be important to voters in the absence of other information.[23] Senate elections, however, have much higher visibility and voters are usually more familiar with the candidates. With more information, voters may make their vote choice based on issues or other information they possess.

So, although women may be more likely to vote for women than are men in some cases, this relationship does not hold in all circumstances. Nor does it hold true all of the time. When each election from 1990 to 2004 is analyzed separately (not shown), women were more likely than men to choose women candidates in House elections in only one year, 1992, the so-called year of the woman. And, interestingly, in 1994, men voters were more likely to choose women candidates in Senate races than were women voters. So, over eight election years, women were more likely to vote for women candidates in

Figure 5.2. Voting for women candidates for U.S. House of Representatives, 1990–2000. *Source:* Dolan 2004.

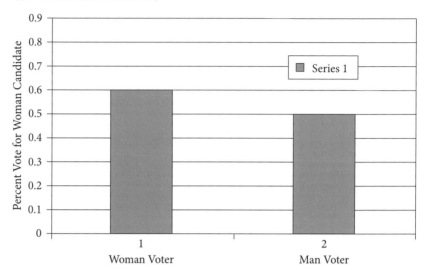

(a) Impact of voter sex on vote for woman

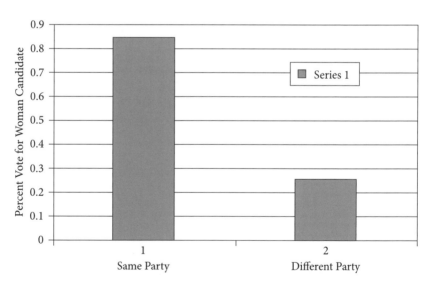

(b) impact of party identification on vote for women candidate

(c) impact of incumbancy on vote for women candidate

only one of those years and for only one chamber, the House. This does not speak to a long-term, enduring gender gap in support for women candidates. Instead, these findings suggest that the potential for women voters to favor women candidates is there, but a simple shared sex identity may not be strong enough to determine women's votes in specific electoral situations.

One of the primary reasons that the affinity effect is not stronger in voting for women candidates is the power of two other important political variables: political party identification and incumbency. From 1990 to 2000, in races for both the House and the Senate, and in each of the individual election years, the most important variables in determining whether a voter would choose a woman candidate were whether the voter and the woman candidate shared the same party identification and whether that woman candidate was an incumbent (Figure 5.2). Election scholars have long understood that these two variables are the most important in shaping vote choice, and this dynamic is no different when women candidates are involved.[24] Voters approach elections predisposed to vote for the candidate of their party and/or the incumbent and often need a strong reason to deviate from that choice. For many voters, even women, candidate sex is not sufficient to pull someone toward a candidate of the other party. In the current time period, when women voters are more likely to identify with Democrats than Republicans, and women candidates are more likely to run as Democrats than Republicans, what appears to be an affinity based on sex may really be an overlap of partisan preferences. Given the power of party identification, it is hard to imagine that many Democratic women voters would choose a Republican candidate simply because she was a woman, or vice versa.

Conclusion

One of the most common intuitive assumptions regarding women candidates is that they attract much, perhaps most, of their support from women voters. Given women's dramatic underrepresentation in elected office in the United States, it makes some sense to think that women voters would try to change this reality by supporting women candidates in large numbers. However, like so much of what we see as "conventional wisdom," there is only limited support for the notion that women favor women candidates at significantly higher levels than do men. The data presented here demonstrate that there are relatively few differences in the attitudes that women and men hold about women candidates, and those differences that do exist tend to be small. Further, those differences tend to be in how women and men evaluated Democratic women candidates, but not Republican women, signaling that candidate party matters alongside candidate sex. Both women and men are generally supportive of women's place in the political world and see politics as an appropriate venue for women's participation. Both women and men voice high levels of support for the (still hypothetical) idea of a woman president. And, in the way that "support" matters most, there is only limited evidence of women voters favoring women candidates at higher rates than men.

All things being equal, many women probably would like to support women candidates. The notion of seeing government bodies becoming more representative could be a powerful motivator. But things are rarely equal in politics. Voters, both women and men, are influenced first and foremost by political party identification and the power of incumbency, whether women candidates are on the ballot or not. Women candidates are not simply women and they present voters with a complex mix of sex, party, and experience considerations that those voters must weigh when deciding their vote. And women voters are not simply women. Instead, they approach political decisions with more than their sex identity to guide them. So although there may well be times when women voters are more likely to support women candidates than are men, this correspondence probably occurs when party, issue, and identity considerations align.

Notes

1. Center for the American Woman and Politics (CAWP), "Women in Elective Office 2006."
2. Rosenthal, "Role of Gender in Descriptive Representation."
3. Sanbonmatsu, "Gender Stereotypes and Vote Choice."
4. Rinehart, *Gender Consciousness and Politics.*
5. Paolino, "Group-Salient Issues and Group Representation."
6. Ibid.
7. Plutzer and Zipp, "Identity Politics, Partisanship, and Voting for Women Candidates."
8. Herrnson et al., "Women Running 'as Women.'"
9. Center for the American Woman and Politics (CAWP). "Women Candidates for Congress 1974–2004."
10. American National Election Studies (ANES), *ANES Guide to Public Opinion and Electoral Behavior.*
11. Seltzer et al., *Sex as a Political Variable.*
12. Cook, "Voter Responses to Women Senate Candidates," in Cook, Thomas, and Wilcox, *Year of the Woman.*
13. Fox, *Gender Dynamics in Congressional Elections.*
14. Ekstrand and Eckert. "Impact of Candidate's Sex on Voter Choice"; Lewis, "Are Women for Women?"; Sigelman and Welch, "Race, Gender, and Opinion toward Black and Female Candidates"; Smith and Fox, "Electoral Fortunes of Women Candidates for Congress."
15. Cook, "Voter Responses to Women Senate Candidates," in Cook, Thomas, and Wilcox, *Year of the Woman*; Dolan, *Voting for Women*; Dolan, "Voting for Women in the 'Year of the Woman.'"
16. Simmons, "Majority of Americans Say More Women in Political Office Would Be Positive."
17. Smith, "Study of Trends in the Political Role of Women."
18. "Ready for a Woman President?" 2006. CBS News, February 5.
19. Moore, "Hillary/Condi Polarize Electorate."
20. Alexander and Andersen, "Gender as a Factor in the Attribution of Leadership Traits"; Huddy and Terkildsen, "Gender Stereotypes and the Perception of Male and Female Candidates"; McDermott, "Voting Cues in Low-Information Elections."
21. Koch, "Gender Stereotypes and Citizens' Impression."
22. Burrell, *Women's Place Is in the House*; Dolan, *Voting for Women*; Seltzer et al., *Sex as a Political Variable.*
23. McDermott, "Voting Cues in Low-Information Elections."
24. Campbell et al., *American Voter*; Jacobson, *Politics of Congressional Elections.*

6

Using Exit Polls to Explore the Gender Gap in Campaigns for Senate and Governor

MARGIE OMERO

Being a political pollster, I regularly ask voters in focus groups and surveys to describe how they make voting decisions and political judgments. In much the way people make other judgments, voters use shortcuts to make sense of the political landscape around them. For example, voters might lament that all elected officials are "liars," or "crooked," or "in the pocket of special interests," with "special interests" referring mainly to organizations with which respondents disagree. And although voters often admit that they should "check the record" of their elected officials to see exactly how they vote, they usually use heuristics such as party affiliation, gender, or, in this last election, allegiance to President Bush to judge whether a candidate shares their own positions. Investigating and measuring these voter shortcuts is part of the responsibility of a pollster.

Not only do voters make assumptions, but campaigns and political operatives make assumptions as well. Some of these assumptions will be about voter preferences and can be easily tested through polling, such as, "Suburban women are concerned about education," or "Older voters care about Social Security," or "Rural men rarely vote Democratic." But other assumptions are about campaign environments and are less frequently examined through research. One common piece of campaign political wisdom is that women make more successful legislative candidates than gubernatorial candidates.[1] The theory is that voters view women as less well-equipped to lead on their own, but are aptly suited to work in a collaborative environment as a legislator. (Certainly that is also the basis of discussion of the attractiveness of a woman presidential candidate.) Another commonly held view is that women will cross party lines to vote for a woman, whether it is a Democratic woman candidate attracting support from Republican women, or a Republican woman candidate attracting Democratic women.

It is not surprising that voters use political shortcuts to make interpretations of their surroundings a bit easier. However, political professionals, whose livelihoods literally depend on the success of campaigns, also use shortcuts when they think about campaigns, perhaps citing a single campaign from their background as "evidence." These shortcuts can inform the decisions of political parties, donors, and candidates themselves. Just as voters rarely "check the record" of their officials to see exactly how they stand on the issues important to them, political operatives do not often "check the research" to see if their assumptions about voters and campaigns hold water.

This article examines some of these heuristics, using the tools commonly used by pollsters and political professionals—results, exit polls, and multivariate analysis. In particular, the success of women candidates for Senate compared to governor and the importance of the party affiliation of a woman candidate to the size of the gender gap, as compared to other variables such as the party leanings of a state and a race's competitiveness, are all examined.

Methodology and Sources

This article analyzes publicly available Voter News Service (VNS) exit polls from 1998 and 2000 and Edison/Mitofsky's 2004 exit polls provided by the media consortium (there were no public exit polls in 2002). Public results from 145 gubernatorial and Senate races in 1998, 2000, and 2004 from CNN and MSNBC reports have all been compiled. Because the data collected and questionnaire wording vary somewhat from election to election and from state to state, analysis is limited to basic information from the exit polls and what is known to be true of the elections (such as the party of the incumbent). Also calculated are additional variables, such as the gender gap itself (defined below) and "switch in party control," in which the election causes a seat to change party hands. Some states, such as Alaska, do not have public exit polling available for their statewide races, and were thus omitted from the data set. States where a third-party candidate won (such as the Minnesota governor's race of 1998) were also omitted from the data set. A variable list is included in an appendix.

There are limitations to this methodology. First, despite their utility in postelection analysis, exit polls themselves have of course come under heavy scrutiny and attack since the 2000 presidential campaign.[2] But even a critical CNN analysis of exit polling in the wake of the 2000 election confirmed exit polls' continued utility in creating postelection analysis.[3] And despite the 2000 incorrect call in the presidential race, there was not a single incorrect call in 2004.[4] Further, exit polls provide a unique ability to examine voting behavior the day it occurs, rather than examining recall influenced by the election outcome itself. Lastly, exit polls can compare subgroups of voters across states and across election years using surveys with comparable methodologies.

Another limitation is the use of aggregate, statewide-level data rather than individual, person-level data. Similar studies on gender and vote choice[5] use National Election Studies (NES) data. The risk, therefore, is the ecological fallacy, in which there are strong subgroup interactions that are unobservable with the current methodology. However, part of the purpose of this study is to show how practitioners and nonacademic political professionals can use easily available data to make judgments about the political climate.

Another limitation is that exit poll data on the gender gap among black or Hispanic voters are inconsistent at best, and are chiefly available only in states with sizable minority populations, preventing comparisons to states with smaller minority populations. As such, this article only examines the overall gender gap rather than the gender gap within white voters or within black or Hispanic voters.

In the tables that follow, even when analysis is limited to factual results rather than exit poll–based results (such as candidate gender and which party's candidate won), only the 145 cases in the data set are used for consistency and ease of comparisons.

The Gender Gap in These Data

Other essays in this book go into great detail about the definition of the gender gap and its previous literature and study. This article is not duplicative. However, it is worthwhile to pause briefly to discuss the gender gap in these data and analysis. The gender gap here is defined as others have—the absolute value of the difference between men and women in their vote for the winning candidate. In the data set this article presents, the gender gap is evident; it ranges from zero to eighteen, with a mean of 7.17 and a median of 7.00. Further, women voters clearly skew Democratic. On average, 51.3 percent of women in these exit polls vote for the Democratic candidate, compared to 44.3 percent of men who do the same. Although the same candidate wins with women as with men in 110 of our 145 cases, in the other thirty-five cases, in only one election does the Republican candidate win with women at the same time the Democratic candidate wins with men (that election was the incredibly close 1998 Nevada Senate race between Senator Harry Reid and Representative [now Senator] John Ensign). Thus, the gender gap in the data set clearly exists, and also clearly shows women favoring Democratic candidates.

Women Candidates for Governor and Senate

One of the benefits of looking at the gender gap in Senate and gubernatorial races is that the role of women candidates in the gender gap can be examined. As noted above, the data set consistently shows that women voters are more likely to vote Democratic than Republican. Similarly, women candidates, at least in this data set, are also more likely to be Democratic. Although the overall percentage of women candidates did not vary much across the three elections measured, there were always more Democratic women candidates than Republican women candidates. That was particularly true in 2004, with only one Republican woman candidate, compared to ten across the aisle. The parties put up essentially even numbers of women candidates in 2000.

But it is not just the presence of women candidates that is of interest, but their ultimate victory. The table below shows that Democratic women candidates fare better than do Republican women candidates. In fact, Democratic women have a higher success rate (55 percent) than any other party/gender grouping. Although Democratic men and Republican men are equally likely to succeed in their efforts, Republican women fare least well. Studying whether Republican women fare better or worse when paired against Democratic women is something explored later in the multivariate analysis.

Table 6.1. The Presence of Women Candidates across Election Cycles in Our Data Set

	1998	2000	2004	Total
Democratic male	50	38	28	116
Democratic female	13	6	10	29
Republican male	57	39	37	133
Republican female	6	5	1	12
Total women candidates for year	63	44	38	145
Percentage of Democratic candidates that are women	21%	14%	26%	20%
Percentage of Republican candidates that are women	10%	11%	3%	8%
Percentage of all candidates that are women	15%	13%	14%	14%

One hypothesis here is that women fare better when they run for Senate as opposed to governor. The table below looks at the data from that perspective. Table 6.3 shows that women candidates indeed fare better than do male candidates. Although both Democratic and Republican women do better in Senate races relative to gubernatorial races, this difference is not statistically significant. Two chi-square tests of type of race by party of winner by candidate gender (one test with Democratic candidate gender, one of Republican candidate gender) show no statistical differences by the type of race.

The Gender Gap across Campaign Scenarios

Regardless of the presence of women candidates, the gender gap pervades the races examined. On average, the 145 races show at least a seven-point gender gap (7.17). Some patterns do emerge; in Democratic-dominated races, where either Democrats have an advantage in party identification or in the race itself or liberals have an advantage in ideology, there is a larger gender

Table 6.2. The Success of Women Candidates in Our Data Set

Candidate	Number	Percentage Winning
Democratic women	29	55%
Democratic men	116	49%
Republican women	12	42%
Republican men	133	50%
Total women	41	51%
Total men	249	50%

Table 6.3 Gender of Candidates by Type of Race by Democratic/ Republican Victories

		Total	Percentage of Democratic Wins
Governor	Democratic male	42	45%
	Democratic female	11	45%
Governor	Republican male	47	57%
	Republican female	6	33%
Senator	Democratic male	74	51%
	Democratic female	18	61%
Senator	Republican male	86	47%
	Republican female	6	50%

gap (7.90, 8.29, and 9.47, respectively). Candidate gender may make a difference because races with a Democratic woman have a higher gender gap (8.59) than in all races. The difference between Senate and gubernatorial races appears small. Regionally, races in the South have a larger gender gap than anywhere else (8.33). Table 6.4 highlights these findings and compares the gender gap across different circumstances.

Also examined is the role of a race's competitiveness in the gender gap. Recall the hypothesis that in a lopsided, noncompetitive campaign, voters will be more likely to vote for a candidate based on their own party identification, as well as for who appears to be the inevitable winner. In a competitive campaign, one might hypothesize that voters will pay closer attention to the campaign and be exposed to more messaging through campaign advertising and heated political coverage, and thus use more varied types of information to make their voting decision. This casting about for information is what could potentially lead women voters to women candidates, as opposed to voting simply on party identification.

Political professionals use a shortcut of 60 percent as a sign of an incumbent's ultimate strength on election day. Incumbents who receive above 60 percent of the vote are far less likely to draw strong competition during their next election. Using that boundary, the 145 cases can be divided almost

Table 6.4. The Gender Gap in Different Campaign Environments

	Gender Gap
Total	7.17
Governor race	6.47
Senate race	7.57
Democratic candidate is a woman	8.59
Republican candidate is a woman	6.83
Republican advantage in Party ID	6.16
Democratic advantage in Party ID	7.90
Conservative advantage in ideology	6.86
Liberal advantage in ideology (or even)	9.47
Republican candidate wins	6.00
Democratic candidate wins	8.29
Winning candidate receives < 60	7.71
Winning candidate receives 60+	6.46
Northeast	7.25
Midwest	5.47
South	8.33
West	7.51

evenly; eighty-two of them can be considered "competitive" while the remaining sixty-three are "noncompetitive." Table 6.4 shows that competitive races have a slightly higher gender gap than those that are not.

Predicting the Gender Gap

Many of the classifications discussed above are interrelated. Obviously, the party identification of a state is related to the outcome of a campaign. Ideology and party identification are also related. As noted above, candidate gender may have an effect on the gender gap among voters, and Democratic candidates are more likely to be women than are Republican candidates.

Deliberately omitted from the model are variables from the initial list that build the definition of the gender gap. That is, omitted is candidates' vote share among men and women of either party, as well as the percentage of men or women in each exit poll. However, included is the difference between the two candidates' overall vote share, and the simpler competitive/noncompetitive variable, as defined above as whether a candidate reaches 60 percent of the vote.

To examine the individual impact of each of these environmental factors, a mixed-effects model is used. Because of the lack of 2002 exit polls, campaigns for Senate seats that occurred in both 1998 and 2004 and governor's races (which are typically four-year terms) that occurred in both 2000 and 2004 are overrepresented. To account for the correlation in error terms associated with observations from the same state in different years, the state of each campaign is treated as a random effect. Cases were also weighted by the sample sizes of each exit poll survey. The results in Table 6.5 shed light on the hypotheses outlined and also yield some unexpected findings.

First, as suspected, candidate gender does play a role in the gender gap. A female Democratic candidate is far more likely to drive the gender gap than a female Republican candidate. However, it is difficult to discern whether a Democratic female candidate encourages independent women to vote more Democratic, or whether a female Democratic candidate suppresses Democratic performance among men. However, the data do suggest that it is unlikely that a Republican female candidate will encourage Democratic women to switch parties in sizeable numbers.

Second, the type of race has no bearing on the gender gap. Gubernatorial races are no more likely to create a gender gap than are Senate races, irrespective of candidate gender. The conventional wisdom—that women candidates do worse with men in particular when they run for executive offices—turns out to not be true, when other environmental factors are held equal. Third, the significance of region and election year raise interesting questions. All other significant predicting variables are, to some extent, additional ways of defining a Democratic-dominated climate. The model shows that races in the South and races in 2000 are more likely to have a larger gender gap. Both environments (the 2000 elections and races in the South) had larger-than-average percentages of Democratic victories, as demonstrated in Table 6.6. But the most interesting of the findings is the relationship between party identification and other environmental factors. As shown in Table 6.4, Dem-

Table 6.5. Mixed-Effects Model

	B	SE
Intercept	7.645**	2.00
South	2.645*	1.05
2000 race	1.967**	0.66
2004 race	−1.354*	0.64
Democratic candidate margin over Republican candidate	0.047**	0.02
Democratic party ID advances over Republican party ID	−0.125**	0.04
Liberal advances over conservative	0.121**	0.04
Democratic candidate is a woman	1.449*	0.65
Democratic candidate is an incumbent	0.752	1.47
Incumbent is defeated	0.460	0.93
West	0.420	0.89
Senate race	0.374	0.57
Republican candidate is an incumbent	0.180	1.34
Open seat	−0.242	1.35
Winner received < 60%	−0.719	0.65
Midwest	−1.046	0.92
Republican candidate is a woman	−1.288	1.02

* Significant at 0.05 level.
** Significant at 0.01 level.

Table 6.6. Victories by Region and Year

	1998	2000	2004	Northeast	Midwest	South	West
Percentage of races with Republican victory	57	36	53	50	55	43	51
Percentage of races with Democratic victory	43	64	47	50	45	57	49

ocratic-dominated environments have a larger gender gap. States where the Democratic candidate won, Democrats had the advantage in party identification, or liberals had the advantage in ideology all had a higher gender gap than more-Republican campaign environments. The mixed-effects model confirms the statistical impact of ideology and a Democratic candidate's lead over their Republican opponent. But the negative relationship between Democratic advantage over Republicans in party identification does not, at first, seem consistent with the results from Table 6.4. If states that were more Democratic have a larger gender gap, then what explains the negative relationship in the model?

To explore this finding further, Table 6.7 compares campaigns where the outcome was consistent with the party leanings of the state to those where the outcome was inconsistent.

Table 6.7 helps explain the results from the mixed-effects model. When a Republican wins the election, there is little difference in the gender gap between Democratic-identified states and Republican-identified states. However, when the Democratic candidate wins, the gender gap is substantially larger in states where more voters identify as Democrats. The substantial gender gap in Democratic-identified states with a Democratic winner confirms earlier results that show a larger gender gap in Democratic-dominated climates. But examining the two scenarios in which the winning candidate is not of the state's dominant political party (Democratic win/Republican state: 6.35 gender gap; Republican win/Democratic state: 5.79 gender gap) suggests that the gender gap influences Democratic wins more than Republican wins.

Conclusion

In conclusion, both women voters and women candidates can be crucial to Democratic successes, regardless of the specific office. Democratic women candidates are the group most likely to succeed in their campaigns and are

Table 6.7. Gender Gap by Party ID and Party of Winner

Winner	Party ID Advantage	Gender Gap
Republican	Republican	6.07
Republican	Democrat	5.79
Democrat	Republican	6.35
Democrat	Democrat	9.08

more likely to create unique support among women than are Republican women candidates. Whether a campaign is for an executive position or a legislative position has no impact on the gender gap. The larger the Democratic candidate's advantage over the Republican opponent, the larger the gender gap, illustrating the importance of women voters to decisive Democratic victories. Other factors, such as region and election year, predict the gender gap to the extent they are favorable climates for Democratic candidates. But the competitiveness of a race has no bearing on the gender gap. Rather than relying on the conventional wisdom of how campaigns work or how voters make decisions, I used tools accessible to other political practitioners to examine past election scenarios. In the process, this study proved wrong the conventional wisdom about women's inability to convince voters that they can lead singly and emphasized the electoral successes available to women candidates.

Appendix: Variables Included In the Data Set and Mixed-Effects Model

Variable name	Description
State	State code
Region	4–way census region
Race	Senate or Governor
Year of election	1998, 2000, 2004
Open seat	No/Yes
Democratic incumbent	No/Yes
Republican incumbent	No/Yes
Total Democratic	Percent Democratic candidate receives in exit poll
Total Republican	Percent Republican candidate receives in exit poll
Sex Democratic	Democratic candidate is male/female
Sex Republican	Republican candidate is male/female
Percent Democratic	Percent self-identified Democrats in exit poll
Percent Independent	Percent self-identified independents in exit poll
Democratic party ID advantage	Democrat advantage over Republican in party identification in exit poll
Percent liberal	Percent self-identified liberals in exit poll
Percent moderate	Percent self-identified moderates in exit poll
Liberal advantage	Liberal advantage over conservatives in ideology in exit poll
Percent male	Percentage male in exit poll
Percent female	Percentage female in exit poll
Male Democrat	Percentage of men voting for Democratic candidate in exit poll
Female Democrat	Percentage of women voting for Democratic candidate in exit poll
Male Republican	Percentage of men voting for Republican candidate in exit poll
Female Republican	Percentage of women voting for Republican candidate in exit poll
Democrat advantage	Democratic candidate lead over Republican candidate in exit poll
Winner	Candidate declared winner in actual results (R/D)
Switch	Was an incumbent voted out (No/Yes)
Competitive	If the winner received more than 60% of the vote

Notes

The author would like to thank Joel Middleton of Yale University for invaluable comments and assistance, and Lindsay Marsh of Momentum Analysis for helpful research assistance.

1. Marlantes, "Year of the Woman Governor?"

2. Traugott, Highton, and Brady, *Review of Recent Controversies.*

3. Konner, Risser, and Watternberg, "Television's Performance on Election Night 2000."

4. Edison Media Research and Mitofsky International, "Evaluation of Edison/ Mitofsky Election System 2004." Prepared for the 2005 National Election Pool.

5. Brians, "Women for Women?"

7

Parenthood and the Gender Gap

LAUREL ELDER AND STEVEN GREENE

Becoming a parent and raising children is one of the most life-changing and enduring adult experiences. Having a child and taking on the role of parent may very well bring about changes in one's political outlook and priorities, and these effects may be mediated by gender. Despite significant changes in gender roles in the latter half of the twentieth century, women and men continue to play different roles in the parenting and child-rearing process, with women more likely to be the primary caregivers and nurturers. Some feminist theorists and political scientists have theorized that women's role as mothers and greater involvement in the parenting experience lies behind women's more liberal views on a range of important political issues. Yet political scientists actually know very little about how parenthood affects political attitudes and whether it affects women and men differently, as these theories posit. Exploring the impact of parenthood on political attitudes is critical to contemporary understandings of the politics of family and whether family life is one of the many factors contributing to the gender gap.

The goal of this article is to develop a better understanding of the politics of parenthood and its implications for the gender gap. To do this, we use original data from a national survey conducted in June 2005 of 516 respondents, half of whom were custodial parents of children under eighteen. The unique aspect of this survey is that it contains valid measures of parenthood and detailed measures of parental involvement, both of which are absent from existing data sets on public opinion. We use these data to assess the role of parenthood and parental involvement in shaping political views on a broad range of economic, social, and use-of-force issues and the degree to which this parental impact affects men and women differently.

In brief, we find that parenthood is political and its impacts are mediated by gender. Parental status and involvement are correlated with attitudes on a range of social welfare issues, most of which directly touch on child rearing, including education, government services, child care, and health care and health care importance, and these effects are much more pronounced for mothers than for fathers. Thus, this research adds another piece to our understanding of the complexities of the gender gap by showing that parenthood is one of many factors contributing to its existence.

The Politics of Parenthood: Literature and Hypotheses

As many of the earlier articles in this book have detailed, women and men differ in their preferences on a range of political issues. Although there is scholarly consensus about the existence and political significance of these gender gaps, their causes remain contested, and many of the possible hypotheses are controversial. One hypothesis, and the one most relevant for this study, is the maternalist hypothesis, which posits that women are more liberal on social welfare and use-of-force issues because of their experiences in having and raising children. Pro-family or social feminists, as they have been referred to, argue that the private sphere, specifically women's experience as mothers, is a powerful and valuable political force long neglected by mainstream theorists and liberal feminists.[1] These pro-family theorists argue that women's role as mother and, more important, the actual act of "mothering" shapes women's political worldview. In her writing on the subject, Sara Ruddick has argued that "distinctive ways of thinking arise out of the work mothers do."[2] Similarly, Jean Bethke Elshtain has argued that women's interests in the preservation, protection, and growth of their children fosters a politics of compassion.[3] Turning to specific issues, social feminists have theorized that mothering fosters more liberal or pacifist attitudes toward the use of military force. Ruddick has stated: "Out of maternal practice a distinctive kind of thinking arises that is incompatible with military strategy but consonant with pacifist commitment to non-violence."[4] Additionally, various scholars have hypothesized that women's experience as mothers and the act of nurturing children might be behind women's more liberal views on social welfare issues.[5] The underlying theory behind the maternalist hypothesis is that it is not just being a parent per se that matters politically, but the actual act of "mothering" or "parenting" that has transformative power.

The broader socialization literature, with its emphasis on the importance of persistent social roles and forces in shaping political attitudes, also lends itself to predictions about the impact of parenthood and how parenthood may affect men and women differently. Several studies have documented that there are attitudinal changes associated with key adult experiences, such as joining the workforce, getting married, growing older, and retiring.[6] It seems reasonable to suppose that parenthood would rival these other adult socialization experiences in its potential to bring about changes in adults' political outlooks. Yet although a number of studies within the socialization literature have examined the impact of having children on the level and type of political *participation* among adults,[7] this research has not been extended to political *attitudes*. Once again, this gap in the literature is surprising because parenthood is associated with fairly dramatic and long-term "life space" changes—changes in one's daily life routine and style of living.[8] Parenthood entails having less free time, dealing with tighter finances, and changing how and with whom one socializes.[9] Additionally, having a child brings about a salient new social role as a mother or father, which brings with it considerable responsibilities, worries, and psychological demands, yet also great rewards and joys.[10]

Much like the maternalist perspective, socialization theory predicts that parenthood effects will be mediated by gender because parenthood is, in the aggregate, a more intense experience and salient role for mothers. Even recent studies show that women and men continue to play significantly different roles in the parenting process.[11] Women continue to be the primary nurturers and caregivers and spend significantly more time on child care activities than do fathers, even in families where both parents work. In comparison, men spend less time with their children and more time at work. Not only are expectations about fathers being the economic providers still widely held, but empirical studies show men also respond to becoming parents by increasing their hours at work outside the home.[12] Finally, work done by social scientists has shown that the effects of children on adults' social resources, daily stresses, and psychological well-being vary by gender.[13]

Taken together, the maternalism and socialization theories lead us to expect that parents will have a unique perspective on a subset of political issues. As parents worry about, care for, and interact with their children year after year, they will become increasingly concerned with the issues that affect children's lives, such as education, child care, health care, and safety. We expect parents to prioritize these issues more highly and support more government action and spending in these areas. Second, both perspectives lead us to expect that parenthood effects should be greater for women than men. More specifically, we expect to see motherhood effects on issues where mothers are most involved and responsible, such as health care and child care. Moreover, the maternalism theory predicts that motherhood will exert a broad liberalizing influence on political orientations and will be seen on issues beyond those directly related to child rearing, including war and defense. Finally, both theories suggest that the politicizing force of parenthood lies not simply in becoming a parent, but in the actual act of engaging in the parental role—nurturing and worrying about children. Although we expect that women will be more involved in parenting than men, we hypothesize that the level of parental involvement will be significant predictors of political attitudes for *both* men and women.

Existing research offers mixed support for these hypotheses. In their detailed empirical analysis of the factors contributing to the gender gap, Susan Howell and Christine Day found that having children contributed significantly to the gender gap on social welfare issues. Analyzing 1996 NES data, Howell and Day found that among those without children, the gender gap on their social welfare index was not even significant, but the gap was significant among those with children. They speculate that these results are the product of women's greater child care responsibilities, which foster women to "see a need for or to actually rely on social welfare programs."[14] On the other hand, studies examining attitudes about the Gulf War found no evidence that mothers held distinctive views on war and defense-related issues.[15]

Although the literature cited above leads us to expect parenting may have a liberalizing impact, there are also some reasons to expect the opposite— that parenthood would be associated with more conservative views, particularly on moral and security issues. An underlying assumption in much of the media coverage about parents and elections has been that parents are an inherently conservative group—they are assumed to be opposed to gay marriage or anything that threatens the traditional family and, in the wake of the 9/11 terrorist attacks, more conservative on national security and defense issues.[16] In the aftermath of the 2004 election, some commentators argued that parents, driven by their more-conservative views on these issues, played a pivotal role in the reelection of Republican president George W. Bush.[17] Some support for a conservatizing effect was found by Laura Arnold and Herbert Weisberg in their study of the 1992 presidential election.[18] They found that the parents of young children were more likely to vote for George H. W. Bush than their childless counterparts, a gap that remained significant even when the usual set of controls was added. They attributed this parental effect to the Republican Party's strong emphasis on conservative family values themes in the 1992 election.

The Survey

Existing attempts to look at the empirical impact of parenthood[19] have been hindered by two factors. First, all lack valid measures of parental status. In most studies, the measure of parenthood is the presence of a child under eighteen in the home. Second, and more problematic, all these studies lack measures of parental involvement. In order to overcome these problems, we created a survey including the best and most commonly accepted measures of political attitudes as well as valid measures of parental status and parental involvement. With these data we are able to explore whether it is child rearing that makes women more liberal than men. Moreover, in analyzing both parental status and parental involvement, we develop a more sophisticated understanding of how having and raising children may contribute to the much-discussed gender gap in attitudes and voting.

Our survey was conducted by Knowledge Networks (KN) using a nationally representative Web-based survey. Given the focus of our research on parenthood, our survey oversampled custodial parents of children under eighteen so that they were half the sample, rather than the roughly one-third that they compose of the overall U.S. population. Our final survey included 256 respondents with custodial children and 260 respondents without.[20]

Measuring Parenthood

Although at first glance parenthood may seem like a fairly easy concept to measure, it is much more difficult in practice. On the National Election Studies (NES) and the General Social Survey (GSS), the primary measures of parenthood are a series of questions asking how many children under the ages of six, twelve, and eighteen are living in the respondent's household.[21] The problems with using such questions as a proxy measure of parenthood are numerous and we designed our survey to overcome those problems. First, our survey not only identified whether there were children under eighteen in the household, but also asked the respondent whether he/she was in fact the parent or stepparent of any of those children. We found that 10 percent of respondents were living with at least one child under eighteen but were not the parent or stepparent of any of these children. Additionally, our survey asked whether there was a child under eighteen living in the household *at least some of the time* to capture parents who have only partial custody of their children. Finally, our survey asked those who said they did not have children under eighteen if they had ever been parents so we could distinguish between parents of grown children and those who have never had children.

Most important, in our survey we sought to measure parental involvement. Both the socialization and maternalist theories argue that it is not parental status that matters, but engaging in the parental role—caring for, worrying about, and tending to the emotional and physical needs of children—that has the potential to generate attitude change. Thus, a dichotomous measure of parenthood is not sufficient to adequately test the hypotheses these theories generate because it does nothing to capture the wide range among adults with children in terms of how much parenting they actually engage in. Some parents spend virtually every hour of their day with their children, know the name of every one of their children's friends, and are responsible for bringing their children to the doctor and dentist, while other parents rely on others (i.e., spouse, nanny, or the child's grandparent) for some or the majority of their child-care responsibilities. Thus, we have created a measure of parental involvement that allows us to differentiate among the full range of parents in terms of their overall commitment to and involvement in rearing their children.

Although a number of studies within these fields have examined parental involvement, there is no "gold standard" measure. Therefore, we created our own measure of parental involvement that draws on measures of parental involvement used in the studies of sociologists, psychologists, and family studies experts.[22] Our parental-involvement scale has two dimensions: parental allocation of time to children and responsibility for children's care. The time measure asks parents how much time they spend with their children on working and nonworking days. The responsibility questions ask the parent to assess on a one-to-five scale the level to which he/she is responsible for various aspects of their child's care, including education, health care, child care, social arrangements, meals, and nurturing. Our questions concerning parental responsibility were designed with a number of different possible examples, so as not to be biased toward parents of children of specific age groups. For parsimony in our analyses and because these two measures of parenthood loaded on a single factor, we combined them into a single parental-involvement index. Complete details on this and all other measures are available in the appendix. Not only do we believe that our measures have significant face validity in assessing parental involvement in child rearing, but also the fact that these measures consistently show prominent gender gaps makes them especially useful in examining how parenthood interacts with gender in shaping political attitudes.

Additional Measures

Our primary interest in parenthood and parental involvement is how well they can explain political issue attitudes. We therefore included a broad assortment of issues addressing economic policy and scope of government, social policy, security policy, and issues of particular relevance to parents. The specific issues we included were: government services, military and defense policy, health care, government support for child care, abortion, the Iraq war, gun control, gay marriage, and presidential vote in 2004. Furthermore, parenthood certainly has the potential to impact not only issue position, but also the priority individuals place on particular issues. We therefore included measures of issue importance for defense spending, heath care, abortion, and education. We used the exact American National Election Studies (ANES) question wording on all issues except abortion, gay marriage, child care, and education.[23] We also included the traditional party identification measure. Complete details on these variables are available in the appendix.

There are a number of important demographic variables that may be correlated with both parenthood and issue attitudes, which we included in our analyses. Studies have shown marriage to have a conservatizing effect above and beyond other variables and that married people are likely to be Republican.[24] Moreover, it is possible that the partisan or political implications of parenthood may be different for married and unmarried people. We therefore included a dummy variable in our regression models indicating married people. Parents of children under eighteen typically fall into a confined age range, so parenthood effects might actually be age or generational effects. We therefore include age measured in years. Others argue that the experience of motherhood is significantly different for nonwhite women because of different family structures, economic positions, and additional issues such as racism.[25] We used a dummy variable to indicate white respondents. Because the social issues are clearly related to religiosity, we use frequency of church attendance (for Christians only) as a control in our multivariate models. Finally, we include the standard demographic controls of education, income, and gender.

The Impact of Parenthood on Political Attitudes: Parents versus Nonparents

We think the most appropriate place to begin our analyses is to simply compare the mean values on the various issues between parents with children in the home and people who have never had children. Although this is a fairly basic analysis, our data set is unique in that it allows us to compare custodial parents to a baseline of persons who have never had children, as opposed to lumping the childless in with those who have grown children.[26] Perhaps the most notable feature of the results in Table 7.1 is that parenthood only has a significant impact on a small subset of issues and priorities. Somewhat surprisingly, there is no relationship between parenthood and defense, the environment, gun control, the Iraq war, and health care, nor with issue priorities on defense, abortion, and health care.[27]

Table 7.1 shows, however, that parenthood is a significant predictor of attitudes on government spending and services, education, and gay marriage. Although Table 7.1 only presents differences of means, it is very important to note that parenthood does appear to play a causal role on these three identified issues because the impact of parenthood remains significant when

Table 7.1. Issue Positions of Parents and Nonparents

	Parents with Children at Home	No Children
Vote for Bush	.53	.46
Government services	4.91*	4.38*
Defense spending	4.07	3.96
Defense importance	3.16	3.26
Health care	3.38	3.53
Health care importance	4.10	3.97
Environment	3.28	3.38
Abortion	2.56	2.43
Abortion importance	3.31	3.19
Education importance	4.11*	3.66*
Child care	3.56	3.86
Opposition to gay marriage	.52*	.38*
Opposition to gun control	2.16	2.13
Support for Iraq War	2.51	2.41

* Indicates means are significantly different at $p \leq .05$.
Note: The impact of parenthood on the variable in question in starred (*) cells remains statistically significant in regression models with controls for age, race, marital status, education, party ID, income, employment status, gender, region, and religiosity.

they are included in a regression model along with race, marital status, age, education, party identification, income, employment status, gender, region, and religiosity. Thus, we can be confident that the "parent gap" is not a by-product of the marriage gap, the confined age range of parents, or other potential confounding variables.

Two of the issues on which parents are distinctive are closely related to the parenting role. Given the role of education in family life, it is not surprising that we find parents placing more emphasis on this issue. Additionally, there is a significant difference between parents and nonparents on government spending and services. Parents are more liberal on this issue, meaning they are more likely than their childless counterparts to think the government should provide more services in areas such as health care and education even if it means an increase in government spending. As others have before us, we speculate that becoming a parent makes people more aware of the need for and immediate benefits of government services such as good public schools and quality health care for children. Although we do not display the results, it is also worth noting that in the models with full multivariate controls, those with grown children were likewise significantly more liberal on government services and education priority, but less so than custodial parents. This suggests that the effects of parenthood are lifelong. Additionally, it underscores the methodological problems inherent in grouping parents of grown children with true nonparents.

Considering the significant attention the issue of gay marriage has received, particularly in the 2004 presidential election, it seemed particularly important to assess whether parents had distinctive attitudes on the issue. Table 7.1 reveals that parents are more opposed to gay marriage than those without children. This finding suggests there is some basis for the assumption that parents are conservative on family values–type issues, and appealing to parents on such issues might be an effective strategy.[28] However, it is important to point out that any parent effect does not extend to abortion; parents are no more conservative than nonparents on this issue. Taken as a whole, Table 7.1 reveals that when parenthood is politically significant, its impact is neither consistently liberal nor conservative, but varies depending on the particular issue. In order for politicians to attract this voting bloc, it may require adopting progressive positions on social welfare issues while taking more conservative stances on gay marriage.

Although the results in Table 7.1 are interesting, the fact that men and women are grouped together could potentially obscure additional findings. As discussed earlier, both the maternalist and socialization theories predict parenthood would have a greater impact on women's attitudes than men's attitudes. Table 7.2, therefore, replicates the analyses in Table 7.1 separately for each gender. On the female side, the pattern of significant results perfectly mirrors that from Table 7.1—women with children have significantly different attitudes than women without children on the issues of government services, education priority, and gay marriage. For men, in contrast, only education importance has a significant difference in the mean comparison, although the differences for men on government services and gay marriage are consistent with those of women and approach significance at the .10 levels.[29] It would certainly appear, then, that the differences attributable to parenthood are driven primarily by women, although to the extent men are impacted by parenthood, it moves their attitudes in an ideological direction consistent with women. Because women are, on the whole, more responsible for attending to their children's education and health care needs, the more pronounced parental effects on those issues for women are not surprising.

The Political Effects of Parental Involvement

The results in Tables 7.1 and 7.2 demonstrate that parental status does play a role in political attitudes on a small set of important issues. Certainly the

Table 7.2. Issue Positions and Parenthood by Gender

	Women without Children	Women with Children	Men without Children	Men with Children
Vote for Bush	0.36	0.49	0.52	0.58
Government services	4.52*	5.09*	4.29	4.69
Defense spending	4.05	3.96	3.91	4.20
Defense importance	3.14	3.19	3.17	3.35
Health care	3.43	3.19	3.59	3.63
Health care importance	4.14	4.17	3.86	4.01
Environment	3.20	3.26	3.49	3.30
Abortion	2.62	2.61	2.31	2.51
Abortion importance	3.53	3.48	2.97	3.09
Education importance	3.78*	4.14*	3.59*	4.08*
Child care	3.64	3.38	4.01	3.79
Opposition to gay marriage	0.25*	0.47*	0.46	0.59
Opposition to gun control	1.86	1.94	2.31	2.43
Support for Iraq War	2.14	2.42	2.58	2.63

* Indicates means are significantly different at $p \leq .05$.

Note: The impact of parenthood on the variable in question in starred (*) cells remains statistically significant in regression models with controls for age, race, marital status, education, party ID, income, employment status, region, and religiosity.

dichotomous change from nonparent to parent can be hugely influential in many aspects of one's life and attitudes, but parenting is not a dichotomy; it is a continuum. The theories discussed earlier suggest that the key factor is the level of parental involvement. Socialization theory emphasizes long-term exposure to new environments and roles, while the maternalism hypothesis focuses on the protection and nurturance of children in accounting for new political priorities and preferences. Our data on parental involvement, therefore, allow us, for the first time, to examine not only the impact of parenthood itself on political attitudes, but also how the degree to which an individual is actually engaged in the tasks of parenting affects political issue attitudes.

Because parental involvement is not exactly a standard variable in political research, we begin with some basic information on our measures. We present descriptive statistics on our parental-involvement measures for all 256 custodial parent respondents as well as separately by gender. The results in Table 7.3 reveal that respondents appear to be fairly engaged in child rearing. The average respondent reports spending nearly twelve hours with children on a nonworkday. The mean for the responsibility measure is between shared responsibility and mostly responsible. As expected, women are significantly more involved in parenting than are men, averaging three and a half more hours per day with children and almost a whole point greater on the five-point responsibility scale. These differences translate into about a point and a half difference on our roughly nine-point parental-involvement summary index.

For present purposes, the truly interesting question is not the levels of parental involvement, but rather how parental involvement may influence attitudes toward political issues. Table 7.4 presents Pearson correlation co-

Table 7.3. Parental Involvement

	Mean	Minimum	Maximum	Standard Deviation
All Respondents				
Non-workday hours	11.76	0	24	6.89
Responsibility	3.55	1	5	0.87
Parental-involvement summary	5.47	1	8.91	1.63
Men Only				
Non-workday hours	9.67	0	24	6.49
Responsibility	3.03	1	5	0.77
Parental-involvement summary	4.56	1	8.91	1.48
Women Only				
Non-workday hours	13.42	0	24	6.72
Responsibility	3.96	1	5	0.73
Parental-involvement summary	6.18	1	8.91	1.38

Note: Differences of means for men and women are significant at $p < .01$ for each variable.

efficients for parental involvement with each of the issues discussed earlier along with vote choice and party identification.[30] Interestingly, the results in Table 7.4 show some expected similarities, but some important differences as well, with earlier analyses examining parenthood as simply a dichotomous variable. Parental involvement is most strongly correlated with government spending and services (as expected, with more involvement related to more liberal attitudes), the issue with which the relationship appeared strongest in Tables 7.1 and 7.2. However, neither opinions on gay marriage nor on education importance are related to the level of parental involvement. It is simply being a parent, rather than the degree of parental involvement, that seems to matter on those two issues.

It is in Table 7.4, though, that we see significant relationships that we might have expected in earlier analyses and did not find. Parental involvement is significantly correlated with support for nationalized health care, government support for child care, and greater salience for the issue of health care. Taken together with the strong and significant effects of parenthood and parental involvement on the government spending and services issue, we believe our results offer some of the first empirical support for the theory advanced in the maternal feminist literature that the actual act of caring for and nurturing children leads one to develop more compassionate and liberal positions on social welfare issues. As these theories suggest and our results support,

Table 7.4. Pearson Correlations between Parental-Involvement Index and Issue Positions

	All	Women Only	Men Only
Vote for Bush	−0.15*	−0.24*	−0.01
Party ID	0.11	0.17	−0.03
Government services	0.22*	0.25*	0.12
Defense spending	−0.03	−0.09	0.12
Defense importance	0.04	0.08	0.10
Health care	−0.16*	−0.21*	−0.01
Health care importance	0.19*	0.24*	0.09
Environment	−0.01	−0.12	0.11
Abortion	0.04	0.05	−0.04
Abortion importance	0.06	−0.10	0.08
Education importance	0.11	0.16	0.03
Child care	−0.21*	−0.29*	−0.08
Opposition to gay marriage	−0.03	0.10	−0.07
Opposition to gun control	−0.09	−0.09	0.14
Support for Iraq War	−0.13*	−0.21*	0.02

* $p < .05$.

it is not just being a parent per se, but actually taking care of children and taking responsibility for their needs and development, that has a politicizing effect. Given the liberalizing impact parental involvement has on social welfare attitudes, it is perhaps not surprising that parental involvement is also significantly, but quite modestly, correlated with voting for Kerry.

Finally, Table 7.4 also shows that parental involvement is significantly, but once again quite modestly, correlated with opposition to the Iraq war. The more involved parents are in their children's lives, the more likely they are to think the United States should have stayed out of the war in Iraq. This correlation offers some empirical support for Sara Ruddick's hypothesis about the antimilitaristic effects of "mothering."[31] It also challenges, to some degree, the notion of "security moms." Parents, including moms, were not significantly different than those without children in terms of their views on defense spending and priority and, if anything, were slightly more liberal in their views on Iraq.

Although informative to consider parents as a whole, socialization and maternalism theories suggest that important distinctions might be lost by grouping men and women together. Table 7.4 therefore also includes these same correlations separately for men and women. In every case of significant correlations for the full sample, the correlations for women only are stronger and statistically significant whereas the correlations for men are smaller and not significant. For example, the correlation on health care is –.21 for women and an utterly insignificant –.01 for men. The extremely small values for the Pearson correlation coefficients for men suggest that the lack of statistical significance is highly unlikely to be a case of type II error and demonstrates that parental involvement simply has negligible impact on the political attitudes of men. It seems safe to say, then, that the significant correlation results for all parents were driven almost exclusively by women.

Taken in conjunction with our earlier analyses, it would seem that for women, both the very fact of parenthood as well as involvement in parenthood help to explain political attitudes, whereas for men, parenthood essentially operates as a dichotomy—once one is a parent, the level of actual involvement seems to have no impact. Why exactly this should be the case remains unclear, but certainly suggests further avenues for study about how gender interacts with parenthood. One possibility is that the relationship between fathers and children may best be captured in different ways than the relationship between mothers and children; for example, centrality of parenthood to self-identity or different types of bonding activities, which we do not measure here. Regardless of the reason, it is clear that parenthood affects the adult political socialization of men differently than women.

Although informative, these correlation coefficients are unable to tell us the truly independent impact of parental involvement while controlling for other related variables. We therefore also ran a series of regression models to ensure that parental involvement serves as a predictor of political attitudes even when controlling for related factors. These models also allow us to gauge the relative effects of parental involvement on the dependent variable. The results from the regression models in Tables 7.5a, b, and c show that parental involvement remains a significant predictor of these issue attitudes with a nontrivial substantive impact. For example, the difference between the least involved and most involved parents would be almost 1.3 on the government services scale and 1.8 on the child care scale. As we might expect from the correlations, the impact for all parents and for women is consistently significant whereas the coefficients for men are never anywhere near significant. The two cases where adding the full range of controls appears to eliminate the effect of parenthood are the Iraq war and presidential vote—perhaps not surprising considering that these were the lowest correlations in Table 7.4.[32] In the case of women, however, parental involvement does come close to significantly explaining vote choice ($p = .07$). Given that we lose even more N because of nonvoters, we are especially sensitive to the possible effects of our small sample size on explaining vote. In sum, though, we can confidently conclude that parental involvement, especially for women, does in fact lead to more liberal issue positions.

Discussion and Conclusion

People have long recognized that becoming a parent is a momentous milestone. Parenthood changes one's life in profound ways—socially, economically, and psychologically. In this article we demonstrated that parenthood is politically significant as well. Although being a parent does not show significant effects across the board on all issue attitudes, parenthood and parental involvement have a significant impact on several policy issues and priorities including education, government spending and services, health care, and gay marriage.

An important feature of the parent gap is the way it seems to reinforce the gender gap. Howell and Day point out that there is no single magic bullet to explain the gender gap, but that the causes vary depending on the issue.[33] Our analysis adds another piece to the complex origins of the gap. Although the impact of parenthood and parental involvement moves the attitudes of men and women in the same ideological direction, our results show mothers are much more affected than fathers, as predicted by the maternalism

Table 7.5a. Regression Models of Parental Involvement

	Government Services			Child Care		
	All	Men	Women	All	Men	Women
Age	.008	.023	−.003	−.012	−.017	−.007
	(.009)	(.016)	(.012)	(.012)	(.020)	(.015)
Education	−.151	−.172	−.092	.199	.255	.109
	(.100)	(.167)	(.128)	(.124)	(.206)	(.159)
Income	−.013	−.031	−.003	.009	.035	−.002
	(.025)	(.043)	(.033)	(.032)	(.053)	(.042)
White	−.165	−.454	.131	.195	.481	−.130
	(.196)	(.317)	(.261)	(.245)	(.391)	(.327)
Married	−.092	−.234	−.049	−.004	.147	−.102
	(.227)	(.368)	(.300)	(.284)	(.454)	(.375)
South	.086	.081	.166	−.334	.036	−.639*
	(.183)	(.294)	(.247)	(.229)	(.362)	(.309)
Employed	.091	.315	−.016	−.519*	−.934	−.409
	(.206)	(.424)	(.242)	(.258)	(.523)	(.303)
Church attendance	−.099	−.089	−.103	.190**	.238*	.169*
	(.045)	(.074)	(.061)	(.056)	(.091)	(.076)
Gender	.075	—	—	−.091	—	—
	(.207)			(.259)		
Party ID	.318**	.276**	.356**	−.277**	−.317**	−.241**
	(.047)	(.074)	(.063)	(.059)	(.091)	(.079)
Parental involvement	.142*	.090	.165+	−.203*	−.075	−.320**
	(.064)	(.098)	(.088)	(.080)	(.121)	(.110)
N	245	108	136	246	108	137
Adjusted R2	.265	195	.282	.214	.217	.194

* $p < .05$, two-tailed test.
** $p < .01$, two-tailed test.
+ $p < .10$, two-tailed test.
Note: Cell entries are OLS coefficients; standard errors are in parentheses.

Table 7.5b. Regression Models of Parental Involvement

	Health Care			Health Care Importance		
	All	Men	Women	All	Men	Women
Age	−.026*	−.014	−.028	.012*	.020*	.006
	(.011)	(.018)	(.015)	(.006)	(.009)	(.008)
Education	.192	.283	.139	−.019	−.037	.010
	(.118)	(.189)	(.156)	(.059)	(.093)	(.081)
Income	.047	.075	.010	−.003	−.007	.000
	(.030)	(.048)	(.041)	(.015)	(.024)	(.021)
White	−.352	−.305	−.302	.155	.050	.259
	(.233)	(.358)	(.321)	(.117)	(.177)	(.166)
Married	−.381	−.542	−.228	.020	−.090	.097
	(.270)	(.415)	(.367)	(.136)	(.205)	(.191)
South	−.300	−.341	−.117	.070	.057	.104
	(.218)	(.331)	(.305)	(.110)	(.164)	(.157)

Table 7.5b. Continued

	Health Care			Health Care Importance		
	All	Men	Women	All	Men	Women
Employed	.118	.465	−.080	.106	.186	.080
	(.246)	(.479)	(.297)	(.124)	(.237)	(.154)
Church attendance	.197**	.205**	.162*	.015	.018	.018
	(.054)	(.084)	(.075)	(.027)	(.041)	(.038)
Gender	−.147	—	—	−.043	—	—
	(.245)			(.124)		
Party ID	−.329**	−.424**	−.237**	.075*	.031	.110**
	(.056)	(.083)	(.077)	(.028)	(.041)	(.040)
Parental involvement	−.128+	−.079	−.233*	.100*	.039	.143*
	(.076)	(.111)	(.108)	(.038)	(.055)	(.056)
N	245	108	136	247	108	138
Adjusted R2	.247	.324	.144	.050	.010	.065

* $p < .05$, two-tailed test.
** $p < .01$, two-tailed test.
+ $p < .10$, two-tailed test.
Note: Cell entries are OLS coefficients; standard errors are in parentheses.

Table 7.5c. Logistic Regression Model of Vote for Bush in 2004

	All	Men	Women
Age	−.033	.003	−.085*
	(.025)	(.041)	(.043)
Education	.120	−.301	.765
	(.283)	(.441)	(.470)
Income	−.197*	−.177	−.321
	(.082)	(.124)	(.172)
White	1.939**	1.669	3.434*
	(.629)	(.903)	(1.366)
Married	−.047	−.125	−.029
	(.641)	(.923)	(1.106)
South	1.421*	1.707	1.787
	(.578)	(.902)	(1.005)
Employed	.984	.741	1.509
	(.602)	(1.214)	(.889)
Church attendance	.061	.056	.127
	(.127)	(.219)	(.193)
Gender	.163	—	—
	(.567)		
Party ID	−1.138**	−1.153**	−1.309**
	(.177)	(.265)	(.310)
Parental involvement	−.288	−.094	−.612+
	(.185)	(.264)	(.342)
N	187	90	97
Pseudo R2	.708	.710	.746

* $p < .05$, two-tailed test.
** $p < .01$, two-tailed test.
+ $p < .10$, two-tailed test.
Note: Cell entries are Logit coefficients; standard errors are in parentheses.

and socialization theories. Thus, on several issues that have historically had a significant gender gap, including government spending, health care, child care, and other social welfare programs, it appears that having and raising children contributes to the gender gap by more strongly pushing women in a liberal direction. Although research by others showed that marriage brings the attitudes of women and men closer together,[34] our research indicates that having children leads to a widening of the gap.

In addition to their theoretical significance, the results presented in this article have practical consequences for twenty-first-century political actors. As the Democratic and Republican parties seek out ways to assemble winning coalitions, an appeal to parents makes strategic sense. Not only is the family "the social institution that is most important to the public," but parents also have distinctive political concerns and priorities to which candidates can appeal.[35] Interestingly, although some commentators have credited the "baby gap" as playing a pivotal role in Bush's victory in 2004,[36] the emergence of parenthood as a significant political identity is not necessarily a boon for Republicans. On the issue of gay marriage, parents are more conservative than their nonparent peers, but on all other issues where there was a parenthood effect, the effect was a liberal one. Moreover, parental status and involvement were associated with greater concern for health care and education, issues on which Democrats have long been perceived as having better ideas and more credibility. What this means on a practical level is that both parties have a viable chance to successfully appeal to parents. Appeals, such as the "compassionate conservatism" embraced by George W. Bush in the 2000 election, which stressed a mixture of progressive ideas on social welfare issues such as education and health care and conservative stances on some social issues, seem to be the best path for attracting parents.

Finally, our findings underscore one of the central arguments made in the article by Susan Carroll about the problematic nature of the frames employed by the media to discuss parents, and mothers in particular. An underlying assumption in recent media coverage about parents and elections has been that parents are an inherently conservative group. As discussed above, our results show such assumptions are inaccurate and that the vast majority of parenthood effects, especially motherhood effects, are liberal. If the media insist on employing catchy labels for parents in their future election coverage, the labels "education parents" or "social welfare moms" would be more accurate than those employed in recent election cycles.

Appendix: Measures and Variables

Custodial Parent: Two-part question: "Do you have any children age 17 or younger living in your home at least part of the time?" and "Are you the parent or legal guardian of any of the children 17 or younger living in your home at least part of the time?" Coded 1 for respondents who answered yes to both questions; 0 for those who answered no to either question.

Parent of Adult Children: "Are you the parent of any children 18 or older?" Asked of those coded 0 for custodial parent. Coded 1 for yes, 0 otherwise.

Government Services: "Some people think the government should provide fewer services even in areas such as health and education in order to reduce spending. Other people feel it is important for the government to provide many more services even if it means an increase in spending. Where would you place yourself on this scale?" 1, decrease spending, to 7, increase spending.

Defense Spending: "Some people believe that we should spend much less money for defense. Others feel that defense spending should be greatly increased. Where would you place yourself on this scale?" 1, decrease spending, to 7, increase spending.

Defense Importance: "How important is the issue of defense spending to you personally? Not at all important, Not too important, Somewhat important. Very important, Extremely important." Coded in increasing importance from 1 to 5.

Health Care: "There is much concern about the rapid rise in medical and hospital costs. Some people feel there should be a government insurance plan which would cover all medical and hospital expenses for everyone. Others feel that all medical expenses should be paid by individuals through private insurance plans like Blue Cross or other company-paid plans. Where would you place yourself on this scale?" 1, government insurance plan, to 7, private insurance plan.

Health Care Importance: "How important is the issue of health care insurance to you personally? Not at all important, Not too important, Somewhat important, Very important, Extremely important." Coded in increasing importance from 1 to 5.

Environment: Standard NES 7-point scale. 1, tougher regulations needed to 7, regulations are too burdensome.

Abortion: "Do you think abortions should be legal under any circumstances, legal under most circumstances, legal only under limited circumstances, or legal in no circumstances?" Coded from 1, always legal to 4, never legal.

Abortion Importance: "How important is the issue of abortion to you personally?" Coded in increasing importance from 1 to 5.

Gay Marriage: "Which comes closest to your view? Same-sex couples should be allowed to legally marry; Same-sex couples should be allowed to form civil unions but not legally marry; or, There should be no legal recognition of a same-sex couple's relationship?" Coded 1 for opposition to gay marriage; 0 otherwise.

Gun Control: Two-part question: "Do you think the federal government should make it more difficult for people to buy a gun than it is now, make it easier for people to buy a gun, or keep these rules about the same as they are now?" Followed by, "A lot more difficult (easier) or somewhat more difficult (easier)?" Coded 1, a lot more difficult, to 5, a lot easier.

Child Care: "Some people think that the government should do more to ensure that there is quality child care available for working parents. Others feel that this is not an area for the federal government to be involved in. Where would you place yourself on this?" 1, government supported child care, to 7, no government support for child care.

Educational Importance: "In thinking about politics, how important is the issue of public education to you?" Coded in increasing importance from 1 to 5.

Iraq War: Two-part question: "Looking back, do you think the United States did the right thing in taking military action against Iraq, or should the U.S. have stayed out?" "Do you feel strongly or not so strongly that the war was the right thing/that the U.S. should have stayed out?" From 1, strong opposition, to 4, strong support.

Nonworkday Hours with Children: For employed: "On a typical day that you do not work for pay, approximately how many hours do you spend taking care of and doing things with your children?" For those not working: "On a typical day, approximately how many hours do you spend taking care of and doing things with your children?" Coded 0 to 24 hours.

Parental Responsibility: "Below are various tasks parents do on behalf of their children. Please tell us whether these tasks are all your responsibility, mostly your responsibility, roughly equal responsibility, mostly another's responsibility, or all another's responsibility." (1) "Making social arrangements for your children, such as play-dates, planning activities, making appointments, and arranging transportation for activities"; (2) "Making decisions regarding your children's health care needs"; (3) "Helping children to learn or helping with homework"; (4) "Making decisions about child care and schooling"; (5) "Setting limits and disciplining"; (6) "Planning appropriate meals and buying food for your children"; (7) "Nurturing your child and tending to their emotional needs." Each item coded from 1, all another's responsibility, to 5, all own responsibility. Index is mean response to the six items.

Parental-Involvement Index: Standardized nonworkday hours + standardized parental-responsibility index. Rescaled for a minimum value of 1. Range from 1 to 8.91.

Party Identification: Standard NES seven-point scale from 1, strong Republican, to 7, strong Democrat.

2004 Presidential Vote: In the 2004 election for president, did you vote for George W. Bush, John Kerry, someone else, or did you not vote in this election? 1, vote for Bush, or 0, vote for Kerry. Respondents indicating they voted for someone else besides Bush or Kerry, or did not vote, were excluded from the analysis.

Gender: 1, male; 2, female.

Employed: 1, currently working for pay; 0, not currently working for pay.

Age: Age in years.

Race: 1, non-Hispanic white; 0, all others.

South: 1, resident of a Southern state; 0, all others. Southern states included the following: Alabama, Arkansas, Florida, Georgia, Kentucky, Louisiana, Mississippi, North Carolina, Oklahoma, South Carolina, Tennessee, Texas, and Virginia.

Education: Ranges from 1, less than high school degree, to 9, doctoral degree.

Marital Status: 1, married; 0, all others.

Income: 19 categories from 1, lowest, to 19, highest.

Religiosity: Church attendance from 1, never, to 6, more than once a week. For Christians only.

Notes

1. Chodorow, *Reproduction of Mothering*; Elshtain, "On Beautiful Souls," in Stiehm, *Women and Men's Wars*; Ruddick, *Maternal Thinking*.

2. Ruddick, "Preservation Love and Military Destruction," in Trebilcot, *Mothering,* 233.

3. Elshtain, *Public Man, Private Woman,* 336.

4. Ruddick, "Preservation Love and Military Destruction," in Trebilcot, *Mothering,* 233.

5. Deitch, "Sex Differences," in Mueller, *Politics of the Gender Gap*; Piven, "Women and the State," in Rossi, *Gender and the Life Course*; Welch and Hibbing, "Financial Conditions, Gender and Voting."

6. For example, see Andersen and Cook, "Women, Work and Political Attitudes"; Jennings and Stoker, "Political Similarity and Influence"; Weisberg, "Demographics of a New Voting Gap."

7. Burns, Schlozman, and Verba, *Private Roots of Public Action*; Jennings, "Another Look at the Life Cycle"; Sapiro, *Political Integration of Women.*

8. Stoker and Jennings, "Life-Cycle Transitions."

9. Gallagher and Gerstel, "Connections and Constraints"; Munch, McPherson, and Smith-Lovin, "Gender, Children, and Social Contacts."

10. McLanahan and Adams, "Parenthood and Psychological Well-Being"; Nomaguchi and Milkie, "Costs and Rewards of Children."

11. Bianchi, "Maternal Employment"; Burns, Schlozman, and Verba, *Private Roots of Public Action*; Downs, *Fertility of American Women.*

12. Burns, Schlozman, and Verba, *Private Roots of Public Action,* 311.

13. See Nomaguchi and Milkie, "Costs and Rewards of Children," for a review of this literature.

14. Howell and Day, "Complexities of the Gender Gap," 869.

15. Conover and Sapiro, "Feminists and the Gender Gap"; Bendyna et al., "Gender Differences in Public Attitudes."

16. Alberts, "Candidates Address 'Security Moms,'" A22; Barnes, "Family Gap"; Feldman, "Why Women Are Edging Toward Bush."

17. Kotkin and Frey, "Parent Trap"; Milbank, "Deeply Divided Country."

18. Arnold and Weisberg, "Parenthood, Family Values."

19. Arnold and Weisberg, "Parenthood, Family Values"; Conover and Sapiro, "Feminists and the Gender Gap"; Bendyna et al., "Gender Differences in Public Attitudes."

20. Knowledge Networks has impaneled a large representative sample of Americans based on a random-digit dialing (RDD) sample of the entire U.S. population. Following this contact, participants for Web-based surveys were recruited in exchange for the provision of WebTV or high-speed Internet access. This panel has proven to be quite representative of the overall U.S. population on most key demographic characteristics as shown in Krosnick and Chang, "Comparison of the Random Digit Dialing Telephone Survey Methodology." Knowledge Networks also has consistently high response rates, in the range of 70 to 80 percent.

21. GSS also includes a question about how many children the respondent has ever had, but includes no information as to whether any of these children are currently minors and/or living in the respondent's household.

22. Bradley et al., "Parents' Socioemotional Investment in Children"; Deutsch, Servis, and Payne, "Paternal Participation in Child Care"; Deutsch, Lozy, and Saxon, "Taking Credit"; Nock and Kingston, "Time with Children"; Whiteside-Mansell, Bradley, and Rakow, "Similarities and Differences in Parental Investment."

23. We use the Gallup question wording for abortion, which we believe is preferable. ANES did not offer the response category of support for civil unions, so we again use Gallup question wording. ANES lacks a seven-point item on child care, so we created our own, emulating the ANES seven-point style as closely as possible. ANES lacks a measure of education importance, so we created our own, emulating the style of the ANES issue importance measures.

24. See Weisberg, "Demographics of a New Voting Gap."

25. Collins, "Shifting the Center," in Bassin, *Representations of Motherhood*; Hill, "Class, Race, and Gender Dimensions."

26. Although it should be noted that simply using people who are not custodial parents as the comparison group yields little difference in substantive findings. Using those with grown children only presents a problematic comparison group on many of these issues because their average age is sixty-three, compared to thirty-eight for the rest of the sample.

27. Because this table is based on data from 256 custodial parents and 114 people with no children, one should be cognizant of the possibility of type II error for some of these issues on which effect sizes might be small. It is entirely possible that a more typically sized survey would pick up some modest but significant differences that our survey was unable to. Even our most significant result is actually substantively rather modest—a mean difference on government services of .53 on the seven-point scale. It may very well be that a larger N survey would find more pervasive effects of parenthood.

28. Barnes, "Family Gap"; Arnold and Weisberg, "Parenthood, Family Values."

29. Again, with the small sample size and risk of type II error, it is important to note that for both gay marriage and government services, the differences for men approach significance at the $p < .10$ level.

30. Because parental involvement was only measured for custodial parents, only these respondents are included in this analysis.

31. Note that Ruddick's argument about the antimilitaristic effects of "mothering" is the major argument advanced in her 1983 book chapter "Preservation Love and Military Destruction" in Trebilcot's *Mothering* and in her 1989 book *Maternal Thinking*.

32. We do not show the Iraq war model because none of the parental-involvement coefficients were significant. We nonetheless include the presidential vote model because of its theoretical importance.

33. Howell and Day, "Complexities of the Gender Gap."

34. Jennings and Stoker, "Political Similarity and Influence."

35. Arnold and Weisberg, "Parenthood, Family Values," 214.

36. Kotkin and Frey, "Parent Trap."

8

Sources of Political Unity and Disunity among Women

Placing the Gender Gap in Perspective

LEONIE HUDDY, ERIN CASSESE,

AND MARY-KATE LIZOTTE

The gender gap has become a staple feature of the political landscape during the past several decades. Women have consistently voted in greater numbers than men for Democratic presidential and congressional candidates since the early 1980s.[1] They have also expressed greater identification with the Democratic Party over the same time period.[2] In the 1980s, Ronald Reagan polarized the genders more than other recent presidents had, which carried over into gender polarization on party identification, resulting in the widely broadcast notion of a "gender gap."[3]

But women's political commonality is far from pervasive. Although women are more inclined than men to support Democratic candidates, they do not act as a cohesive political force. Political group unity is typically marked by homogeneity of vote choice among group members and a sharp divergence from nongroup members. Such unity is highly visible among blacks, among whom 80 to 90 percent have supported Democratic presidential candidates in recent elections and have done so to a far greater degree than whites, whose support for Democratic candidates is closer to 40 percent.[4] Women do not form a cohesive, unified political force in this way. The gender gap in vote choice between men and women has hovered around ten percentage points over the last several decades, resulting, for example, in 54 percent of women supporting Bill Clinton in 1996 as compared to 43 percent of men, according to exit poll data.[5] This is very far from the unanimity exhibited by black voters in recent elections.[6]

Group-based political solidarity or cohesion is also typically marked by the degree to which a group's common interests motivate political commonality. But women's political cohesion also appears weak when examined from this perspective.[7] There is no evidence that the electoral "gender gap" reflected political unity among women by originating in a distinctive response to women's shared interests. In the 1930s and 1940s, women were substantially more supportive than men of liberalized roles for women, particularly their suitability for paid work and political office. However, such gender differences diminished through the 1960s, so that contemporary research typically turns up almost no major gender differences in support for such women's issues. The gender difference in support for the Equal Rights Amendment, which most explicitly promoted women's collective interests, was negligible during the late 1970s and early 1980s, when it was receiving the most publicity and its fate was largely determined. Similarly, much research has shown that men and women have not differed significantly in recent years on other women's issues, such as whether "a woman's place" is properly in the home, whether women should be drafted, how much discrimination there is against women, favorability toward women's organizations, and support for legalized abortion, issues on which both women and men are divided.[8]

Group members may also evince political cohesion through a greater political emphasis on group-linked issues. But women fail to pass the cohesion test in this respect. Ronald Reagan and the Republican Party took unsympathetic stances on women's issues in the 1980s, and leaders of the women's movement were outspokenly opposed to the Reagan administration. So women might well have been more inclined than men to vote for candidates who support women's issues. But here, too, the evidence suggests disunity rather than solidarity. Klein found large gender differences in the impact of women's issues on the presidential vote in 1980.[9] But others have not found such gender differences. Indeed, Mansbridge refutes the notion that the ERA had greater impact on women's than men's vote choice in the 1980 presidential election; the impact of the ERA was minimal among both genders.[10] Frankovic reported that support for women's issues such as the ERA and abortion had about the same small influence on women's job approval ratings of Reagan as it did on men's in the 1980–82 era.[11] And both Klein and Mueller report no gender differences in 1972 and 1976 surveys.[12] The weight of this and recent evidence is against strong gender differences on women's issues or in their political impact.[13]

Thus, when taken as a whole, there is little evidence that women are very unified politically. There are political differences between men and women.

But these differences are modest and seem unrelated to gender-linked issues such as legalized abortion, the ERA, or other women's issues.[14] Our goal in this article is to look more closely at different kinds of women across diverse employment, marital, economic, and religious backgrounds to account for women's shared political commonality and scrutinize further the sources of their political disunity.[15] We favor a sociological approach in which we focus on demographic and religious factors rather than attitudes or subjective beliefs in order to assess the origins of the gender gap in women's real-life circumstances. We do not want to suggest, however, that attitudes are unimportant. Indeed, they are critical to the existence of the gender gap.

We also ask the following questions about women's admittedly limited political unity: Is it exhibited across the board, regardless of women's circumstances? Or is the gender gap confined to specific subgroups of women? We examine these issues across a broad time frame—from 1980 to 2004—in order to uncover general trends across a number of different presidential elections. This article serves to update an earlier analysis of the 1984 ANES data in which we found considerable disunity among women, revolving around their general political beliefs.[16]

Women's Political Unity

The electoral and partisan gender gap is fueled by women's somewhat different positions than men on several political issues.[17] Women's stronger (or men's weaker) support of government social welfare spending is the most consistent explanation for the gender gap over time.[18] The centrality of social welfare issues to the gender gap raises questions about whether women's political unity is observed among all women or is confined to specific subgroups. One obvious possibility is that the gender gap is isolated among economically vulnerable women. In the aftermath of welfare reform in 1996, low-income women have had to rely on government assistance with child care to obtain employment and undertake job retraining. Prior to 1996, they were also more dependent on direct government assistance through Aid to Families with Dependent Children (AFDC). They may also have more invested in programs directed at low-income children such as Head Start.[19] Box-Steffensmeier and colleagues find that in the aggregate, the gender gap in Democratic Party identification increases over time with an increase in the number of single women in American society, a potentially vulnerable group economically.[20] The gender gap and political unity may thus be especially pronounced among low-income women. We refer to this as the "economic vulnerability" hypothesis.

Alternatively, the gender gap might be driven by those who are economically autonomous from men (not economically vulnerable women) as Carroll has suggested.[21] From this perspective, the gender gap is confined to single women or well-educated women who are in professional employment because, in part, women are especially likely to be employed in the public sector (education, health care, etc.), and so have more to gain from the success of the Democratic Party.[22] This argument can be extended to working women more generally who may have more to gain than nonemployed women from Democratic administrations that are inclined to actively support assistance to working parents and promote affirmative action programs that help women's advancement in the workforce. And, finally, women employed in higher-status, male-dominated occupations may benefit the most from specific legislation concerning job discrimination and affirmative action and court decisions mandating redress of pay inequities. These considerations suggest that professional or well-educated working women may have the most to gain from the Democratic Party and Democratic candidates. We refer to this as the "economic autonomy" hypothesis.

Women's Political Disunity

Overall, women and men alike show considerable political disunity when it comes to partisanship and electoral choice; these political differences are sizeable and largely independent of gender. We thus turn from women's common interests, or interests shared by specific subgroups of women (but not men), to focus more squarely on gender-neutral life situations and interests that divide men and women equally. We consider a number of demographic factors that have served as important lines of cleavage in American electoral politics, including race and ethnicity, religiosity and religion, and economic factors. When taken together, these characteristics account for a good deal of diversity in electoral choice and partisanship.

RACE

One of the most visible sources of division in American politics revolves around race. African Americans vote overwhelmingly for Democratic candidates and identify largely with the Democratic Party. Among whites, support for the Democratic Party is far more tepid. Voting studies conducted in the 1940s and 1950s demonstrated that blacks were more likely than whites to support Democratic candidates and identify as Democrats.[23] And blacks continue to display tremendous political unity in an era characterized by a marked decline in the political cohesion of many other sociodemographic groups.[24] Blacks' continued identification as Democrats goes hand in hand with widespread racial differences across a broad range of racial and social issues.[25] Overall, there are sizeable racial differences in support of government economic policy, social welfare spending, and explicit racial issues that are associated, in turn, with large racial differences in vote choice and partisanship.[26]

RELIGION AND RELIGIOSITY

From Ronald Reagan's 1980 election victory onward, there has been much discussion of the role of religiosity and the religious Right as a source of support for Republican candidates. In fact, it was not Ronald Reagan but rather Bill Clinton who triggered the most powerful religious cleavage in recent electoral history, resulting in strong support for Republican candidates among highly religious individuals that has persisted over time.[27] The political role of religion came to a head in the 2004 presidential election when pundits were quick to conclude that Christian fundamentalists had handed President Bush his reelection victory, leading in turn to demands by fundamentalist leaders for political payback.[28] Pew researchers conclude that religious voters, especially white fundamentalists, formed a powerful base of support for Bush in both 2000 and 2004 (http://people-press.org/commentary/display .php3?AnalysisID=103). This trend began earlier, with a steady increase in the percentage of white Protestant fundamentalists who identified with the Republican Party through the 1980s and early 1990s.[29]

Christian fundamentalists' strong support for the Republican Party stands in marked contrast to the political inclinations of Jews, who have typically supported the Democratic Party, a tendency that was apparent in the very first electoral studies and that has continued through the 1990s.[30] However, it is insufficient to look only at gross differences between major religious denominations to assess the political effects of religion. The frequency and nature of religious practice and belief are also politically consequential. The effect of religion or religious identity on partisanship and electoral behavior is likely most pronounced among individuals who frequently attend religious service—particularly those who attend weekly as opposed to attendance solely on religious holidays.

But one can expect diversity in political attitudes and behavior, even among individuals who report frequent religious practice. Several scholars have argued that the primary religious cleavages have shifted from those dividing major religious denominations to more cross-cutting cleavages that pit orthodox subdenominations against progressive or liberal subdenominations.[31] For example, we expect smaller differences in partisanship and electoral choice between mainline Protestants and respondents reporting no religious affiliation than between mainline Protestants and fundamentalist Protestants—and this seems to be borne out in the examples offered above. Overall, religion—denominational affiliation, religious practice, and religious beliefs—forms an important source of cleavage in both partisanship and vote choice among men and women, and has done so from the early 1980s. Religion and religiosity thus form a potentially powerful source of political division among women.

ECONOMIC FACTORS

Economic factors also influence vote choice and partisanship independently of gender, and must be considered as a further gender-neutral source of disunity among women. The traditional Democratic New Deal coalition included members of the working class and union households. There has been some decline over time in support for the Democratic Party among members of union households, although they are still more likely to identify as Democrats than Republicans.[32] And there is a continued link between household income, with wealthier households supporting Republican candidates and identifying as Republicans, and low-income households supporting Democratic candidates and identifying as Democrats.[33] We note above the possibility that economic factors may unite women and exacerbate differences with men of the same economic background, but they are also likely to divide women and men equally. We examine both possibilities empirically in this study.

REGION

Finally, geographic region and urbanism also influence vote choice and partisanship. The South, once a Democratic stronghold, has slowly drifted toward the Republican Party. In the past, Southerners were distinctive politically in their strong identification as Democrats. But they may now look very similar to other regions of the country.[34] In recent years, another political divide has emerged between urban and nonurban voters, with increasingly strong support for Democrats in urban areas.[35]

We examine several key propositions concerning political unity and disunity among women. First, we examine whether the gender gap in support of Democratic presidential candidates and identification with the Democratic Party is pervasive among all women and men regardless of their demographic characteristics or whether it is confined to specific subgroups. We examine two distinct sources of unity: (1) economic vulnerability and (2) affluence and economic autonomy. Second, we evaluate the size of the gender gap in relation to several broader sources of disunity among women and men, including race, religious preference, level of religiosity, income, region, and other demographic characteristics. Overall, our expectation is that the sources of disunity among women outweigh their commonalities.

Data and Analytic Approach

SAMPLE

Our data come from the pooled ANES data set for the seven presidential elections between 1980 and 2004 (N = 23,290; ranging from N = 1,212 in 2004 to N = 2,485 in 1992).[36] Each election year is analyzed separately to identify trends that are stable across elections. Analyses focus on two key dependent variables: (1) Democratic versus Republican vote choice and (2) partisanship split three ways in which leaning independents are collapsed with partisans (Democrat, Republican, independent).[37] The sample is confined to individuals who voted for one of the two major party candidates in analyses predicting vote choice. The percentage voting for a Republican or Democratic candidate ranges from a low of 54 percent of the sample in 1980 when John Anderson ran as an independent presidential candidate (N = 877) to a high of 67 percent in 2004 (N = 811).

KEY VARIABLES

We examine the impact of various demographic factors on presidential vote choice and partisanship to uncover sources of political unity and disunity among women. Multivariate analyses are conducted with a series of dummy variables derived from standard demographic factors in the data including respondent gender, respondent race (white, black, and other race),[38] respondent religion (Protestant, Catholic, Jewish, and other),[39] frequency of church attendance (almost weekly and more than weekly attendance, monthly attendance, or less-frequent religious service attendance), whether the respondent endorses a fundamentalist interpretation of the Bible, and respondent education (high school degree or less, some college or an associate's degree, a bachelor's degree, or an advanced degree).[40]

A variety of economic factors are also considered. Multivariate models include respondent's current employment status, whether the respondent holds a professional position, household union membership, and whether the respondent reported a high, medium, or low household income.[41] In addition to these economic considerations, marital status, the presence of children in the household,[42] and birth cohort—whether respondents reached their late teens/early adulthood during WWII (born between 1895 and 1944), the postwar period (baby boomers; born between 1943–58), or after the baby boom (born after 1958)—are included.[43] In addition, we consider the political effect of region (residence in the Northeast, West, South, or Midwest), and urbanism (rural, suburban, or urban residence). These variables were assessed in all presidential elections between 1980 and 2004 with a few exceptions, making it possible to run exactly the same analytic model in all years.[44]

ANALYTIC STRATEGY

We first examine the size of the gender gap in Democratic candidate support and identification, then delve into sources of unity and disunity among women by employing a multivariate technique—logistic regression. We use a multivariate approach to examine the gender gap because some of the factors thought to influence vote choice and partisanship are linked to gender. Women tend to be more religious than men, for example, which might incline them toward the Republican Party. But they also tend to reside in lower-income households, which should steer them toward the Democratic Party. An analysis of the gender gap based solely on cross-tabulations of exit poll results does not allow researchers to demonstrate decisively that the gender gap is a result of gender and not other demographic factors, such as religion or income, with which it may be confounded.

The ANES studies included between one and two thousand respondents in each survey (fewer actually voted), but even that sample is insufficient to assess the effects of gender while still controlling for a number of other demographic factors. A table that depicted vote choice by all possible combinations of gender, race, education, age, religion, and religiosity would quickly exceed the sample size of ANES studies. A multivariate technique such as logistic regression gets around this problem by controlling simultaneously for many factors that influence vote choice in order to isolate the electoral effect of gender independently of the other factors with which it is related.

Logistic regression has one other important feature: It allows for the construction of predicted probabilities—that is, predictions as to how particular groups of people with one characteristic in common (such as gender) would vote, controlling for a number of other characteristics (such as religiosity, race, or income). Calculated on the basis of a logistic regression equation, predicted probabilities allow for the isolation of the "pure" effect of gender among specific groups of people, such as highly religious white Protestants, and permit us to estimate the electoral effects of one single factor (such as gender) within the same demographic group. They also allow for a careful comparison of the effects of gender among specific subgroups of women and men across all presidential elections between 1980 and 2004.

Gender Gap, 1980–2004

There is a consistent gender gap in support of presidential Democratic candidates between 1980 and 2004, as depicted in Table 8.1. In all years, women demonstrate greater support than men for the Democratic candidate. As noted elsewhere, this does not always translate into majority female support. For example, a majority of women in the ANES sample preferred Ronald Reagan to his Democratic opponents in 1980 and 1984 (out of the two major-party candidates), although by a smaller majority than found among men. In all other presidential elections, however, a majority of women in the ANES sample voted for the Democratic over the Republican candidate. In contrast, a majority of men supported only one Democratic presidential candidate— Bill Clinton in 1992 and 1996—expressing a preference for the Republican candidate in all other elections. And even this support for Clinton among men is inflated because of the omission of voters who supported third-party candidate Ross Perot. In exit poll data, somewhat more men than women voted for Perot in both 1992 and 1996.[45] The gender gap in Democratic support is smallest in 1988 and 1992 and largest in 1996. It is also slightly larger in 2004 than in 2000, a finding that is at odds with evidence of a smaller gender gap in 2004 than in 2002 in exit poll data.[46]

The gender gap in Democratic partisanship (examined with and without partisan leaners) is presented in Table 8.1 and is similar in magnitude to the gender gap in support of Democratic presidential candidates. Excluding partisan leaners (independents who lean toward one of the parties), women were more likely than men to identify as Democrats in all presidential election years between 1980 and 2004. This gender partisan gap was modest in size, ranging from twelve percentage points in 2004 to seven points in 1980, 1983, and 1992. A comparable gender gap in support of Democratic candidates emerges when leaners are added to partisans. Once again, women are more inclined than men to identify as Democrats, with the gender gap ranging from a low of seven to a high of twelve points. Overall, Table 8.1 demonstrates a decline over time in the strength of Democratic identification among both men and women (when leaners are excluded), but no decline in the simple percentage who identify as Democrats (including leaners).

Table 8.1. Gender Gap in Democratic Vote Choice and Partisanship

	1980	1984	1988	1992	1996	2000	2004
Vote Choice (N)	(877)	(1,376)	(1,195)	(1,357)	(1,034)	(1,120)	(811)
Women	47	45	50	61	64	57	57
Men	39	38	44	55	51	47	45
Democratic Gap (Women-Men)	*8*	*7*	*6*	*6*	*13*	*10*	*12*
Party Identification (N)							
Democratic party ID (no leaners)							
Women	45	41	40	39	43	39	38
Men	38	34	30	32	34	30	26
Democratic Gap (Women-Men)	*7*	*7*	*10*	*7*	*9*	*9*	*12*
Democratic party ID (plus leaners)							
Women	56	51	51	55	58	54	54
Men	50	46	43	45	46	46	45
Democratic Gap (Women-Men)	*4*	*5*	*8*	*10*	*12*	*8*	*9*
Republican party ID (no leaners)							
Women	24	28	28	23	25	23	28
Men	22	28	29	28	32	29	30
Republican Gap (Women-Men)	*2*	*0*	*-1*	*-5*	*-7*	*-6*	*-2*
Republican party ID (plus leaners)							
Women	32	39	39	34	33	34	37
Men	35	42	46	43	46	44	44
Republican Gap (Women-Men)	*-3*	*-3*	*-7*	*-9*	*-13*	*-10*	*-7*

Source: ANES pooled data set.
Note: Data are unweighted. Entries are percentage who supported the Democratic candidate or identified with the Democratic Party in each year. Cross-tabulations for vote choice are confined to respondents who reported voting for one of the two major party candidates. Leaners are independents who identify with either the Democratic or Republican Party. Missing values are excluded in the calculation of percentages.

The decline in Democratic identification is coupled with an increase in Republican identification among men but not women, fueling a symmetrical gender gap in Republican identification. This difference is most pronounced when leaners are included in the analyses, replicating the findings reported by Barbara Norrander.[47] The number of women Republicans did not increase dramatically between 1980 and 2004 (with or without leaners). But the number of Republican men did increase (although the biggest increase occurs between 1980 and 1984). By 2004, similar percentages of men (including leaners) identified with the Democratic and Republican parties, whereas substantially more women identified as Democrats. This resulted in a sizeable gender gap in Republican partisanship, ranging from a low of three points in 1980 to a high of thirteen points in 1996.

Overall, the gender gap in vote choice and partisanship is relatively modest, with somewhere between 6 and 12 percent more women than men voting for the Democratic than Republican presidential candidate in the past seven elections, and between 7 and 12 percent more women than men identifying with the Democratic Party. Although modest in size, women's greater support of Democratic candidates remains important. Even a gap of eight to ten points matters in a tight electoral contest, and is further amplified by higher levels of voter turnout among women than men in recent elections.[48]

Isolating the Gender Gap Within Specific Subgroups

The gender gap is thus robust across vote choice and partisanship—but does the gap extend to all women? Or is it concentrated among a subset of women and men, indicating the existence of specific economic or life circumstances that especially incline women to support the Democratic Party or vote for Democratic candidates?

Initial analyses suggest that the gender gap is relatively uniform among women and men of different economic, racial, and social backgrounds. Simple bivariate cross-tabulations are presented in Table 8.2 for vote choice and Table 8.3 for partisanship. In these analyses, the gender gap is examined among subgroups of women sharing similar interests in government policy (based on income, work status, occupation, education, marital status, and children) to test the economic vulnerability and economic autonomy hypotheses. We also added generation (baby boom, pre–baby boom, and post–baby boom) to control for any possible greater support of the Democratic Party among women who came of age during the women's movement of the 1960s and 1970s (baby boomers).

Consider vote choice first. As a baseline, the overall gender gap is presented in the top section of Table 8.2 and is significant in all years (as indicated by a chi-square test of association). Looking further down the table, there are only minor variations in the size of this gap in a given year. There is a slightly greater preference for the Democratic Party between professional men and women than among men and women in general, consistent with the economic autonomy hypothesis. But the gap is largely driven by professional men's weaker support of Democratic candidates, not women's stronger support (2004 is the exceptional year in which male professionals were more supportive of Kerry than men overall).

In other groupings the gap is a little larger in some years, smaller in others, but generally tracks the overall gender gap. At odds with the economic vulnerability hypothesis, the gender gap is no greater among low-income than high-income individuals. Low-income women, single women, and mothers

Table 8.2. Support for Democratic Presidential Candidate within Specific Subgroups

	1980	1984	1988	1992	1996	2000	2004
All							
Women	47	45	50	61	64	57	52
Men	39	38	44	55	51	47	45
Democratic Gap	*8**	*7***	*6**	*6**	*13***	*10***	*7**
Professional occupation							
Women	48	45	50	64	61	59	60
Men	33	32	40	50	46	44	52
Democratic Gap	*15**	*13***	*10**	*14***	*15***	*15***	*8*
High income							
Women	38	35	43	54	51	51	47
Men	34	27	34	47	44	44	39
Democratic Gap	*4*	*8**	*9+*	*7*	*7*	*7*	*8*
Low income							
Women	58	54	59	66	76	65	63
Men	51	63	54	75	71	54	51
Democratic Gap	*7*	*-9*	*5*	*-9*	*5*	*11**	*12**
Not married							
Women	54	51	54	67	69	65	63
Men	46	46	50	72	61	54	52
Democratic Gap	*8**	*5*	*4*	*-5*	*8*	*11**	*11**
At least one child in household							
Women	45	46	47	57	71	54	54
Men	30	31	41	46	60	43	48
Democratic Gap	*15***	*15***	*6*	*11*	*11*	*11**	*6*
Baby boomer cohort							
Women	47	46	50	63	65	59	47
Men	33	35	44	54	53	51	40
Democratic Gap	*14**	*11***	*6*	*9*	*12**	*8*	*7*

* *p* < .05.
** *p* < .01.
Source: ANES pooled data set.
Note: Data are unweighted. Entries are the percentage of respondents who supported the Democratic candidate in each year. Cross-tabulations for vote choice are confined to respondents who reported voting for one of the two major party candidates, and subject to a chi-square test of association.

are somewhat more supportive of Democratic candidates than their male counterparts, but a comparable gap is also found among high-income women and men.

Generational explanations for the gap are also unsupported by the data; female baby boomers are more likely than males of their generation to identify as Democrats, but not more so than women in general. In a similar vein, there are few demographic differences in the magnitude of the gender gap in partisanship, as seen earlier in Table 8.3. Professional men and women are the most politically divergent (although the gap among them is not significantly larger than the overall gap in subsequent multivariate analyses). And professional women are actually slightly less, not more, supportive of Democratic candidates than women overall in most years (with the exception of 1996 and 2004). There is thus little support here for the autonomy hypothesis. The economic vulnerability hypothesis also fares poorly. The gender gap is of comparable size regardless of men and women's income level. Low-income women are more likely than low-income men to identify as Democrats in five of the seven elections, but no more so than women in general. If anything,

Table 8.3. Democratic Partisan Identification within Specific Subgroups

	1980	1984	1988	1992	1996	2000	2004
Women	56	51	51	55	58	54	54
Men	50	46	43	45	46	46	45
Total Democratic Gap	*6**	*5*	*8***	*10***	*12***	*8***	*9***
Professional occupation							
Women	*53*	*50*	*49*	*54*	*59*	*51*	*63*
Men	*42*	*42*	*37*	*41*	*38*	*40*	*47*
Democratic Gap	*11**	*8*	*12***	*13***	*21***	*11***	*16***
High income							
Women	51	45	43	48	46	50	56
Men	41	37	39	37	36	42	39
Democratic Gap	*10**	*8**	*4*	*11***	*10**	*8*	*17***
Low income							
Women	62	58	58	57	65	59	59
Men	65	56	50	57	61	54	50
Democratic Gap	*−3*	*2*	*8*	*0*	*4*	*5*	*9*
Not married							
Women	60	55	55	59	63	59	61
Men	57	51	46	51	54	51	53
Democratic Gap	*3*	*4*	*9**	*8**	*9**	*8**	*8*
At least one child in household							
Women	60	52	49	49	64	51	51
Men	42	40	42	39	51	42	50
Democratic Gap	*8***	*12***	*7**	*10**	*13*	*9**	*1*
Baby boomer cohort							
Women	57	49	49	56	57	56	48
Men	45	41	42	45	48	46	42
Democratic Gap	*12***	*8**	*7**	*11***	*9**	*10**	*6*

* *p* < .05.
** *p* < .01.
Source: ANES pooled data set.
Note: Data are unweighted. Entries are the percentage of respondents who identified with the Democratic Party in each year (including independent leaners). All cross-tabulations are subject to a chi-square test of association.

the gender gap is a little more consistent among high-income Americans. Overall, the gender gap in both partisanship and vote choice is widespread and cannot be isolated among specific subgroups of women and men.

Multivariate Analyses

Does the gender gap in vote choice and partisanship persist with controls for various other factors linked to gender, such as low income or single marital status, which might actually account for the observed gender gap? To answer this question, we ran a series of multivariate analyses (logistic regression models) in which we assessed the extent to which vote choice varied by gender and a number of other sociodemographic and religious factors for each election between 1980 and 2004. Similar analyses were conducted to examine the origins of Democratic and Republican identification (using ordered probit analyses). In these analyses, individuals who describe themselves as politically independent but lean toward one of the two parties were included as partisans. The analyses for electoral choice are presented in Table 8.4, and the findings for partisanship in Table 8.5.

The gender gap in party identification in vote choice holds even when we control for possible differences among men and women based on the demographic and religious characteristics listed in Tables 8.3 and 8.4. The effects of gender are positive in each election except 1992, the only year in which the gender gap (of roughly six points) disappears (and this is because of other factors). The gender gap in partisanship persists in multivariate analyses in all years from 1988 onward, but it is not statistically significant in either 1980 or 1984. In sum, the gender gap is not simply an artifact of related factors such as economic vulnerability, work status, professional occupation, or educational level that promote support for the Democratic Party regardless of gender. The gender gap exists independently of a slew of demographic and religious factors.

We also expanded the multivariate models in Tables 8.3 and 8.4 by adding a series of interaction terms between gender and other factors. In essence, this approach provides a rigorous test of the economic vulnerability and autonomy hypotheses to determine whether the gender gap is bigger in some groups than others. In these analyses, gender is interacted with variables that tap economic factors and women's life circumstances: professional occupation, income, marital status, the presence of children, and generation. Analyses were run for vote choice and partisanship in each election year. We do not show the analyses here because very few of the interactions were significant, indicating that the gender gap was of roughly the same size in all of these subgroups.

In confirmation of findings reported earlier in Tables 8.2 and 8.3, the gender gap did not vary consistently in size across specific subgroups of men and women. There was no year in which the gender gap in partisanship varied significantly in size within specific religious, occupational, union, income, marital status, birth cohort, or regional subgroups in the expanded multivariate analyses. None of the interaction terms with gender reached significance (at the .05 level in a two-way test) out of a total of eighty-one coefficients (thirteen coefficients in seven elections).

There were a few instances in which the gender gap in vote choice varied significantly among demographic and religious groupings. For instance, women baby boomers and pre-boomers were substantially more inclined than men in the same birth cohorts to support Jimmy Carter in 1980. White women were significantly more likely than white men to support Michael Dukakis in 1988. Married women were much more likely than married men to support Bill Clinton in 1992. And employed women were especially likely to vote for Clinton in 1996 when compared to employed men. But none of these instances of a heightened gender gap in vote choice represent a consistent trend across elections, and overall there were only four elections in which there was a statistically significant heightened gender gap in one of these subgroups (out of a total of eighty-one possible instances). This is no greater than what might be observed by chance. Efforts to examine more complex combinations of background factors (such as single professional women or single mothers) also fail to uncover any consistent trends in vote choice.[49]

Table 8.4. The Determinants of Democratic Presidential Vote Choice

	1980	1984	1988	1992	1996	2000	2004
Female	.40*	.34*	.39**	.21	.67**	.47**	.42*
	(.18)	(.14)	(.14)	(.14)	(.16)	(.14)	(.17)
White	-1.84**	-1.54**	-1.87**	-1.52**	-1.75**	-1.38**	-1.61**
	(.28)	(.20)	(.22)	(.21)	(.24)	(.20)	(.23)
Protestant	-.35	-.83**	-1.25**	-.86**	-1.01**	-.71**	-.07
	(.29)	(.23)	(.28)	(.25)	(.26)	(.24)	(.26)
Catholic	-.09	-.46	-.87**	-.47	-.63*	-.74**	.22
	(.32)	(.25)	(.30)	(.27)	(.29)	(.25)	(.28)
Weekly Church	-.18	-.14	.00	-.66**	-.80**	-.48**	-.50*
Attendance	(.18)	(.16)	(.16)	(.16)	(.18)	(.17)	(.21)
Monthly Church	.42	.28	.13	-.47*	-.03	.09	-.64*
Attendance	(.28)	(.21)	(.23)	(.23)	(.24)	(.21)	(.25)
Fundamentalist	-.19	-.23	-.32*	-.79**	-.43*	-.44**	-.69**
	(.18)	(.15)	(.16)	(.16)	(.18)	(.17)	(.21)
Some College	-.38+	-.18	-.50**	-.26	-.54**	.31	-.29
	(.22)	(.17)	(.18)	(.18)	(.21)	(.25)	(.21)

Table 8.4. Continued

	1980	1984	1988	1992	1996	2000	2004
College Degree	−.75**	−.07	−.80**	−.84	−.59*	.22	−.19
	(.28)	(.22)	(.23)	(.21)	(.24)	(.19)	(.25)
Post Graduate Degree	.28	.60*	−.05	−.19	−.43	.10	n.a.
	(.37)	(.30)	(.30)	(.27)	(.29)	(.25)	
Professional	.17	.07	.30	−.01	.05	.00	.72**
	(.21)	(.18)	(.18)	(.17)	(.19)	(.16)	(.20)
Currently Working	.08	−.12	.15	.12	.29	−.33	.07
	(.19)	(.17)	(.17)	(.17)	(.20)	(.18)	(.23)
Union Member	.86**	1.14**	.78**	.56**	1.31**	.74**	.95**
	(.20)	(.16)	(.18)	(.19)	(.20)	(.20)	(.22)
High Income	−.12	−.66**	−.45**	−.37*	−.36*	−.32	−.44*
	(.21)	(.17)	(.17)	(.17)	(.19)	(.19)	(.21)
Low Income	.51*	.53**	.15	.06	.68**	.24	.29
	(.23)	(.18)	(.20)	(.21)	(.23)	(.20)	(.24)
Missing Income	−.05	.02	.09	−.27	−.03	−.24	−.42
	(.31)	(.26)	(.26)	(.31)	(.29)	(.23)	(.32)
Married	.14	−.06	.10	−.43**	−.14	−.39*	−.47**
	(.20)	(.15)	(.16)	(.16)	(.18)	(.16)	(.18)
Children	−.32	−.14	−.38*	−.17	.45	−.14	.24
	(.18)	(.17)	(.18)	(.18)	(.33)	(.17)	(.21)
Baby Boomer	−.42	.26	.15	.30	.24	.36*	−.12
	(.42)	(.24)	(.22)	(.18)	(.20)	(.17)	(.20)
Pre–Baby Boomer	−.44	.36	.04	.33	.18	.12	.39
	(.41)	(.24)	(.23)	(.20)	(.22)	(.22)	(.25)
Northeast	−.13	−.16	−.36	.32	.47*	−.16	−.15
	(.25)	(.20)	(.21)	(.20)	(.24)	(.21)	(.26)
West	−.07	.32	−.09	−.31	−.08	−.08	−.11
	(.26)	(.19)	(.19)	(.20)	(.23)	(.21)	(.24)
South	.35	.07	−.01	.29	.26	−.41*	−.06
	(.21)	(.18)	(.18)	(.18)	(.20)	(.18)	(.22)
Urban	.72**	.58**	.36*	.43*	.21	n.a.	n.a.
	(.21)	(.18)	(.19)	(.17)	(.20)		
Rural	.00	.12	.10	.08	.06	n.a.	n.a.
	(.19)	(.15)	(.17)	(.16)	(.18)		
Constant	1.37*	.99*	2.36**	2.83**	2.33	2.29**	1.47**
	(.60)	(.45)	(.49)	(.45)	(.50)	(.18)	(.48)
N	818	1233	1097	1165	989	1027	766
Pseudo R²	.15	.15	.15	.16	.20	.11	.14

Source: ANES pooled data set. * $p < .05$, ** $p < .0$.

Note: Entries are logit coefficients with robust standard errors in parentheses. All variables are coded on a 0 to 1 scale.

Sources of Women's (and Men's) Disunity

Our analysis of the gender gap demonstrates its persistence across specific demographic groups; it also clearly illuminates factors that divide women (and men) politically. A closer examination of Tables 8.4 and 8.5 highlights the powerfully divisive influence of race, religion, and economics on men and women's political preferences.

RACE

Whites have been significantly more likely than nonwhites to support Republican presidential candidates in every election between 1980 and 2004. When blacks are broken out from other nonwhites in Table 8.5, it is clear that they are much more likely to identify as Democrats than any other racial group. Whites are also somewhat more likely to identify with the Republican Party than individuals in the "other" racial grouping (the omitted category). To flesh out these findings for vote choice, we calculated the predicted probability of Democratic support for the "average" voter (with modal characteristics) who is Protestant, nonfundamentalist, has a high school degree or less, is nonprofessional, is employed, lives in a medium-income household, is married with at least one child at home, is a baby boomer, and is living in a suburb in the Northeast. We varied race and gender in the calculation of predicted probabilities to see how these factors shape support for the Democratic presidential candidate in a given election. These predicted probabilities better illustrate the impact of race on vote choice than coefficients in the logistic regressions (which are difficult to interpret).

Table 8.5. The Determinants of Democratic Party Identification

	1980	1984	1988	1992	1996	2000	2004
Female	.10	.10	.19**	.25**	.35**	.22**	.30**
	(.08)	(.06)	(.07)	(.06)	(.07)	(.06)	(.08)
White	−.21	−.35**	−.44**	−.24*	−.27**	−.14	−.16
	(.17)	(.11)	(.11)	(.10)	(.10)	(.10)	(.11)
Black	.76**	.52**	.65**	.75**	.79**	1.18**	1.41**
	(.21)	(.15)	(.16)	(.13)	(.15)	(.15)	(.17)
Protestant	−.05	−.32**	−.38**	−.29**	−.40**	−.19*	−.27*
	(.13)	(.11)	(.12)	(.09)	(.10)	(.10)	(.13)
Catholic	.33*	.03	−.09	.15	−.02	−.03	.05
	(.14)	(.12)	(.13)	(.10)	(.12)	(.11)	(.13)
Jewish	1.22**	.65**	.37	.94**	.60*	.96**	.64*
	(.31)	(.24)	(.24)	(.27)	(.29)	(.25)	(.28)
Weekly Church	−.22**	−.07	−.13	−.33**	−.29**	−.27**	−.19*
Attendance	(.08)	(.07)	(.08)	(.07)	(.08)	(.08)	(.10)

Table 8.5. Continued

	1980	1984	1988	1992	1996	2000	2004
Monthly Church	−.14	.02	−.05	−.12	−.02	−.09	−.31**
Attendance	(.13)	(.09)	(.10)	(.06)	(.10)	(.10)	(.12)
Fundamentalist	.04	−.13	.00	−.07	−.17*	−.14	−.26**
	(.08)	(.07)	(.07)	(.06)	(.08)	(.07)	(.10)
Some College	−.11	−.11	−.14	−.18*	−.16*	−.11	−.17+
	(.09)	(.08)	(.08)	(.07)	(.08)	(.11)	(.10)
College Degree	−.16	−.21	−.37**	−.34**	−.22*	−.19*	−.16
	(.13)	(.11)	(.11)	(.09)	(.11)	(.09)	(.12)
Post Graduate Degree	.15	.07	−.02	−.10	−.05	−.18	*n.a.*
	(.18)	(.16)	(.16)	(.12)	(.14)	(.13)	
Professional	−.09	.09	.04	.04	.06	−.06	.32**
	(.10)	(.09)	(.09)	(.07)	(.08)	(.08)	(.10)
Currently Working	−.00	.06	.07	.07	.11	−.04	.09
	(.09)	(.08)	(.08)	(.07)	(.09)	(.08)	(.11)
Union Membership	.36**	.47**	.39**	.46**	.41**	.43**	.38**
	(.08)	(.08)	(.08)	(.08)	(.09)	(.10)	(.11)
High Income	−.16	−.28**	−.08	−.31**	−.36**	−.01	−.15
	(.09)	(.08)	(.08)	(.07)	(.09)	(.09)	(.11)
Low Income	.23*	.21*	.16	.01	.10	.13	.12
	(.10)	(.08)	(.09)	(.08)	(.09)	(.09)	(.11)
Missing Income	.02	−.06	.17	−.11	−.13	−.15	−.17
	(.13)	(.11)	(.12)	(.11)	(.12)	(.10)	(.14)
Married	−.02	−.04	−.02	−.08	−.05	−.14*	−.26**
	(.08)	(.07)	(.07)	(.06)	(.07)	(.07)	(.09)
Children	.03	.01	−.04	−.13	.15	−.11	.03
	(.08)	(.07)	(.08)	(.08)	(.12)	(.08)	(.10)
Baby Boomer	−.13	.09	.24**	.24**	.16*	.10	−.09
	(.15)	(.09)	(.09)	(.07)	(.08)	(.08)	(.09)
Pre–Baby Boomer	−.10	.22*	.35**	.27**	.17	.10	.12
	(.15)	(.10)	(.10)	(.08)	(.09)	(.10)	(.12)
Northeast	−.16	−.09	−.04	.13	−.01	−.03	−.03
	(.10)	(.09)	(.09)	(.08)	(.10)	(.10)	(.12)
West	.18	.14	.03	−.04	.09	−.01	.06
	(.11)	(.09)	(.10)	(.09)	(.10)	(.09)	(.11)
South	.27**	.30**	.36**	.22**	.03	−.10	−.02
	(.09)	(.08)	(.08)	(.07)	(.08)	(.08)	(.11)
Urban	.24**	.17*	.17	.39**	.24**	*n.a.*	*n.a.*
	(.10)	(.08)	(.09)	(.07)	(.09)		
Rural	.00	−.01	−.05	.05	.18*	*n.a.*	*n.a.*
	(.08)	(.07)	(.08)	(.06)	(.08)		
Cut point 1	−.37	−.33	−.29	−.40	−.42	−.58	−.35
	(.27)	(.20)	(.20)	(.18)	(.19)	(.17)	(.22)
Cut point 2	−.01	−.04	.01	−.05	−.17	−.26	−.08
	(.27)	(.21)	(.20)	(.18)	(.19)	(.17)	(.22)
N	1264	1718	1600	2089	1607	1598	1116
Pseudo R²	.08	.08	.09	.10	.10	.09	.12

Source: ANES pooled data set. **p<.05, **p<.01.*

Note: Entries are ordered logit coefficients with robust standard errors in parentheses. All variables are coded on a 0 to 1 scale.

Figure 8.1 depicts the gender gap in vote choice for the "average" voter
who is either black or white and male or female across all election years. The
divergence between black and white females is made plain by this graph. The
largest racial difference among women occurs in 1980 when 70 percent of
black and only 25 percent of "average" white women voters supported Jimmy
Carter, the Democratic candidate. Among the same group of women, racial
differences reach their lowest value, just under twenty points, in 1996 (although once again it is worth remembering that Clinton support is inflated
because of the exclusion of Perot voters). The difference between "average"
black and white women voters is enormous, but so is the difference between
comparable black and white men. There is simply a large racial divide in support of Democratic candidates that swamps the gender gap in every presidential election studied in this data set.

Figure 8.1 also makes clear the persistence of a small gender gap among
whites and blacks, respectively. Across all election years, the mean gender

Figure 8.1: Predicted support for Democratic candidates by race and gender.

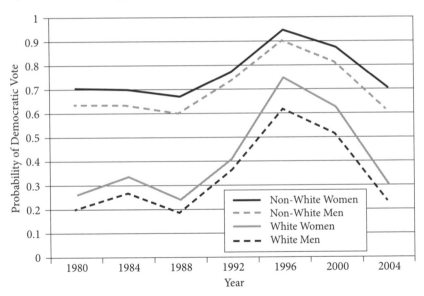

Note: Predicted values are based on logit equations in Table 8.4 and are calculated for respondents
with modal sample characteristics (Protestant, nonfundamentalist, monthly church attendance, high
school educated, nonprofessional, employed, medium household income, married with at least one
child at home, baby boomer, living in a suburb in the Northeast), who vary in terms of their race
and gender.

gap between "average" white men and white women voters is roughly eight percentage points. The comparable gap among black men and women is six percentage points. In other words, even with very large racial differences in vote choice, both black and white women are somewhat more likely to support Democratic candidates than their male counterparts.

RELIGION

Race produces the greatest divide in American politics among women and men. But religion is close behind and has had a growing influence on both vote choice and partisanship in recent elections. Protestants have consistently supported Republican candidates when compared to individuals who describe their religion as "other" (the omitted category), as can be seen in the multivariate analyses presented in Table 8.4 (with the exception of 1980 and 2004). Catholics were once part of the Democratic coalition, but they too have been more inclined to support Republican candidates in these data than those with an "other" religion, although these effects are less consistent. The effects of religion also emerge in analyses of partisanship in Table 8.5. It is possible to further separate Jews from Christians and other religions in this larger sample, which includes nonvoters. And analyses in Table 8.5 make clear that Protestants identify less as Democrats, Jews identify more, and Catholics about the same as individuals in the "other" religion category, although once again effects vary in strength across elections.[50] These findings are consistent with the expected impact of religion on partisan leanings.

Religiosity (independent of specific religion) has more fully consistent political effects than religion, especially on vote choice. As seen in Table 8.4, individuals who attend religious services at least weekly have been substantially less likely than those who attend services infrequently to support Democratic candidates since the 1992 presidential election. They have also been less likely to identify as Democrats over the same time period, a trend that emerged initially in 1980 (Table 8.5). Individuals who believe in a fundamentalist or literal interpretation of the Bible have been consistently more supportive of Republican candidates since the 1988 election, although they are not consistently less Democratic in identification.[51]

When considered together, religion and religiosity produce a second large divide among American women and men. To illustrate this divide, we calculated the predicted probability of support for the Democratic presidential candidate among "average" Protestant men and women who are either secular (nonfundamentalists who attend religious services infrequently) or very religious (fundamentalists who attend services at least weekly). We calculate these probabilities for Protestants although we expect similar findings for other

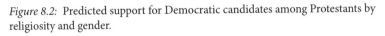

Figure 8.2: Predicted support for Democratic candidates among Protestants by religiosity and gender.

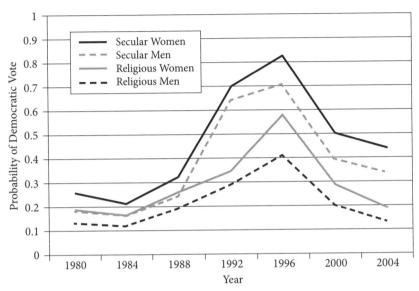

Note: Predicted values are based on logit equations in Table 8.4 and are calculated for respondents with modal sample characteristics (white, Protestant, high school educated, nonprofessional, employed, medium household income, married with at least one child at home, baby boomer, living in a suburb in the Northeast), who vary in terms of their religiosity and gender. Secular respondents do not hold a literal interpretation of the Bible and attend religious services rarely or never. Religious respondents attend services weekly or more often and believe in the literal interpretation of the Bible.

religions based on the analyses presented in Tables 8.4 and 8.5. The magnitude of both the gender and religiosity gap over time is evident in Figure 8.2. Prior to 1988, there was almost no "religiosity" gap in support of Democratic candidates. But it emerged quite visibly in 1992, resulting in a gap of roughly thirty-five percentage points between secular and religious women, a gap that has persisted over time at somewhere between twenty-two and twenty-five points. A comparable religiosity gap is observed among men.

In contrast, the gender gap is present among religious and nonreligious individuals, but is much smaller. There has been a persistent gender gap among religious men and women that was smallest in 1984 (four points) and largest in 1996 (seventeen points). A gender gap of similar magnitude emerges among secular women, as can be seen in Figure 8.2. Our findings reveal that, despite their differences, religious and secular women have something in common: they are more likely to support Democratic candidates than their male counterparts.

Social Class

Conventional political wisdom tends to minimize the importance of class in contemporary American politics. However, evidence presented in both Tables 8.4 and 8.5 contradicts this conclusion. Union membership, household income, and, to a lesser extent, education all influence electoral choice and partisanship. The political effects of living in a union household may have subsided over time but they still remain a strong source of Democratic identification and support for Democratic candidates. Members of union households have been more likely than others to support Democratic candidates and identify as Democrats in every presidential election between 1980 and 2004. These effects are large and statistically significant.

Income and education also influence electoral choices, although less consistently. Individuals in high-income households (the top third) were more supportive than those in mid-income households of Republican presidential candidates in all years except 1980 and 2000, and were more likely to identify as Republicans in 1984, 1992, and 1996. In contrast, low income increased support for Democratic candidates and Democratic partisanship in some but not all years. Having at least some college education or a college degree inclines Americans toward greater support of Republican candidates and the Republican Party when compared to those with no more than a high school degree. But once again these effects are sporadic, as can be seen in Tables 8.4 and 8.5. Those with at least a college education or a college degree evince some greater support of Republican candidates or the party in 1980, 1988, 1992, 1996, and 2000, but only eleven out of a total of twenty-eight coefficients (for some college or a college degree) reach statistical significance.[52] This is clearly better than chance but is not a consistent trend. It is important to note that these effects do not extend to Americans with postgraduate degrees, who are no different in their support for Democratic candidates or the party than those with a high school education (except in 1984, when they supported Mondale).

Both women and men are therefore also divided by class-related factors, especially residence in a union household. The magnitude of class differences becomes clearer in examination of the predicted probabilities of support for a Democratic presidential candidate. Predicted probabilities were calculated for the "average" voter who varied in gender, household income, and union membership. These probabilities are depicted in Figure 8.3 and illustrate the large class gap among women (and men). The gap among women ranges from a low of eighteen points in 1996 to a sizeable thirty-four points in 2004. In all instances, medium-income women in a union household are more likely to support Democratic candidates than wealthier nonunion women. The "class" gap is equally pronounced among men, ranging from a low of eighteen points to a high of thirty-two. For the years under examination, the percentage of respondents living in a union household ranged from a high of 26 percent (in 1980) to a low of 15 percent (in 2000). An even smaller percentage of respondents live in medium-income union households (7 percent on average). Thus, some of the differences depicted in Figure 8.3 do not reach statistical significance because of small sample sizes and large standard errors. Nonetheless, the trend is consistent over time and in the expected direction for all years.

In comparison, the gender gap is relatively small within both class groupings. When averaged across all years, the gender gap is eight points among both low-income individuals living in a union household and among indi-

Figure 8.3: Predicted support for Democratic candidates by income, union household, and gender.

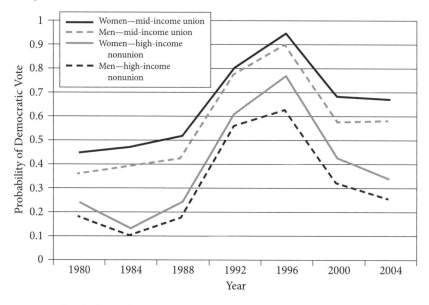

Note: Predicted values are based on logit equations in Table 8.4 and are calculated for respondents with modal sample characteristics (white, Protestant, nonfundamentalist, high school educated, nonprofessional, employed, married with at least one child at home, baby boomer, living in a suburb in the Northeast), who vary in terms of their income, residence in a union household, religiosity, and gender. High income is the top third of the distribution of household income in each year, and low is the bottom third.

viduals in high-income, nonunion households. Overall, women are more supportive of Democratic candidates than their male counterparts.

Finally, there are a few other sources of disunity among women and men in Tables 8.4 and 8.5 that deserve mention. Living in an urban area is fairly consistently linked to support of Democratic candidates and the Democratic Party, although we lack data on this for the most recent election years. In contrast, the effects of geographic region are very weak. Southerners were still more likely to identify as Democrats up until 1992 but have not differed in partisanship since, and there are no consistent effects of region on vote choice over time. Thus, urban women (and men) are likely to differ from nonurban women (and men) in their stronger support of Democratic candidates and the Democratic Party. But there are no obvious regional differences that currently divide women politically.

Conclusion

Race, religion, and economics form powerful sources of cleavage among women (and men) that vastly outweigh women's commonality, a finding observed in our research and elsewhere.[53] These differences emerge, in part, from the persistence of the traditional Democratic coalition. Black women are more supportive than white women of the Democratic Party; both black and Jewish women are more likely to identify as Democrats than other women; and women in union households are more supportive than others of Democratic candidates and more inclined to identify with the Democratic Party. A more recent Republican coalition of high-income and religious individuals is also apparent in our data, producing further cleavages among women. Women in wealthier households support Republican candidates and identify with the Republican Party. Women who believe in the Bible as the literal word of God and frequently attend religious services, regardless of denomination, are more supportive than secular women of Republican candidates. And women who frequently attend religious services are also more inclined to identify as Republicans. Women's political differences based on race, religion, and economics are larger, on average, than the gender gap and place it in needed perspective.

Nonetheless, there is a small, stable gender gap in vote choice and partisanship of roughly eight to ten percentage points that exists even after controlling for a variety of sociodemographic and religious characteristics, and cannot be isolated among one or more subgroups of women and men in these analyses. A robust difference of this magnitude has obvious electoral importance and its origins deserve careful scrutiny. It is not a product of women's shared material interests in the ANES pooled data because it is observed among men and women across a very broad array of sociodemographic and religious groupings. This raises an obvious question. What are the origins of the gender gap if not in women's shared economic interests?

Attitudinal factors that transcend material circumstances, such as political beliefs or specific policy positions, are an obvious alternative source of the gender gap. We noted earlier that the gap is often traced empirically to women's greater support of social welfare spending.[54] But this finding does not clearly illuminate the origins of the gender gap, raising instead a second pertinent question as to why women are more supportive of welfare spending. We can rule out any greater reliance among women on government policies because the gender gap is apparent across a broad spectrum of women who vary in household wealth, occupation, and work and family status.

The gap might be because of women's greater compassion and concern for the poor, consistent with evidence of sociotropic voting among women and pocketbook voting among men.[55] But this political compassion hypothesis raises a number of additional questions. Are women, in fact, more concerned about the plight of the poor than men? Do they rate themselves as more socially compassionate? Are they more forgiving and understanding when it comes to the origins and solutions to poverty? Does the impact of compassion have limits so that it is more focused on the protection of the young and elderly than on poverty more generally? And do women translate this compassion into support for specific candidates and policies? Schlesinger and Heldman provide partial supportive evidence, observing gender differences in emotional response to social problems, awareness of them among one's own family, and the perceived fairness of social institutions.[56] The compassion hypothesis would gain stronger support from evidence that the gender gap is fueled by women who score highly on empathy scales, rate themselves as compassionate, or who express sympathy with the plight of disadvantaged people.

Other factors also sporadically figure into the gender gap. Women's greater opposition to the use of force has fueled the gender gap in some years.[57] But these effects are variable over time and are unlikely to consistently drive the gender gap across elections. Others argue for the existence of a feminist gap, in which the gender gap is driven largely by women who identify as feminists.[58] It is important to remember, however, that traditional women's issues do not drive the gender gap, raising questions about whether the feminist gap conveys the impact of broader nongender political beliefs such as egalitarianism.

One clear political consequence of a robust gender gap is its likely future persistence, regardless of specific election year, salient issues, or particular candidates. Our analyses suggest that the gender gap in partisanship has solidified since 1988, and may now be firmly ensconced in American politics. It remains to be seen whether politicians can successfully manipulate the gap to further alter the current partisan balance. Men have clearly veered away from the Democratic Party while women remain loyalists, helping to explain the greater success of Republicans in recent decades. If the gender gap revolves centrally around social compassion, the Republican Party must determine how to pursue a conservative economic agenda while not appearing overly hard-hearted in order to attract additional women voters. George W. Bush's simple adoption of the term "compassionate conservative" obviously did little to undermine the gender gap. Democrats face the equally difficult challenge of appealing to men who are less supportive of social welfare spending without losing their image as concerned about the disadvantaged, a feat mastered successfully by Bill Clinton with the passage of welfare reform in 1996.

In sum, women are more divided than united politically, but they also display some limited political commonality. And although their political differences are large and suggest substantial caveats on the notion of the "women's vote," their commonalities are sufficient to determine electoral outcomes. More probing research is thus needed on the gender gap to better understand its origins and responsiveness to specific electoral forces. Perhaps the gap will persist regardless of the actions of the Republican and Democratic parties and their standard-bearers. But if the gender gap widens or narrows in the future, it could have a long-lasting impact on the American political landscape.

Notes

1. Brooks and Manza, "Social Cleavages and Political Alignments"; Carroll, "Voting Choices," in Carroll and Fox, *Gender and Elections*.

2. Box-Steffensmeier, Bouf, and Lin, "Dynamics of the Partisan Gender Gap"; Chaney, Alvarez, and Nagler, "Explaining the Gender Gap"; Adell Cook and Wilcox, "Women Voters in the Year of the Woman," in Weisberg, *Democracy's Feast*.

3. Carroll, "Voting Choices," in Carroll and Fox, *Gender and Elections*.

4. Tate, *From Protest to Politics*.

5. Carroll, "Voting Choices."

6. Tate, *From Protest to Politics*.

7. Huddy, "Group Identity and Political Cohesion," in Sears, Huddy, and Jervis, *Oxford Handbook of Political Psychology*.

8. Chaney, Alvarez, and Nagler, "Explaining the Gender Gap"; Klein *Gender Politics*; Shapiro and Mahajan, "Gender Differences in Policy Preferences"; Mansbridge, "Myth and Reality."

9. Klein, *Gender Politics.*

10. Mansbridge, "Myth and Reality."

11. Frankovic, "Sex and Politics."

12. Klein, *Gender Politics*; Mueller, "Empowerment of Women," in Mueller, *Politics of the Gender Gap.*

13. Chaney, Alvarez, and Nagler, "Explaining the Gender Gap"; Adell Cook and Wilcox, "Feminism and the Gender Gap"; Manza and Brooks, "Gender Gap in U.S. Presidential Elections."

14. Chaney, Alvarez, and Nagler, "Explaining the Gender Gap"; Adell Cook and Wilcox, "Feminism and the Gender Gap"; Mansbridge, "Myth and Reality."

15. Sapiro, "Theorizing Gender in Political Psychology Research," in Sears, Huddy, and Jervis, *Oxford Handbook of Political Psychology.*

16. Sears and Huddy, "On the Origins of the Political Disunity," in Tilly and Gurin, *Women, Politics, and Change.*

17. Chaney, Alvarez, and Nagler, "Explaining the Gender Gap."

18. Gilens, "Gender and Support for Reagan"; Kaufmann and Petrocik, "Changing Politics of American Men"; Manza and Brooks, "Gender Gap in U.S. Presidential Elections."

19. Piven, "Women and the State," in Rossi, *Gender and the Life Course.*

20. Box-Steffensmeier, Bouf, and Lin, "Dynamics of the Partisan Gender Gap."

21. Carroll, "Women's Autonomy and the Gender Gap," in Mueller, *Politics of the Gender Gap*; Carroll, "Voting Choices."

22. Erie and Rein, "Women and the Welfare State," in Mueller, *Politics of the Gender Gap*; Rosenbluth, Salmond, and Thies, "Welfare Works"; Manza and Brooks, "Gender Gap in U.S. Presidential Elections."

23. Berelson, Lazarsfeld, and McPhee, *Voting*; Campbell et al., *American Voter.*

24. Huddy, "Group Identity and Political Cohesion," in Sears, Huddy, and Jervis, *Oxford Handbook of Political Psychology.*

25. Jackman, *Velvet Glove*; Kinder, and Sanders, *Divided by Color*; Kinder and Winter, "Exploring the Racial Divide"; Schuman et al., *Racial Attitudes in America*; Sigelman and Welch, *Black Americans' Views of Racial Inequality*; Tate, *From Protest to Politics*; Tuch, Sigelman, and Martin, "Fifty Years After Myrdal," in Tuch and Martin, *Racial Attitudes in the 1990s*; Welch et al., *Race and Place.*

26. Tate, *From Protest to Politics.*

27. Fiorina, Abrams, and Pope, *Culture War?*

28. Huddy, Feldman, and Dutton, "Role of Religion."

29. Stanley and Niemi, "Demise of the New Deal Coalition," in Weisberg, *Democracy's Feast.*

30. Berelson, Lazarsfeld, and McPhee, *Voting*; Campbell et al., *American Voter;*

Stanley and Niemi, "Demise of the New Deal Coalition," in Weisberg, *Democracy's Feast.*

31. Hunter, *Culture Wars.*

32. Berelson, Lazarsfeld, and McPhee, *Voting*; Campbell et al., *American Voter;* Stanley and Niemi, "Demise of the New Deal Coalition," in Weisberg, *Democracy's Feast.*

33. Huddy, Feldman, and Dutton, "Role of Religion."

34. Stanley and Niemi, "Demise of the New Deal Coalition," in Weisberg, *Democracy's Feast.*

35. Sperry, *Are Republican Sprawlers.*

36. All analyses are unweighted because the ANES data set only contains weights for data collected from 1992 onward. There were only minor differences in our findings when the data are reanalyzed using weights, and these are noted in the relevant section of text.

37. Voters who supported independent candidates were removed from the vote tally in all years in order to compare across elections.

38. For the presidential voting models, there is insufficient racial diversity in the years from 1980 to 2004 to distinguish between multiple racial categories. For these models, a dummy variable is included to indicate the effect of white identification relative to identification as nonwhite. The enhanced sample size for partisanship models allows for greater racial differentiation. In these analyses, other race/ethnicity is treated as the missing category.

39. Because of reduced sample size, Jews were only distinguished in the analyses of partisanship, not vote choice. Other religion was the missing category in multivariate analyses.

40. High school or less was the omitted category in multivariate analyses.

41. Income categories are based on respondent reports of household income. Reported income was transformed from dollars to income percentiles. The income ranges corresponding to each percentile varied by year (see the National Election Studies Cumulative Data File Appendix for more details). Here, low income corresponds to family incomes in the 0–33 percentile. Medium income reflects family incomes in the 34–67 percentile. In this analysis, medium income is the baseline category for the income variables. High income corresponds to household incomes in the 68–100 percentile range. In addition, we included a dummy variable for missing income to avoid list-wise deletion of these observations.

42. The question wording for the item about the number of children living in the respondent's household varied from the standard item in 1994 and 2000. Observations for these years are not included in the National Election Studies Cumulative Data File. Instead, this information was taken from the individual data sets for 1994 and 2000.

43. The post–baby boom cohort was treated as the missing category in analyses.

44. It was not possible to evaluate the influence of holding a postgraduate degree

in 2004 because there were no respondents in this category. In addition, the effects of urban and rural residence could not be assessed in 2000 because it was not asked of respondents who were interviewed by phone or in 2004 because the question was not asked of any respondent.

45. Pomper, "Presidential Election," in Pomper, *Election of 2000*.

46. The slightly larger gender gap in 2004 holds up when the data are weighted.

47. For a similar finding, see Norrander, "Independence Gap and the Gender Gap," and Norrander's article in this volume.

48. Conway, Steurnagel, and Ahern, *Women and Political Participation*.

49. Single professional women were more supportive of Bill Clinton in 1992 than single professional men but that was the only year in which the coefficient was significant.

50. These effects are slightly weaker when the data are weighed. With weights, the coefficient for Catholic is no longer significant for vote choice in 1996, and coefficients for Protestant in 2000 and Jewish in 1996 and 2004 are no longer significant for partisanship.

51. The impact of fundamentalism is not significant in 1996 once the data are weighted.

52. The number of significant coefficients for some college or college education diminishes slightly with the addition of weights to eight.

53. Brooks and Manza, "Social Cleavages and Political Alignments"; Mattei and Mattei, "If Men Stayed Home"; Sapiro and Conover, "Variable Gender Basis of Electoral Politics."

54. Gilens, "Gender and Support for Reagan"; Kaufmann, "Culture Wars, Secular Realignment, and the Gender Gap"; Kaufmann and Petrocik, "Changing Politics of American Men"; Mattei, "Gender Gap in Presidential Evaluations."

55. Chaney, Alvarez, and Nagler, "Explaining the Gender Gap"; Welch and Hibbing, "Financial Conditions, Gender, and Voting."

56. Schlesinger and Heldman, "Gender Gap or Gender Gaps?"

57. Chaney, Alvarez, and Nagler, "Explaining the Gender Gap"; Frankovic, "Sex and Politics"; Gilens, "Gender and Support for Reagan."

58. Conover, "Feminists and the Gender Gap."

9

The Gender Gap

A Comparison across Racial and Ethnic Groups

M. MARGARET CONWAY

The term "gender gap" has been used to describe differences between men and women in vote choice, voter turnout, other types of political
participation, policy preferences, and public opinion differences. Regardless
of the topic studied, almost all research focusing on the United States has
examined the gender gap either exclusively among whites or just within the
white and African American groups. In part this paucity of research can be
attributed to the small numbers of minority group members included in most
national surveys. Only a few studies have expanded analysis of the political
gender gap to include Hispanics, Asian Americans, and Native Americans.
The extent to which a political gender gap occurs within different racial and
ethnic groups merits further study.

This article focuses on the gender gap among several racial and ethnic
groups in the United States, comparing patterns found within those groups.
It first reviews prior research on the political gender gap; then the gender
gap patterns within white, African American, Hispanic, Asian American,
and American Indian racial or ethnic groups are examined, using data from
several surveys conducted between 1990 and 2004.

Prior Research

Survey data collected since 1952 in the American National Election Studies
(ANES) provide evidence for the existence of the political gender gap among
whites and of change over time in its patterns. For example, prior to 1964,
women more frequently voted for Republican Party presidential candidates

than did men.[1] After 1964, women were more likely than men to vote for the Democratic Party presidential candidates.[2] Examining the gender gap in the 1992 presidential election, Franco Mattei suggests the most powerful contributor to the gender gap in voting behavior is beliefs about the proper role of federal government.[3] Other research based on survey data collected during the 1984, 1988, and 1992 elections points out that different levels of salience on economic issues contributed to the gender gap in voting behavior.[4] Since 1980, a gender gap has existed in voting for members of the House of Representatives, with women being more supportive of Democratic Party candidates.[5]

Previous research suggests that a gender gap also exists in other forms of political participation. In their study of political activity, Burns, Schlozman, and Verba found whites to be more politically active than African Americans, who were more politically active than Latinos. Within each racial or ethnic group, men were more politically active than women.[6] However, the disparities between groups in factors affecting political activity were structured more by race or ethnicity than by gender.[7]

Differences have also existed in patterns of party identification. Since 1964, a greater proportion of women than men have identified with the Democratic Party, and, since 1988, a greater proportion of men than women have reported a Republican Party identification.[8] Other studies have examined political ideology and party support among racial and ethnic groups. A study of Hispanic Americans using data from exit polls conducted in 1980, 1984, and 1988 concluded that Hispanic women were more liberal and more supportive of the Democratic Party than were Hispanic men.[9] Another study of the gender gap suggests that the shift in male-female differences in both partisanship and presidential voting may be explained by differences in policy attitudes. An alternative explanation points to the shifts occurring because of different weights that men and women apply to selected attitudes when making decisions about partisan identification and presidential vote choice. Research using survey data from the 1992 and 1996 election studies provides evidence that both explanations contribute to understanding citizens' choices.[10] Other factors besides the gender gap, including educational attainment, level of income, religious affiliation and religiosity, and organizational memberships, appear to influence party identification.[11]

Differences in men's and women's evaluations of presidents also exist. What might explain a gender gap in presidential evaluations? An examination of variations in support for Ronald Reagan, using data from the 1982 NES study, concludes that the most important component of the gender gap in presidential approval was generated by differences in opinions on social and military issues.[12]

These differences in political attitudes may arise from a variety of sources. Possible sources include gender-based social roles, socioeconomic status, and value differences. Gender differences in political attitudes may arise because of compositional effects, which exist when women and men differ on an explanatory variable. A gender gap could also occur as a result of conditional effects that occur when a variable has differential effects on the political orientations of men and women.[13] Lending support to the compositional explanation is research that emphasizes women's autonomy, with increased autonomy resulting from women's increased participation in the labor force.[14]

How might a gender gap in support for government programs be explained? Women might be expected to be more supportive of government programs because they tend to be more compassionate in their reactions to social problems or because they are more aware of such problems among family and friends. Women may perceive gender differences in economic opportunities, with a greater perceived need for effective social programs. Women's personal experiences may also lead them to perceive more unfairness in the operation of social institutions, or they may be more likely to perceive government-sponsored social programs as ineffective.[15]

Another explanation for political gender gaps emphasizes differences in political interest, information, and efficacy. Prior research suggests that women tend to be less politically interested, informed, and efficacious than men. That could contribute to differences in both levels and patterns of political participation.[16]

PRIOR RESEARCH ON THE POLITICAL GENDER GAP WITHIN ETHNIC AND RACIAL GROUPS

The research discussed above focused primarily on white Americans. Do political gender gaps exist within racial and ethnic minorities? As noted above, research on the existence of a political gender gap among racial and ethnic minorities has been limited because few data sets contain large enough samples of minorities to permit valid generalizations. Exceptions are studies that use the U.S. Bureau of the Census Current Population Surveys conducted after the November general elections in even-numbered years. Research by Pei-te Lien compared patterns of voter registration and turnout across racial and ethnic groups using data from the 1992 postelection Current Population Survey. Her analysis of voter turnout rates found small but significant gender differences in voter registration rates among whites and blacks, but not among Latinos and Asians.[17] Subsequent research by Lien used data from the postelection studies conducted by the Bureau of the Census after both the 1992 and 1996 presidential elections. The samples were large enough to permit comparisons among non-Hispanic whites, blacks, Latinos, Asian and Pacific Islanders, and American Indians as well as between men and women within each racial group. Differences in levels of registration and turnout were far less distinct between men and women within each racial and ethnic group than they were between racial and ethnic groups. For example, Asian American men and women had acquired citizenship, registered, and voted at approximately the same rates. Comparing patterns of registration and voting between men and women among blacks, whites, American Indians, and Hispanics, black women were significantly more likely to register and vote than black men, and in 1992, American Indian women had significantly higher registration rates than American Indian men. When controls are applied for socioeconomic conditions and social connections, only among both blacks and whites were women more likely than men to register and vote.[18] To summarize, Lien's research suggests that differences in electoral participation between ethnic and racial groups in registration and voting may be greater than differences in electoral participation between men and women within a racial or ethnic group.

Data

To examine gender differences in political behavior, attitudes, and policy preferences within ethnic and racial groups, the research reported here uses data from several surveys. One data set used is an ANES data file that combines the 1990, 1992, 1994, 1996, 1998, and 2000 data files. This data set permits research on the gender gap within the white, African American, Hispanic, Asian American, and American Indian racial and ethnic groups. Also used in the analysis are the 2004 ANES and the Pew Hispanic Center (PHC) 2004 political survey. The 2004 ANES data set enables additional analysis of the gender gap within white, black, and Latino populations. The PHC data set permits analysis of the gender gap within white, black, and Latino racial and ethnic groups. In addition, inferences about the gender gap contained in the Joint Center for Political and Economic Studies' (JCPES) 2000 *National Opinion Poll* report and the center's *The Black Vote in 2004* are discussed. Gender differences in Asian Americans' political participation and political attitudes based on analyses of data collected in late 2000 and early 2001 by the Preliminary National Asian American Study (PNAAPS) are also presented.[19]

Four topics are considered in this article: (1) the extent to which gender gaps exist in voter registration and turnout; (2) other forms of political participation; (3) orientations toward government and public affairs; (4) and policy preferences on several issues. The discussion focuses on gender gaps within an ethnic or racial group that are statistically significant.

VOTING TURNOUT

Does a gender gap exist in voter turnout within each racial and ethnic group? Based on the ANES data sets used here, the answer would be no. Although a gender gap in turnout existed among whites during 1990 to 2000, it did not occur among the other groups studied. In contrast, analysis of the PHC 2004 data indicates that Hispanic women were significantly more likely than Hispanic men to vote in 2004. The report on the black vote in 2004 by JCPES, using data from the postelection U.S. Bureau of the Census Current Population Survey, suggests that a gender gap in turnout existed between black men and black women, with black women being more likely to vote. In other words, the evidence about a gender gap in voter turnout is mixed, varying both across time and among racial and ethnic groups (see Tables 9.1 and 9.2).

OTHER TYPES OF POLITICAL PARTICIPATION

Other forms of political participation are also possible. One is to engage in campaign activities, such as volunteering in a campaign, donating money, and attending political meetings. Based on the ANES 1990 to 2000 data set, it appears that men more frequently than women in the white, African

Table 9.1. Political Participation by Gender by Racial or Ethnic Group, 1990–2000

	White		African American		Asian American		Native American		Latino	
	Men	Women	Men	Women	Men	Women	Men	Women	Men	Women
Voted	69.2	66.3[a]	60.2	57.0	57.6	57.3	50.7	49.4	50.4	47.7
Engaged in at least one campaign activity	36.5	27.2[c]	30.5	19.8[c]	26.3	18.2	29.0	27.6[a]	32.8	18.7[c]

[a] = $p < .05$
[b] = $p < .01$
[c] = $p < .001$
Source: American National Election Study Combined File, 1990–2000.
Chi-square test of significance is indicated by the following (absence of indicator = not significant).

Table 9.2. Political Participation by Gender by Racial or Ethnic Group, 2004

	White		African American		Other		Latino	
	Men	Women	Men	Women	Men	Women	Men	Women
Voted	79.3	80.1	61.8	59.3	71.3	70.9	65.0	75.0
Engaged in at least one non-voting political activity	35.9	26.4b	27.8	32.6	29.6	31.8	31.5	29.5

Chi square test of significance is reported.
Chi square: a = $p < .05$; b = $p < .01$; c = $p < .001$.
Data source: Pew Hispanic Center Survey 2004.

American, Native American, and Latino racial and ethnic groups participate in at least one campaign activity (see Table 9.1). Examining different types of campaign activity, white, black, and Latino men attend political meetings more frequently than did women, and white men more frequently reported giving money to political candidates or parties. In contrast, the Pew 2004 data suggest that gender differences in political activity occur only among whites.

PARTY IDENTIFICATION

Does a gender gap exist in party identification? During 1990 to 2000, a gender gap in party identification existed among both Hispanics and American Indians as well as among whites. However, no gender gap in party identification existed within either the African American or Asian American groups. The PHC 2004 survey also provides evidence of a gender gap in party identification among American Indians, with women significantly more likely to identify as Democrats than men and less likely to identify as Republicans. However, in that survey, women and men in the white, black, and Hispanic racial and ethnic groups did not differ significantly in party identification.

ATTENTIVENESS TO GOVERNMENT AND PUBLIC AFFAIRS

Are gender differences evident within racial and ethnic groups in their attentiveness to government and public affairs, their concern with election outcomes, and their political attitudes? Analysis of the combined 1990 to 2000 ANES data set suggests that a gender gap in attentiveness to politics exists among not only whites and African Americans but also among Hispanics and American Indians. In all four groups, women are less likely than men to pay attention to what is going on in government and public affairs.

A gender gap in attention paid to politics occurred among African Americans and whites in 2004, but not among Hispanics. When the question is interest in the current election, in the 1990s, gender differences exist within African American, Asian American, and Hispanic groups, with women being less interested than men.

Turning to identifying as a liberal or a conservative, in all groups but Hispanics, men were significantly more likely than women to indicate that they were politically conservative (see Table 9.3). Why are Latino women more frequently identifying as conservative than Latino men? Several explanations are possible. Religiosity may be greater among Latino women, and that may influence their self-identification as politically conservative. It may reflect significant differences on policy issues, such as legalization of abortion. Also noteworthy is the significant difference in the proportion of Native American men and women who identify as conservative; the gender gap in ideological identification is larger among Native Americans than for any other group. That may reflect greater dissatisfaction among Native American men with government policies that affect Native Americans or more frequent unsatisfactory contact with federal government officials who significantly affect life on Indian reservations. Or it might reflect stronger support for more traditional Native American values. Further exploration of these gender gap differences among ethnic groups in ideological identification is warranted.

Table 9.3. Political Attitudes by Gender and Racial or Ethnic Group, 1990–2000

	White		African American		Asian American		Native American		Latino	
	Men	Women	Men	Women	Men	Women	Men	Women	Men	Women
Follow public affairs some or most of the time	72.8	58.3[c]	71.2	55.8[c]	66.5	51.2	66.5	55.8[b]	60.4	44.1[c]
Care who wins election a good deal	77.6	77.1	76.6	76.9	71.7	70.9	76.5	81.8	73.3	69.4
Election interest very much	31.8	27.2[c]	37.9	23.9[c]	30.6	14.7[a]	32.3	26.2	21.9	17.9a
Trust in government low	69.4	70.2	70.7	67.5	55.7	64.8	72.3	69.0	55.5	54.7
Ideology										
Percent liberal	22.3	26.0	30.0	33.8	27.2	30.0	18.4	31.4	27.1	15.6
Percent conservative	49.6	38.4[c]	29.3	24.9	45.7	31.7	51.5	33.3[a]	33.7	40.9[a]

Chi square test of significance is indicated by the following (absence of indicator = not significant): [a] = $p < .05$; [b] = $p < .01$; [c] = $p < .001$.

Source: American National Election Studies Combined File, 1990–2000.

Are there gender differences in political trust within any of the racial and ethnic groups? Not during the 1990s. However, there are differences between groups in levels of political trust. Although a majority of all groups are distrustful of government, the proportion in the lower two levels of trust range from 54 percent among Latinos to 70 percent among Native Americans.

Are there gender differences related to election outcomes? Analyses of the ANES 1990–2000 data found no significant gender differences in caring who won the presidential and congressional elections. In 2004, only among whites did a gender gap exist in caring who won the presidential election, with men caring more than women.

Does a gender gap exist in identifying oneself as a liberal or a conservative? During the 1990s, a gender gap existed among whites and Latinos, with men in both groups more frequently labeling themselves as conservatives.

Policy Preferences

One issue that stirs controversy and policy debate is abortion policy. Are there gender differences on abortion policy within each racial and ethnic group? When provided with four choices on the issue of abortion policy, with the choices ranging from "by law, abortion should never be permitted" to "by law, a women should always be able to obtain an abortion as a matter of personal choice," a gender gap in abortion policy preferences was evident in 1990 to 2000 among both Hispanics and whites, but not among Asian Americans, African Americans, and American Indians. Hispanic men were more supportive than Hispanic women of abortion as a matter of personal choice. White women were slightly more supportive than white men of the two extremes of the abortion policy options. In contrast, in 2004, no significant differences existed between men and women within any of the racial and ethnic groups on the abortion policy question.

Another controversial policy issue is the provision of health insurance. Asked to indicate whether they preferred a government insurance plan or a private insurance plan, in the 1990–2000 ANES combined data file, white women were more likely to prefer a government insurance plan than were white men. No significant differences between men and women occurred in any of the other racial and ethnic groups. In 2004, a similar pattern prevailed, with white women preferring governmental provision of health insurance and white men preferring private provision of health insurance. No significant gender differences occurred on that policy issue within the Hispanic and African American groups in 2004.

Are there gender differences within these groups on the issue of the appropriate roles for women in contemporary society? When asked to place themselves on a seven-point scale, with "women and men should have an equal role" at one end of the continuum and "women's place is in the home" at the other, gender differences existed between men and women among both blacks and whites in the 1990–2000 ANES data set. In both groups, women were significantly more supportive of an equal role for women. In contrast, in the 2004 ANES survey, 55 percent of black men and 65 percent of black women supported the view that women and men should have an equal role, compared to approximately 60 percent of both white men and women supporting an equal role for women.

Controversy swirls around the role of government in American society. Does a gender gap exist in opinion on that issue? Should the government cut spending and reduce services or increase spending and services? Both black women and men and white women and men differed on that issue during the 1990s. Women were more supportive of the role of government, preferring higher levels of spending and more provision of government services. A gender gap did not exist on that issue among Asian Americans, Native Americans, and Latinos. In the 2004 PHC survey, the question focusing on that issue was worded differently and a gender gap on that issue was not present among Hispanic, black, and white survey respondents, but it was among respondents in the "other" ethnic group.

In the 2004 PHC study, survey respondents were queried as to their policy preferences on the issue of gay marriage. The survey item asked if they favored or opposed a constitutional amendment that would define marriage as a union between one man and one woman, thereby prohibiting legally sanctioned marriages for same-sex couples. A gender gap did not exist on that issue in any of the racial and ethnic groups.

Is there a gender gap in political participation, party identification, and policy preferences among Asian Americans? Another study, focusing only on Asian Americans, provides additional evidence that some differences do exist. The gender gap patterns reported here focus on Asian Americans as a group.[20] The survey that provided the data for the analysis by Lien, Conway, and Wong sampled six Asian American ethnic groups—Chinese, Japanese, Vietnamese, Filipinos, Indians, and Korean Americans.

Asian American men have higher levels of political knowledge and political interest than Asian American women. The men are also more likely to report identifying with the Republican Party than are the women, but both men and women are more likely to identify as Democrats than as Republicans. Men are more likely to report being contacted in political mobilization efforts, but men and women do not differ in political organization memberships. Men have higher levels of trust in state and local governments and are more likely than women to perceive local governments as responsive to citizens' complaints.

To some extent, gender gap differences among Asian Americans are a function of nativity. For example, foreign-born men express greater interest in politics than do foreign-born women. In contrast, native-born Asian American men and women do not differ in their levels of political interest. When foreign-born Asian Americans are queried about the extent to which they trust the U.S. government compared to the government in their home country, men are more likely than women to report they trust the U.S. government more. Men are also more likely than women to believe they have more influence over the U.S. government than they had over the home country government. Among native-born Asian Americans, men are more likely than women to perceive government as responsive to their concerns.

Despite these differences in beliefs about American government, the Asian American men and women surveyed in the PNAAPS study in 2000 and 2001 do not differ in their levels of voter turnout. Men and women also do not differ in their levels of participation in other forms of political activity.[21]

Among the differences that prior research suggest as relevant in influencing patterns of political behavior and political orientations are levels of political interest, information and efficacy, awareness of social problems, and compassion for those who face such problems. Individuals also differ in economic opportunities, personal values, social status, and social roles.

The next step in the analysis of the political gender gap among racial and ethnic groups is to test models incorporating relevant variables. That would permit comparison of their effects on men and women within racial and ethnic groups, across racial and ethnic groups, and across time.[22]

A Preliminary Test of a Model of Voting Turnout

Do attitudes, policy preferences, and sociological characteristics have similar effects in stimulating participation of both men and women in different racial/ethnic groups? A preliminary examination of that issue, using regression analysis, is presented in Tables 9.4 and 9.5. The tables report the results of an analysis of the effects of a variety of frequently discussed influences on patterns of voter registration and turnout of both men and women within each racial/ethnic group. The analysis uses data from the American National Election Studies from 1990 through 2000. The dependent variable, a measure of voter registration and turnout, is scored 0 if the individual is not registered and did not vote in the previous election, 1 if registered but did not vote, and 2 if he or she voted in the election. Several attitude measures are included as explanatory variables; these are trust in government, assessment of personal economic well-being during the prior year, party identification (Democratic, independent, or Republican), strength of party identification, and indicators of the strength of self-identification as a liberal or a conservative. Policy orientation measures include an abortion policy preference measure, support for government spending less, support for the government providing more services, and an assessment of past national economic conditions. Sociological variables include marital status, employment status, being in a professional or clerical occupation, having a union member in one's family, educational attainment, length of residence in the community, length of residence in the home, family income level, frequency of church attendance, and two measures of religious denomination affiliation (Protestant and Catholic). Also included are frequency of following what happens in government and politics and an assessment of personal financial well-being during the previous year.

Table 9.4. Did a Gender Gap Exist in Policy Preferences? 1990–2000

	White	African American	Asian American	Native American	Latino
Equal role for women	yes	no	no	no	no
Government role in health insurance	yes	no	no	no	no
Abortion legal by law	yes	no	no	no	yes
Government spending and services level	yes	yes	no	no	no

Yes indicated chi square significant at $p < .05$.
Source: American National Election Study File 1990–2000.

Table 9.5. Gender Gap in Policy Preferences by Racial/Ethnic Group, 2004

	White	African American	Hispanic	Other
Abortion	ns	ns	ns	$p < .05$
Gay Marriage	ns	ns	ns	ns
Health Insurance	$p < .05$	ns	ns	ns
Tax Cuts v. More Services	ns	ns	ns	$p < .01$

Chi Square Test of Significance: ns = not significant.
Data source: Pew Hispanic Center Survey 2004.

Variables significant in accounting for both white men's and white women's voting participation include preferences on abortion policy, assessment of the previous year's performance of the economy, strength of a conservative political identity, and strength of party identification. A number of personal characteristics are also significant; those include having a family member in a union, being married, level of educational attainment, length of residence in the home, income level, frequency of church attendance, and Protestant religious affiliation. A Catholic religious affiliation and being a liberal were also significant in explaining voting turnout among white men but not among white women. Among white women, employment in a clerical occupation also contributes to explaining voting participation.

In contrast, fewer of the variables predicted electoral participation among African American men and women. Among African American men, preferences on abortion policy laws, strength of party identification, and following what occurs in government and politics are significant predictors of participation, as were membership in a union household, frequency of church attendance, and length of residence in the household. Still fewer variables included in the analysis were significant predictors of voter turnout among African American women; those variables include level of trust in government, length of residence in the home, level of educational attainment, frequency of church attendance in the home, and strength of party identification.

Variables in the participation model are least effective in accounting for electoral participation patterns among Native Americans. Only one of the included variables (level of educational attainment) is statistically significant in explaining voting registration and turnout among men. Only three are significant in explaining electoral participation among Native American women (following government and politics, being married, and level of income.) Among both Latino Americans and Asian Americans, more variables in the analysis were significant in accounting for participation by women than by men.

Several general conclusions can be drawn from the analysis of the impact of these variables on the patterns of men's and women's electoral participation within and between racial/ethnic groups. The variables included in this analysis are more useful in explaining voter registration and turnout among white Americans than among members of other groups. Prior research on electoral participation has for the most part used data sets that primarily include white Americans. Thus, it is not surprising that the variables included in the model used here are better at explaining election participation among both white women and men.

Fourteen of the twenty-three explanatory variables are significant in accounting for electoral participation among both white men and women. Only five of the twenty-three are significant for both men and women among Latinos, four for African Americans, two for Asian Americans, and none for both men and women among Native Americans. Gender differences in the impact of these variables varies within racial/ethnic groups; for example, among Asian American women, ten are significant, but only five among Asian American men, and, as noted above, only two are the same variables. One inference that might be drawn is that whatever gender gaps exist within each of the racial/ethnic group examined here, explanatory models more focused on the experiences, relevant attitudes, and policy concerns within each group need to be specified and examined.

Statistical analyses using the same variables to account for participation in campaign activities were even less successful. Campaign participation is undoubtedly stimulated by both the context of the campaign and by citizens' involvement in organizations that make them more likely to be recruited by campaign organizers. A much wider variety of issue concerns also provides a stimulus to campaign participation.

Discussion and Conclusions

The research presented here suggests that the political gender gap varies across ethnic and racial groups, across time, and across political objects (vote choice, voter turnout, other forms of political participation, political attitudes, and policy preferences) as the conditions stimulating a gender gap change. The political, social, and economic contexts of citizens' lives change over time, and the salience of the components of those contexts also change over time. Conditional effects exist; variables can have differential effects on women and men. Compositional differences also exist; women and men may differ on the explanatory variables. Obviously, relevance is also a function of personal characteristics such as gender and race or ethnicity and how those identified are internalized and integrated.

Future research examining differences in racial and ethnic patterns of political participation needs to draw more specifically on the experiences and social circumstances of racial and ethnic minorities. Additional data sets that include a broader and more appropriate set of variables, reflecting the life experiences of racial and ethnic minorities, need to be collected.

Notes

1. Clark and Clark, "Gender Gap in 1996," in Whitaker, *Women in Politics,* Table 2.22.
2. Clark and Clark, "Gender Gap in 1996," in Whitaker, *Women in Politics,* Table 2.22; Seltzer, Newman, and Leighton, *Sex as a Political Variable,* Table 3.1.
3. Mattei, "Gender Gap in Presidential Evaluations."
4. Chaney, Alvarez, and Nagler, "Explaining the Gender Gap."
5. Selzer, Newman, and Leighton, *Sex as a Political Variable,* Tables 3.3 and 3.4.
6. Burns, Schlozman, and Verba, *Private Roots of Public Action,* Figure 11.1, 278.
7. See ibid., Chapter 11.
8. Selzer, Newman, and Leighton, *Sex as a Political Variable,* Table 3.5.
9. Welch and Sigelman, "Gender Gap among Hispanics?"
10. Kaufmann and Petrocik, "Changing Politics of American Men."
11. Mattei and Mattei, "If the Men Stayed Home," Table 3, 425, and Table 4.
12. Gilens, "Gender and Support for Reagan."
13. Howell and Day "Complexities of the Gender Gap."
14. Manza and Brooks, "Gender Gap in U.S. Presidential Elections."
15. Schlesinger and Heldman, "Gender Gap or Gender Gaps."
16. Verba, Burns, and Schlozman, "Knowing and Caring about Politics"; Conway, Steuernagel, and Ahern, *Women and Political Participation,* 52, Table 3–6.
17. Lien, "Does the Gender Gap in Political Attitudes and Behavior Vary?"
18. Lien. "Who Votes in Multiracial America?" in Alex-Assensoh and Hanks, *Black and Multiracial Politics.*
19. Combining the ANES data files provides enough cases to permit analysis of the gender gap within white, African American, Asian American, American Indian, and Hispanic groups. The 2004 Pew Hispanic Survey (PHS) permits analysis of the gender gap among Hispanics, whites, and African Americans. The PNAAPS and JCPES surveys are studies of just one racial group and do not permit comparisons across ethnic and racial groups within the context of those surveys.
20. The U.S. Bureau of the Census identifies twenty-eight different Asian Pacific Islander ethnic groups in the United States. The groups vary in the timing of group patterns of immigration to the United States, religion, historical experiences in the home country and in the United States, and socioeconomic characteristics.
21. Lien and Conway, "Are There Gender Gaps in Political Attitudes and Behavior Patterns?"; Lien, Conway, and Wong, *Politics of Asian Americans,* Chapter 5.
22. For examples of the testing for the effects of different variables on the gender gap at one point in time, see Burns, Schlozman, and Verba, *Private Roots of Political Action,* Tables 11.11 and 11.14; Lien, Conway, and Wong, *Politics of Asian Americans,* Tables 6.4 and 6.5b.

Conclusion

When Women Vote,
Are Women Empowered?

LOIS DUKE WHITAKER

This book has explored the gender gap in voting and the differences found in men and women in issue preferences, candidate choice, and partisan association. As we have seen from the articles in this volume, and certainly other scholarly studies bear this out, the gender gap is influenced by many societal, demographic, and regional factors; varies from one race to another based on issues, candidates, political parties, and so on; and thus is a complex issue to isolate and draw firm conclusions that withstand the test of time. As Niemi and Weinberg contend, "It must be admitted that we do not yet fully understand voting and elections."[1]

So what is really going on with the gender gap? To start with the obvious, neither women nor men are anything like a solid bloc. Gender differences in voting are easily dwarfed by other gaps, including the racial divide.[2] As Fitzpatrick has noted, "Age, geography, religion, participation, education level, household income and investments, and use of technology also may influence a woman's priorities. The most insightful research into the way women think combines any number of these characteristics."[3]

Still another political pollster has described the gender gap as, "It's candidate-based, it's issue-based, and it's partisan-based."[4] Other researchers have found that, as a group, women are significantly more likely to be on the left in their views on political issues; this, they argue, is the major factor explaining their differing electoral choices.[5]

Political psychologist Pamela Johnston Conover maintains that some women with a particularly strong or transformative kind of gender consciousness, which she calls "feminist consciousness," have clearly distinct preferences and goals in the political process that stem from their advanced group identification with other women. Conover believes that it is the behavior and attitudes of this subset of women that drives the gender gap.[6] Other observers and studies have found that one has to recognize, when women vote on the basis of their gender consciousness, that women are generally more dovish than men on foreign policy and more inclined to favor an active role for government in economic and social life.[7]

In general terms, the Center for the American Woman and Politics (CAWP) has found, when compared to men, woman are:

Less militaristic on issues of war and peace
More often opposed to the use of force in nonmilitary situations
More likely to favor measures to protect the environment and to check the growth of nuclear power
More often supportive of efforts to achieve racial equality
More likely to favor laws to regulate and control various social vices (e.g., drugs, gambling, pornography)
Less likely to be optimistic about the country's future[8]

Despite this, however, perhaps the biggest overriding question scholars and pundits should ask about the gender gap and its importance to American politics is whether the gender gap (voting differences in men and women) can result in increased political empowerment for women in U.S. politics. That is, when women vote in increasing numbers as contrasted with men, can we assume there will be an increase in the numbers of women in the American political realm?

If one looks at statistics, we do know that we now have more women in political office since women voted in larger numbers in 1980. And women are represented more in launching positions traditionally used by men to advance to our nation's highest offices. For example, in 2006, women held eighty-one or 15.1 percent of the 535 seats in the 109th U.S. Congress. Fourteen women (nine Democrats and five Republicans) served in the U.S. Senate. Sixty-seven or 15.4 percent of the 435 seats in the House of Representatives were occupied by women. Also, in 2006, seventy-nine women held statewide elective executive offices across the country, including eight women governors. In 2006, 1,686 or 22.8 percent of the 7,382 state legislators in the United States were women.[9]

Further, a total of thirty women have held cabinet or cabinet-level appointments in the history of our nation. Of the thirty, twenty-two had cabinet posts, including two who headed two different departments and who held both a cabinet post and a position defined as cabinet-level. Sixteen of these women were appointed by Democratic presidents and fourteen by Republicans.[10]

Assuming that the gender gap does matter and that there is a linkage between voting and political empowerment for women, why is it that women currently do not vote in larger numbers and are not more involved in the American political process? One could use an example from ancient Greece to illustrate a paradox in which historically women were uneducated and excluded from most of society, yet used their limited political influence to have a real impact on an important political issue. This example can then be contrasted with American women in the United States today. Women are highly educated, free to make professional choices, and, for the most part, represented in all major social institutions. Yet women only use their political clout minimally to influence public policy and the outcome of political elections.

The example comes from ancient Greece and a comic play, *Lysistrata*, written by Aristophanes in the 5th century B.C. Women had no public role in society at the time and were excluded from the process of policy-making. The plot of the play centers on a group of women led by Lysistrata (pronounced lie-SEE-strata) and their successful efforts to turn the tables on the men, who have excluded their wives from this process of policy making. Fantastic as the idea was, the heroine, Lysistrata, who feels in some way frustrated or victimized by the operations of contemporary society, manages to evade or alter the situation of which she initially complains and proceeds to effect a triumph of wish-fulfillment over reality.[11]

One has to remember the role of women in Greek society of the time. By law, they were defined as "incapable of a self-determined act, as almost . . . an un-person, outside the limits of those who constitute society's responsible and representative agents."[12] Women had no formal political representation and were for a great part of the time confined to the *gunaikeion,* the women's quarters of the house. Marriage was conceived as the "taming" of the wild young woman, as can be seen from the language used of it and the representations on vases of young males "hunting" the fleeing girl.[13]

At the time the play was produced, it was a bad time for Athens. The grandiose armada invasion of Sicily had proved a disaster. She lost her fleet, her army, and a great deal of money. Meanwhile, the Spartans were on her doorstep and many of her allies were seizing the opportunity to defect from the Athenian hegemony.[14]

To put an end to war, Lysistrata hits on a startlingly simple way of forcing husbands to stay at home and become pacifists: deny them sex. Not all the husbands, of course, are immediately subject to this radical treatment because they are away fighting, but even these men would come home on leave—with one thought on their minds. Withholding sex from panting young husbands is the strategy Lysistrata has devised for their wives, but she has a different one for the older women: to make an assault on the acropolis (the upper fortified part of an ancient Greek city). The older women would thus seize the public building and freeze the assets that fund the war. Thus, this Athenian citizen called Lysistrata, which means "disbander of armies," organizes and successfully prosecutes a Panhellenic conspiracy of citizen wives that forces the chief combatants (Athens and Sparta) and their allies to negotiate a peaceful settlement of the war and promise never again to fight one another.[15]

It should be pointed out that Lysistrata is identified neither as a housewife nor as an elderly woman. No details about her age or marital status appear. In the strike and in the seizure of the citadel she is the strategist and spokesman, and the other women are her agents. She understands and makes use of her helpers' talents but does not herself share in them. In fact, she pointedly differentiates herself from the other women, especially the young wives. Moreover, she is not merely a representative of her own sex but also an advocate of traditional values for all Greeks, male and female. She is endowed with a degree of intelligence, will, and eloquence that would have been considered extraordinary in a citizen of either sex and emerges triumphant on all fronts.[16] This characterization of Lysistrata has prompted speculation that our heroine was modeled on an actual contemporary.[17]

Whether this play is based on fantasy and wishful thinking,[18] it serves as an example of how women creatively used resources available to them to alter the public agenda. One has to wonder what could happen with the more professional and more educated women of today using resources that the ancient Greek women did not have to set the political agenda and alter contemporary American public policy. As Nicholas D. Kristof, writing in the New York Times, points out, "A smart and ambitious woman graduating from college in 1970 often ended up as a third-grade teacher; today, she ends up as a surgeon or senator."[19]

And, as Speaker of the House Nancy Pelosi noted as she took the oath of office, "This is an historic moment for the Congress and for the women of this country and a moment for which we have waited more than 200 years."[20] In this same article, Pelosi thanked her husband and five children "for giving me their love, support and the confidence to go from the kitchen to the Congress."[21] Thus, as more and more women achieve success in our nation's top policy-making roles, more young women will aspire to achieving these goals.

Thus, women today not only have role models and mentors, but their resources also include networking and the use of technology. A current example of this is the use of the Web and Internet to form grassroots groups to educate voters and create a vision for the idea that a women can actually be elected president this day and age (see www.womanforpresident2008.org). The leaders of this group are advocating measures, including starting book clubs on women and politics and forming groups of young women who will turn eighteen and be able to vote for the first time in 2008. The latter idea has particular merit because we know that eighteen-year-olds represent a very poor voting bloc demographically. Current resources also include groups that seek to encourage the recruitment and financial support of women candidates, including Emily's List, the White House Project, and the Women's Campaign Fund. Emily's List's "Early Money Is Like Yeast" delivered $7.5 million in the 1998 election cycle and contacted millions of women in get-out-the-vote activities.[22]

To take the elective office to the highest in the land, one of the big questions for 2008 is whether Senator Hillary Rodham Clinton will become our first female president. If she is successful, we know there has been a huge shift in national attitudes about whether the country is ready to elect a female president. In an article in *Parade* magazine entitled "Is It Time for a Woman President?" Winik points out that, on the eve of World War II, two-thirds of Americans wouldn't even consider voting for a female president, according to a Gallup poll. Today, Gallup says, nearly 90 percent would.[23] And, as Mark McKinnon, media director of President George W. Bush's victorious 2004 reelection campaign, states, "The country is more than ready to elect a women. . . . But, it has to be the right woman."[24]

Despite the successes and advancement of American women in politics, as Susan J. Carroll points out, the potential for women voters to influence politics has not yet been fully realized. She explains this will require more involvement of certain subgroups of women who have traditionally been uninvolved in the political process and the involvement of other women whose concerns are not being addressed by candidates.[25] Parity will come only with the participation of more women, not only in voting, but in all other avenues of political activism as well.

Notes

1. Niemi and Weisberg, *Controversies in Voting Behavior*, 4.
2. Young, "Venus at the Ballot Box," 17.
3. Fitzpatrick, "Why the Gender Gap Should Get a Pink Slip," 4.
4. Feldman, "Clinton Reelection Motto," 1, 1C.

5. Studlar and McAllister. "Explaining the Gender Gap in Voting."

6. Conover, "Feminists and the Gender Gap," in O'Connor, Brewer, and Fisher, *Gendering American Politics*.

7. Young, "Venus at the Ballot Box"; Conover, "Feminists and the Gender Gap," in O'Connor, Brewer, and Fisher, *Gendering American Politics*.

8. Center for the American Woman and Politics, CAWP Fact Sheet, September 1992, as quoted in Nancy E. McGlen et al., *Women, Politics, and American Society*, 80.

9. Fact Sheet, Center for American Women and Politics, Eagleton Institute of Politics, Rutgers University, www.cawp.rutgers.edu.

10. Ibid.

11. Henderson, *Aristophanes: Lysistrata*.

12. Bloom, *Aristophanes*, 95.

13. Ibid.

14. Roche, *Aristophanes: The Complete Plays, the New Translations*, 417

15. Ibid., 418–19; Henderson, *Aristophanes: Lysistrata*, xxv–xxvi.

16. Henderson, *Aristophanes: Lysistrata*, xxv–xxvi.

17. Ibid., xxxviii.

18. Ibid.

19. Kristof, "Opening Classroom Doors," WK 15.

20. From wire reports in *The State* (Columbia, S.C.), Friday, January 5, 2007, 1A.

21. Ibid.

22. Kirchhoff, "Dollars and Sensitivities."

23. Winik, "Is It Time for a Woman President?" 4–5.

24. As quoted in ibid., 4.

25. Carroll, "Voting Choices," 94.

Bibliography

Abramowitz, Alan I., and Kyle L. Saunders. "Ideological Realignment in the U.S. Electorate." *Journal of Politics* 60 (1998): 634–52.

Abzug, Bella, with Mim Kelber. *Gender Gap: Bella Abzug's Guide to Political Power for American Women.* Boston: Houghton Mifflin, 1984.

Adams, Greg D. "Abortion: Evidence of Issue Evolution." *American Journal of Political Science* 41 (July 1997): 718–37.

Adell Cook, Elizabeth, Ted G. Jelen, and Clyde Wilcox. *Between Two Absolutes: Public Opinion and the Politics of Abortion.* Boulder, Colo.: Westview Press, 1992.

———, Sue Thomas, and Clyde Wilcox, ed. *The Year of the Woman: Myths and Realities.* Boulder, Colo.: Westview Press, 1994.

———, and Clyde Wilcox. "Feminism and the Gender Gap: A Second Look." *Journal of Politics* 53, no. 4 (November 1991): 1111–22.

———, and Clyde Wilcox. "Women Voters in the Year of the Woman." In *Democracy's Feast: Elections in America,* edited by Herbert Weisberg, 195–219. Chattam, N.J.: Chatham House, 1995.

Alberts, Sheldon. "Candidates Address 'Security Moms.'" *The Gazette,* Montreal: October 18, 2004, A22.

Alexander, Deborah, and Kristi Andersen. "Gender as a Factor in the Attribution of Leadership Traits." *Political Research Quarterly* 46 (1993): 527–45.

American National Election Studies (ANES). *The ANES Guide to Public Opinion and Electoral Behavior.* Ann Arbor: University of Michigan, Center for Political Studies, 2006. www.electionstudies.org.

Andersen, Kristi. "Gender and Public Opinion." In *Understanding Public Opinion,* edited by Barbara Norrander and Clyde Wilcox, 19–36. Washington, D.C.: CQ Press, 1997.

———, and Elizabeth A. Cook. "Women, Work and Political Attitudes." *American Journal of Political Science* 29 (1985): 606–25.

Arnold, Laura W., and Herbert F. Weisberg. "Parenthood, Family Values, and the 1992 Presidential Election." *American Politics Quarterly* 24 (1996): 194–220.

Atkeson, Lonnie Rae. "Not All Cues Are Created Equal: The Conditional Impact of Female Candidates on Political Engagement." *Journal of Politics* 65 (November 2003): 1040–61.

Ballou, Janice. "Respondent/Interviewer Gender Interaction Effects in Telephone Surveys." Paper presented at the 1990 International Conference on Measurement Errors in Surveys, Tucson, Ariz.

Banaszak, Lee Ann. *Why Movements Succeed or Fail: Opportunity, Culture, and the Struggle for Woman Suffrage.* Princeton, N.J.: Princeton University Press, 1996.

Barber, Lionel. "Bush Gambles the Presidency on Mobilising the Faithful." *Financial Times,* October 30, 2004.

Barnes, Fred. "The Family Gap." *Reader's Digest* (July 1992): 48–54.

Baxter, Sandra, and Marjorie Lansing. *Women and Politics: The Visible Majority,* 2nd ed. Ann Arbor: University of Michigan Press, 1983.

Bendyna, Mary E., Tamara Finucane, Lynn Kirby, John P. O'Donnell, and Clyde Wilcox. "Gender Differences in Public Attitudes Toward the Gulf War: A Test of Competing Hypotheses." *Social Science Journal* 33 (1996): 1–22.

Berelson, B. R., P. F. Lazarsfeld, and W. N. McPhee. *Voting: A Study of Opinion Formation in a Presidential Campaign.* Chicago: University of Chicago Press, 1954.

Berenson, Bernard R., Paul F. Lazarsfeld, and William N. McPhee. *Voting: A Study of Opinion Formation in a Presidential Campaign.* Chicago: University of Chicago Press, 1954.

Beutal, Ann, and Margaret Marini. "Gender and Values." *American Sociological Review* 60 (June 1995): 436–48.

Bianchi, Suzanne. "Maternal Employment and Time with Children: Dramatic Change or Surprising Continuity?" *Demography* 37(2000): 401–14.

Bloom, Harold, ed. *Aristophanes.* Broomall, Pa.: Chelsea House Publishers, 2002.

Bord, Richard J., and Robert E. O'Connor. "The Gender Gap in Environmental Attitudes: The Case of Perceived Vulnerability to Risk." *Social Science Quarterly* 78 (December 1997): 830–40.

Box-Steffensmeier, Janet M., Suzanna DeBoef, and Tse-Min Lin. "The Dynamics of the Partisan Gender Gap." *American Political Science Review* 98, no. 3 (2004): 515–28.

Bradley, Robert H., Leanne Whiteside-Mansell, Judith A. Brisby, and Bettye M. Caldwell. "Parents' Socioemotional Investment in Children." *Journal of Marriage and the Family* 59 (1997): 77–90.

Brians, Craig Leonard. "Women for Women? Gender and Party Bias in Voting for Female Candidates." *American Politics Research* 33 (2005): 357–75.

Brooks, C., and J. Manza. "Social Cleavages and Political Alignments: U.S. Presidential Elections, 1960 to 1992." *American Sociological Review* 62, no. 9 (1997): 937–46.

Burns, Nancy, Kay Lehman Schlozman, and Sidney Verba. *The Private Roots of Public Action: Gender, Equality, and Political Participation.* Cambridge, Mass.: Harvard University Press, 2001.

Burrell, Barbara. *A Woman's Place Is in the House: Campaigning for Congress in the Feminist Era.* Ann Arbor: University of Michigan Press, 1994.

Caldicott, Helen. *Missile Envy: The Arms Race and Nuclear War.* New York: Bantam, 1986.

Campbell, Angus, Philip E. Converse, Warren E. Miller, and Donald E. Stokes. *The American Voter.* New York: John Wiley and Sons, 1960.

Carroll, Susan J. "The Dis-Empowerment of the Gender Gap: Soccer Moms and the 1996 Elections." *PS: Political Science and Politics* 32 (March 1999): 7–11.

———. "Gender Politics and the Socializing Impact of the Women's Movement." In *Political Learning in Adulthood: A Sourcebook of Theory and Research,* Roberta S. Sigel, 306–39. Chicago: University of Chicago Press, 1989.

———. "Voting Choices: Meet You at the Gender Gap." In *Gender and Elections: Shaping the Future of American Politics,* edited by Susan J. Carroll and Richard L. Fox, 74–96. Cambridge: Cambridge University Press, 2006.

———, ed. *Women and American Politics New Questions, New Directions.* Oxford: Oxford University Press, 2003.

———. "Women's Autonomy and the Gender Gap: 1980 and 1982." In *The Politics of the Gender Gap: The Social Construction of Political Influence,* edited by Carol M. Mueller, 236–257. Newbury Park, Calif.: Sage Publications, 1988.

———. "Women Voters and the Gender Gap." Washington, D.C.: American Political Science Association (APSA). http://www.apsanet.org/content_5270.cfm, 2005.

———, and Richard L. Fox, eds. *Gender and Elections: Shaping the Future of American Politics.* New York: Cambridge University Press, 2006.

———, and Debbie Walsh. "Gender Gap Persists in the 2004 Election.," Center for American Women and Politics (CAWP) Advisory. New Brunswick, N.J.: Center for American Women and Politics, Eagleton Institute, 2004, www.cawp.rutgers.edu.

Center for American Women and Politics. "Gender Gap Persists in 2004 Election." Press advisory, 2004, www.cawp.rutgers.edu/Facts/Elections/GG2004Facts.pdf.

———. "The Gender Gap: Voting Choices in Presidential Elections." Fact Sheet, 2005, www.cawp.rutgers.edu/Facts/Elections/GGPresVote.pdf.

———. "Women Candidates for Congress 1974–2004." New Brunswick, N.J.: Center for the American Woman and Politics, Eagleton Institute, Rutgers University, 2006.

———. "Women in Elective Office 2006." New Brunswick, N.J.: Center for the American Woman and Politics, Eagleton Institute, Rutgers University, 2006.

Chaney, Carole K., R. Michael Alvarez, and Jonathan Nagler. "Explaining the Gender Gap in U.S. Presidential Elections, 1980–1992." *Political Research Quarterly* 51, no. 2 (June 1998): 311–39.

Chodorow, Nancy. *The Reproduction of Mothering: Psychoanalysis and the Sociology of Gender.* Berkeley: University of California Press, 1978.

Clark, Cal, and Janet Clark. "The Gender Gap in 1996: More Meaning Than a 'Revenge of the Soccer Moms.'" In *Women in Politics: Outsiders or Insiders?*, 3rd ed., edited by Lois Duke Whitaker, 68–84. Upper Saddle River, N.J.: Prentice-Hall, 1999.

———, and Janet Clark. "The Gender Gap in the Early 21st Century: Volatility from Security Concerns." In *Women in American Politics: Outsiders or Insiders?*, 4th ed., edited by Lois Duke Whitaker, 45–64. Englewood Cliffs, N.J.: Prentice-Hall, 2005.

———, Janet Clark, and Rooney Patterson. "The Evolving Issue Base of the Gender Gap." Paper presented at the annual meeting of the Southern Political Science Association, New Orleans, 2004.

Clark, Janet, and Cal Clark. "The Gender Gap: A Manifestation of Women's Dissatisfaction with the American Polity?" In *Broken Contract? Changing Relationships between Citizens and their Government in the Untied States*, edited by Stephen C. Craig, 167–82. Boulder, Colo.: Westview Press, 1996.

Collins, Patricia Hill. "Shifting the Center: Race, Class, and Feminist Theorizing about Motherhood." In *Representations of Motherhood*, edited by Donna Bassin, Margaret Honey, and Meryle Mahrer Kaplan, 56–74. New Haven, Conn.: Yale University Press, 1994.

Conover, Pamela Johnston. "Feminists and the Gender Gap." *Journal of Politics* 50, no. 4 (November 1988): 985–1010.

———. "Feminists and the Gender Gap." In *Gendering American Politics*, edited by Karen O'Connor, Sarah E. Brewer, and Michael Philip Fisher, 111–20. New York: Pearson, Longman, 2006.

———, and Virginia Gray. *Feminism and the New Right: Conflict over the American Family.* New York: Praeger, 1983.

———, and Virginia Sapiro. "Gender, Feminist Consciousness, and War." *American Journal of Political Science* 37, no. 4 (November 1993): 1079–99.

Conway, M. Margaret, David W. Ahern, Gertrude A. Steuernagel. *Women and Public Policy: A Revolution in Progress*, 3rd ed. Washington, D.C.: Congressional Quarterly Press, 2005.

———, Gertrude A. Steuernagel, and David W. Ahern. *Women and Political Participation: Cultural Change in the Political Arena.* Washington, D.C.: Congressional Quarterly Press, 1997.

———, Gertrude A. Steuernagel, and David Ahern. *Women and Political Participation*, 2nd ed. Washington, D.C.: CQ Press, 2005.

Cook, Elizabeth. "Voter Responses to Women Senate Candidates." In *The Year of the Woman: Myths and Realities*, edited by Elizabeth Adell Cook, Sue Thomas, and Clyde Wilcox, 217–36. Boulder, Colo.: Westview Press, 1994.

Cook, Rhodes. "Democratic Clout Is Growing as the Gender Gap Widens." *Congressional Quarterly Weekly Report* 50, no. 41 (October 27, 1992): 3265.

Costain, Anne N. *Inviting Women's Rebellion: A Political Process Interpretation of the Women's Movement.* Baltimore: Johns Hopkins University Press, 1992.

———. "The Mobilization of the Women's Movement and the American Gender Gap in Voting." Paper presented at the annual meeting of the American Political Science Association, San Francisco, 1996.

Cuniberti, Betty. "The Power of the Security Mom Is Not Entirely Secure." *St. Louis Post-Dispatch,* October 6, 2004.

Davidson, Debra J., and William R. Freudenburg. "Gender and Environmental Risk Concerns: A Review and Analysis of Available Research." *Environment and Behavior* 28 (1996): 302–39.

Deitch, Cynthia. "Sex Differences in Support for Government Spending." In *The Politics of the Gender Gap,* edited by Carol M. Mueller, 192–216. Newbury Park, Calif.: Sage Publications, 1988.

Delli Carpini, Michael X., and Scott Keeter, "Measuring Political Knowledge: Putting First Things First." *American Journal of Political Science* 37 (November 1993): 1179–1206.

———, and Scott Keeter. *What Americans Know About Politics and Why It Matters.* New Haven, Conn.: Yale University Press, 1996.

Deutsch, Francine M., Jennifer L. Lozy, and Susan Saxon. "Taking Credit: Couples' Reports of Contributions to Child Care." *Journal of Family Issues* 14 (1993): 421–37.

———, Laura J. Servis, and Jessica Payne. "Paternal Participation in Child Care and Its Effects on Children's Self-Esteem and Attitudes Toward Gender-Roles." *Journal of Family Issues* 22 (2001): 1000–1024.

Dolan, Julie, Melissa Deckman, and Michele L. Swers. *Women and Politics: Paths to Power and Political Influence.* Upper Saddle River, N.J.: Pearson Education, 2007.

Dolan, Kathleen. "Voting for Women in the 'Year of the Woman.'" *American Journal of Political Science* 42 (1998): 272–93.

———. *Voting for Women: How the Public Evaluates Women Candidates.* Boulder, Colo.: Westview Press, 2004.

Douglas, Susan J., and Meredith W. Michaels. *The Mommy Myth: The Idealization of Motherhood and How It Has Undermined All Women.* New York: Free Press, 2004.

Downs, Barbara. *Fertility of American Women: June 2002.* Washington, D.C.: U.S. Census Bureau, 2003.

Duverger, Maurice. *The Political Role of Women.* Paris: UNESCO, 1955.

Edlund, Lena, and Rohini Pande. "Why Have Women Become Left-Wing? The Political Gender Gap and the Decline in Marriage." *Quarterly Journal of Economics,* 117, no. 3 (2002): 917–61.

Ekstrand, Laurie, and William Eckert. "The Impact of Candidate's Sex on Vote Choice." *Western Political Quarterly* 34 (1981): 78–87.

Elshtain, Jean Bethke. "On Beautiful Souls, Just Warriors and Feminist Consciousness." In *Women and Men's Wars,* edited by Judith Stiehm, 342–49. Oxford: Pergamon Press, 1983.

———. *Public Man, Private Woman*. Princeton, N.J.: Princeton University Press, 1981.

Entman, Robert M. "Framing: Toward Clarification of a Fractured Paradigm." *Journal of Communication* 43, no. 4 (1993): 51–58.

———. "Framing U.S. Coverage of International News: Contrasts in Narratives of the KAL and Iran Air Incidents." *Journal of Communication* 41, no. 4 (1991): 6–27.

Erie, Steven P., and Martin Rein. "Women and the Welfare State." In *The Politics of the Gender Gap: The Social Construction of Political Influence*, edited by Carol M. Mueller, 173–91. Newbury Park, Calif.: Sage Publications, 1988.

Erikson, Robert S., and Kent L. Tedin. *American Public Opinion*, 6th ed. New York: Longman, 2001.

Erskine, Hazel. "The Polls: Women's Role." *Public Opinion Quarterly* 35 (Summer 1971): 275–90.

Fan, David P., Kathy A. Keltner, and Robert O. Wyatt. "A Matter of Guilt or Innocence: How News Reports Affect Support for the Death Penalty in the United States." *International Journal of Public Opinion Research* 14, no. 4 (2002): 439–52.

Feldman, Linda. "A Clinton Reelection Motto for '96: 'It's Gender, Stupid,'" *Christian Science Monitor*, February 6, 1996, 1, 1C.

———. "Why Women Are Edging toward Bush." *Christian Science Monitor*, September 23, 2004, 1.

Fiorina, Morris P., Samuel J. Abrams, and Jeremy C. Pope. *Culture War? The Myth of a Polarized America*, 2nd ed. New York: Pearson Longman, 2006.

Fite, David, Marc Genest, and Clyde Wilcox. "Gender Differences in Foreign Policy Attitudes: A Longitudinal Analysis." *American Politics Quarterly* 18 (1990): 492–512.

Fitzpatrick, Kellyanne. "Why the Gender Gap Should Get a Pink Slip." *Human Events* 56, no. 28 (August 4, 2000): 4.

Flanigan, William H., and Nancy H. Zingale. *Political Behavior of the American Electorate*, 11th ed. Washington, D.C.: Congressional Quarterly Press, 2006.

Flexner, Eleanor, and Ellen Fitzpatrick. *Century of Struggle: The Woman's Rights Movement in the United States*. Cambridge: Belknap Press of Harvard University Press, 1996.

Fox, Richard. *Gender Dynamics in Congressional Elections*. Thousand Oaks, Calif.: Sage Publications, 1997.

Frankovic, Kathleen A. "The Ferraro Factor: The Women's Movement, the Polls and the Press." In *The Politics of the Gender Gap: The Social Construction of Political Influence*, edited by Carol M. Mueller, 102–23. Newbury Park, Calif.: Sage Publications, 1988.

———. "Public Opinion Polls." In *The Politics of News, the News of Politics*, edited by Doris Graber, Pippa Norris, and Denis McQuail, 150–70. Washington, D.C.: CQ Press, 1998.

———. "Sex and Politics—New Alignments, Old Issues." *Political Science* 15, no. 3 (Summer 1982): 439–48.

———. "Why the Gender Gap Became News in 1996." *P.S. Political Science and Politics* 32, no. 1 (March 1999): 20–22.

Frazer, Elizabeth, and Kenneth Macdonald. "Sex Differences in Political Knowledge in Britain." *Political Studies* 51, no. 1 (2003): 67–83.

Freeman, Jo. *The Politics of Women's Liberation: A Case Study of an Emerging Social Movement and Its Relation to the Policy Process.* New York: McKay, 1975.

———. *A Room at a Time.* Lanham, Md.: Rowman and Littlefield, 2000.

Fukuyama, Francis E. "Women and the Evolution of World Politics." *Foreign Affairs* 77, no. 5 (1998): 24–40.

Gallagher, Sally K., and Naomi Gerstel. "Connections and Constraints: The Effects of Children on Caregiving." *Journal of Marriage and the Family* 63 (2001): 265–75.

Gilens, Martin. "Gender and Support for Reagan: A Comprehensive Model of Presidential Approval." *American Journal of Political Science* 32, no. 1 (February 1988): 19–49.

Gilligan, Carol. *In a Different Voice: Psychological Theory and Women's Development.* Cambridge, Mass.: Harvard University Press, 1982.

Gilson, Dave. "Wild Cards: A Field Guide to the American Swing Voter." *Mother Jones,* September 9, 2004, http://www.motherjones.com/news/featurex/2004/09/09_400 .html.

Gitlin, Todd. *The Whole World Is Watching.* Berkeley: University of California Press, 1980.

Goldberg, Gertrude Schiffner, and Eleanor Kremen, eds. *The Feminization of Poverty: Only in America?* New York: Greenwood Press, 1990.

Greenberg, Anna. "A Gender Divided: Women as Voters in the 2000 Presidential Election." *Women's Policy Journal of Harvard* 1 (2001).

———. "Race Religiosity, and the Women's Vote." *Women and Politics* 22, no. 3 (2001): 59–82.

———. "Re: The Security Mom Myth—Updated." Memo. Greenberg Quinlan Rosner Research, September 29, 2004. www.greenbergresearch.com/publications/ reports/r_security_mom_myth092804.pdf.

Greenberg, Stanley B. *The Two Americas: Our Current Political Deadlock and How to Break It.* New York: St. Martin's Press, 2004.

Hansen, Susan. "Talking About Politics: Gender and Contextual Effects on Political Proselytizing." *Journal of Politics* 59 (1997): 73–103.

Hastings, Philip K. "Hows and Howevers of the Woman Voter." *New York Time Magazine,* June 12, 1960, 14, 80–81.

Henderson, Jeffrey, ed. *Aristophanes: Lysistrata.* Oxford: Oxford University Press, 1991, xv–xxx.

Herek, Gregory M. "Gender Gaps in Public Opinion about Lesbians and Gay Men." *Public Opinion Quarterly* 66 (2002): 40–66.

Herrnson, Paul, J. Celeste Lay, and Atiya Stokes. "Women Running 'as Women':

Candidate Gender, Campaign Issues, and Voter-Targeting Strategies." *Journal of Politics* 65 (2003): 244–55.

Hill, Shirley A. "Class, Race, and Gender Dimensions of Child Rearing in African American Families." *Journal of Black Studies* 31 (2001): 494–508.

Howell, Susan E., and Christine L. Day. "Complexities of the Gender Gap." *Journal of Politics,* 62, no. 3 (August 2000): 858–74.

Huddy, Leonie. "Group Identity and Political Cohesion." In *Oxford Handbook of Political Psychology,* edited by David O. Sears, Leonie Huddy and Robert Jervis, 511–58. New York: Oxford University Press, 2003.

———, Stanley Feldman, and Sarah Dutton. "The Role of Religion in the 2004 Presidential Election." *Public Opinion Pros* (March 2005).

———, Francis K. Neely, and Marilyn Lafay. "Trends: Support for the Women's Movement." *Public Opinion Quarterly* 64 (Fall 2000): 309–50.

———, and Nayda Terkildsen. "Gender Stereotypes and the Perception of Male and Female Candidates." *American Journal of Political Science* 37 (1993): 119–47.

Hunter, James Davison. *Culture Wars: The Struggle to Define America.* New York: Basic Books, 1991.

Hutchings, Vincent L., Nicholas A. Valentino, Tasha S. Philpot, and Ismail K. White. "The Compassion Strategy: Race and the Gender Gap in Campaign 2000." *Public Opinion Quarterly* 68 (Winter 2004): 512–41.

Hyman, Herbert H., William J. Cobb, Jacob J. Feldman, Clyde W. Hart, and Charles H. Stember. *Interviewing in Survey Research.* Chicago: University of Chicago Press, 1954.

Jackman, M. *The Velvet Glove: Paternalism and Conflict in Gender, Class, and Race Relations.* Berkeley, Calif.: University of California Press, 1994.

Jacobson, Gary. *The Politics of Congressional Elections.* New York: Longman, 2004.

Jennings, M. Kent. "Another Look at the Life Cycle and Political Participation." *American Journal of Political Science* 23 (1979): 755–71.

———, and Laura Stoker. "Political Similarity and Influence between Husbands and Wives." Paper presented at the annual meeting of the American Political Science Association, Washington D.C., August 30–September 2, 2000.

Jones, Robert, and Riley Dunlap. "The Social Bases of Environmental Concern: Have They Changed Over Time?" *Rural Sociology* 5 (Spring 1992): 28–47.

Kahn, Kim Fridkin, and Patrick J. Kenney. *The Spectacle of U.S. Senate Campaigns.* Princeton, N.J.: Princeton University Press, 1999.

Kane, Emily W., and Laura J. Macauley. "Interviewer Gender and Gender Attitudes." *Public Opinion Quarterly* 57 (1993): 1–28.

Kanthak, Kristin, and Barbara Norrander. "The Enduring Gender Gap." In *Models of Voting in Presidential Elections,* edited by Herbert F. Weisberg and Clyde Wilcox, 141–60. Stanford, Calif.: Stanford University Press, 2004.

Kaptur, Marcy. *Women of Congress: A Twentieth Century Odyssey.* Washington, D.C.: Congressional Quarterly Press, 1996.

Katz, Daniel. "Do Interviewers Bias Poll Results?" *Public Opinion Quarterly* 6 (1942): 248–68.

Kaufmann, Karen M. "Culture Wars, Secular Realignment, and the Gender Gap in Party Identification." *Political Behavior* 24, no. 3 (September 2002): 283–307.

———. "The Partisan Paradox: Religious Commitment and the Gender Gap in Party Identification." *Public Opinion Quarterly* 68 (Winter 2004): 491–511.

———, and John R. Petrocik. "The Changing Politics of American Men: Understanding the Sources of the Gender Gap." *American Journal of Political Science* 43, no. 3 (July 1999): 864–87.

Kemp, Alice Abel. *Women's Work: Degraded and Devalued.* Englewood Cliffs, N.J.: Prentice-Hall, 1994.

Kenski, Henry C. "The Gender Factor in a Changing Electorate." In *The Politics of the Gender Gap: The Social Construction of Political Influence,* edited by Carol M. Mueller, oo–oo. Newbury Park, Calif.: Sage Publications, 1988.

Kenski, Kate, and Kathleen Hall Jamieson. "The Gender Gap in Political Knowledge: Are Women Less Knowledgeable Than Men About Politics?" In *Everything You Think You Know About Politics . . . And Why You're Wrong,* edited by Kathleen Hall Jamieson, 83–90. New York: Basic Books, 2000.

Kinder, D. R., and L. M. Sanders. *Divided by Color: Racial Politics and Democratic Ideals.* Chicago: University of Chicago Press, 1996.

———, and N. Winter. "Exploring the Racial Divide: Blacks, Whites, and Opinion on National Policy." *American Journal of Political Science* 45 (2001): 439–56.

Kirchhoff, Sue. "Dollars and Sensitivities: Finessing the Gender Gap." *CQ Weekly* 57, no.17 (April 24, 1999): 22–24.

Klein, Ethel. *Gender Politics: From Consciousness to Mass Politics.* Cambridge, Mass.: Harvard University Press, 1984.

Klein, Joe. "How Soccer Moms Became Security Moms." *Time,* February 17, 2003, 23.

Koch, Jeffrey. "Gender Stereotypes and Citizens' Impression of House Candidates' Ideological Orientations." *American Journal of Political Science* 46 (2002): 453–62.

Konner, Joan, James Risser, and Ben Wattenberg. "Television's Performance on Election Night 2000: A Report for CNN." January 2001. http://i.cnn.net/cnn/2001/ ALLPOLITICS/stories/02/02/cnn.report/cnn.pdf. Accessed 9/12/07.

Kotkin, Joel, and William Frey. "Parent Trap." *The New Republic Online,* December 2, 2004, www.tnr.com/doc.mhtml?pt=sKzRTBxZkbnZ3RuMocWdfh%3D%3D.

Kristof, Nicholas D. "Opening Classroom Doors." *New York Times,* Op-Ed section, Sunday, April 30, 2006, WK 15.

Krosnick, Jon A., and Lin Chiat Chang. "A Comparison of the Random Digit Dialing Telephone Survey Methodology with Internet Survey Methodology as Implemented by Knowledge Networks and Harris Interactive." Stanford, Calif.: Stanford University, 2001, http://communication.stanford.edu/faculty/krosnick.html.

Ladd, Everett Carl. "Media Framing of the Gender Gap." In *Women, Media and Politics,* edited by Pippa Norris, 114–28. New York: Oxford University Press, 1997.

———. "1996 Vote: The 'No Majority' Realignment Continues." *Political Science Quarterly* 112, no. 1 (Spring 1997): 9.

Lane, Robert. *Political Life: Why People Get Involved in Politics.* Glencoe, Ill.: Free Press, 1959.

Leege, David, Kenneth D. Wald, Brian S. Krueger, and Paul D. Mueller. *The Politics of Cultural Differences: Social Change and Voter Mobilization Strategies in the Post–New Deal Period.* Princeton, N.J.: Princeton University Press, 2002.

Lewis, Carolyn. "Are Women for Women? Feminist and Traditional Values in the Female Electorate." *Women and Politics* 20 (1999): 1–28.

Lien, Pei-te. "Does the Gender Gap in Political Attitudes and Behavior Vary Across Racial Groups?" *Political Research Quarterly* 51, no. 4 (December 1998): 869–94.

———. "Who Votes in Multiracial America?" In *Black and Multiracial Politics in America,* edited by Yvette M. Alex-Assensoh and Lawrence J. Hanks, 199–224. New York: New York University Press, 2000.

———, and M. Margaret Conway. "Are There Gender Gaps in Political Attitudes and Behavior Patterns among Asian Americans? Evidence from the PNAAPS." Paper presented at the American Political Science Association annual meeting, Boston, Mass., August 28–September 1, 2002.

———, M. Margaret Conway, and Janelle Wong. *The Politics of Asian Americans.* New York: Routledge, 2004.

Luker, Kristen. *Abortion and the Politics of Motherhood.* Berkeley: University of California Press, 1984.

Maccoby, Eleanor. *The Psychology of Sex Differences.* Stanford, Calif.: Stanford University Press, 1974.

Mansbridge, Jane E. "Myth and Reality: The ERA and the Gender Gap in the 1980 Election." *Public Opinion Quarterly* 49 (Summer 1985): 164–78.

Manza, Jeff, and Clem Brooks. "The Gender Gap in U.S. Presidential Elections: When? Why? Implications?" *American Journal of Sociology* 103, no. 5 (March 1998): 1235–66.

Marlantes, Liz. "Year of the Woman Governor?" *Christian Science Monitor,* August 5, 2002, 1.

Mattei, Franco. "The Gender Gap in Presidential Evaluations: Assessments of Clinton's Performance in 1996." *Polity* 33, no. 2 (Winter 2000): 199–228.

Mattei, Laura R. Winsky, and Franco Mattei. "If Men Stayed Home: The Gender Gap in Recent Congressional Elections." *Political Research Quarterly* 51, no. 2 (June 1998): 411–36.

McDermott, Monika. "Voting Cues in Low-Information Elections: Candidate Gender as a Social Information Variable in Contemporary United States Elections." *American Journal of Political Science* 41 (1998): 270–83.

McGaw, Dickinson, and George Watson. *Political and Social Inquiry.* New York: John Wiley, 1976.

McGlen, Nancy E., and Karen O'Connor. *Women, Politics, and American Society.* Upper Saddle River, N.J.: Prentice-Hall, 1998.

——, Karen O'Connor, Laura van Assendelft, and Wendy Gunther-Canada. *Women, Politics, and American Society,* 4th ed. New York: Pearson Longman, 2005.

McLanahan, Sara, and Julia Adams. "Parenthood and Psychological Well-Being." *Annual Review of Sociology* 5 (1987): 237–57.

Micklethwait, John, and Adrian Woolridge. *The Right Nation: Conservative Power in America.* New York: Penguin, 2004.

Miedaian, Myriam. *Boys Will Be Boys: Breaking the Link Between Masculinity and Violence.* New York: Doubleday, 1991.

Milbank, Dana. "Deeply Divided Country Is United in Anxiety." *Washington Post,* November 4, 2004, A28.

Misciagno, Patricia S. *Rethinking Feminist Identification: The Case for De Facto Feminism.* Westport, Conn.: Praeger, 1997.

Mohai, Paul, and Bunyan Bryant. "Is There a 'Race' Effect on Concern for Environmental Quality?" *Public Opinion Quarterly* 62 (Winter 1998): 475–505.

Mondak, Jeffery J., and Mary R. Anderson. "The Knowledge Gap: A Reexamination of Gender-Based Differences in Political Knowledge." *Journal of Politics* 66 (May 2004): 492–512.

Moore, David. "Hillary/Condi Polarize Electorate." Gallup Poll, January 25, 2006.

Morin, Richard. "Swing Voters Who Hang Real Loose." *Washington Post,* October 3, 2004.

Mueller, Carol M. "The Empowerment of Women: Polling and the Women's Voting Bloc." In *The Politics of the Gender Gap: The Social Construction of Political Influence,* edited by Carol M. Mueller, 16–36. Newbury Park, Calif.: Sage Publications, 1988.

——, ed. *The Politics of the Gender Gap: The Social Construction of Political Influence.* Newbury Park, Calif.: Sage Publications, 1988.

Mueller, John. *Policy and Opinion in the Gulf War.* Chicago: University of Chicago Press, 1994.

——. *War, Presidents and Public Opinion.* New York: Wiley, 1973.

Munch, Allison, J. Miller McPherson, and Lynn Smith-Lovin. "Gender, Children, and Social Contacts: The Effects of Childrearing for Men and Women." *American Sociological Review* 62 (1997): 674–89.

Niemi, Richard G., and Herbert F. Weisberg, eds. *Controversies in Voting Behavior,* 4th ed. Washington, D.C.: Congressional Quarterly Press, 2001.

Nincic, Miroslav, and Donna J. Nincic. "Race, Gender, and War." *Journal of Peace Research* 39, no. 5 (2002): 574–68.

Nock, Steven L., and Paul William Kingston. "Time with Children: The Impact of Couples' Work-Time Commitments." *Social Forces* 67 (1988): 59–85.

Nomaguchi, Kei M., and Melissa A. Milkie. "Costs and Rewards of Children: The Effects of Becoming a Parent on Adults' Lives." *Journal of Marriage and Family* 65 (2003): 356–74.

Norrander, Barbara. "The Evolution of the Gender Gap." *Public Opinion Quarterly* 63, no. 4: (Winter 1999): 566–76.

———. "The Independence Gap and the Gender Gap." *Public Opinion Quarterly* 61, no. 3 (Fall 1997): 464–76.

———. "Is the Gender Gap Growing?" In *Reelection 1996: How Americans Voted,* edited by Herbert F. Weisberg and Janet M. Box-Steffensmeier, 145–61. New York: Chatham House, 1999.

———, and Clyde Wilcox. "The Gender Gap in Ideology." Paper presented at the Western Political Science Convention, Portland, Oreg., March 11–13, 2004.

Norris, Pippa. "The Gender Gap: A Cross-National Trend?" In *The Politics of the Gender Gap: The Social Construction of Political Influence,* edited by Carol M. Mueller, 217–34. Newbury Park, Calif.: Sage Publications, 1988.

———. "Introduction: Women, Media, and Politics." In *Women, Media, and Politics,* edited by Pippa Norris, 1–18. New York: Oxford University Press, 1997.

———, ed. *Women, Media, and Politics.* New York: Oxford University Press, 1997.

Page, Benjamin I., and Robert Y. Shapiro. *The Rational Public: Fifty Years of Trends in American Policy Preference.* Chicago: University of Chicago Press, 1992.

Paolino, Phillip. "Group-Salient Issues and Group Representation: Support for Women Candidates in the 1992 Senate Elections." *American Journal of Political Science* 39 (1995): 294–313.

Penn, Mark J. "It's the Moderates, Stupid." *Washington Post,* November 6, 2004.

Peterson, V. Spike. *Gendered States: Feminist (Re)visions of International Relations.* Boulder, Colo.: Lynne Rienner, 1994.

Piven, Frances F. "Women and the State: Ideology, Power and the Welfare State." In *Gender and the Life Course,* edited by Alice S. Rossi, 265–87. New York: Aldine, 1985.

Pomper, Gerald M. "The Presidential Election." In *The Election of 2000,* edited by Gerald M. Pomper, 125–54. New York: Chatham House, 2001.

———. *Voter's Choice: Varieties of American Electoral Behavior.* New York: Harper & Row, 1975.

Plutzer, Eric, and John Zipp. "Identity Politics, Partisanship, and Voting for Women Candidates." *Public Opinion Quarterly* 60 (1996): 30–57.

Poole, Keith T., and L. Harmon Zeigler. *Women, Public Opinion, and Politics: The Changing Political Attitudes of American Women.* New York: Longman, 1985.

Popkin, Samuel. *The Reasoning Voter.* Chicago: University of Chicago Press, 1991.

Purdum, Todd S. "Threats and Responses: Washington Memo; Surreal Time of Waiting Amid the Talk of War." *New York Times,* March 7, 2003.

"Ready for a Woman President?" CBS News, February 5, 2006.

Rinehart, Sue Tolleson. *Gender Consciousness and Politics.* New York: Routledge, 1992.

———, and Jyl J. Josephson, eds. *Gender and American Politics Women, Men, and the Political Process,* 2nd ed. Armonk, N.Y.: M. E. Sharpe, 2005.

Roche, Paul. *Aristophanes: The Complete Plays, the New Translations.* New York: Penguin, 2005.

Romano, Lois. "Female Support for Kerry Slips: Polls Show Women View Bush as Stronger on National Security." *Washington Post,* September 23, 2004.

Rosenbluth, Frances, Rob Salmond, and Michael F. Thies. "Welfare Works: Explaining Female Legislative Representation." *Politics and Gender* 2 no. 2 (2006): 165–92.

Rosenthal, Cindy Simon. "The Role of Gender in Descriptive Representation." *Political Research Quarterly* 48 (1995): 599–611.

Rosenthal, Jack. "Ruth Clark: The Right Questions." *New York Times Sunday Magazine,* (January 4, 1998): 41.

Ruddick, Sara. "Maternal Thinking." *Feminist Studies* 6 (Summer 1980): 342–47

——. *Maternal Thinking: Toward a Politics of Peace.* Boston: Beacon Press, 1989.

——. "Preservation Love and Military Destruction: Some Reflections on Mother and Peace." In *Mothering: Essays in Feminist Theory,* edited by Joyce Trebilcot, 231–62. Totowa, N.J.: Rowman and Allanheld, 1983.

Sanbonmatsu, Kira. "Gender Stereotypes and Vote Choice." *American Journal of Political Science* 46 (2002): 20–34.

Sapiro, Virginia. *The Political Integration of Women: Roles, Socialization, and Politics.* Urbana: University of Illinois Press, 1983.

——. "Theorizing Gender in Political Psychology Research." In *Oxford Handbook of Political Psychology,* edited by David O. Sears, Leonie Huddy, and Robert Jervis, 601–34. New York: Oxford University Press, 2003.

——, and Pamela Johnston Conover. "The Variable Gender Basis of Electoral Politics: Gender and Context in the 1992 U.S. Election." *British Journal of Political Science* 27, no. 4 (1997): 497–523.

Schlesinger, Mark, and Caroline Heldman. "Gender Gap or Gender Gaps? New Perspectives on Support for Government Action and Policies." *Journal of Politics* 63, no. 1 (February 2001): 59–92.

Schuman, H., C. Steeh, L. D. Bobo, and M. Krysan. *Racial Attitudes in America: Trends and Interpretations.* Cambridge, Mass.: Harvard University Press, 1997.

Schwindt-Bayer, Leslie A., and William Mishler. "The Nexus of Representation: An Integrated Model of Women's Representation." *Journal of Politics* 67 (May 2005): 407–28.

Sears, David O., and Leonie Huddy. "On the Origins of Political Disunity Among Women." In *Women, Politics, and Change,* edited by Louise A. Tilly and Patricia Gurin, 249–77. New York: Russell Sage, 1990.

Seelye, Katharine Q. "Kerry in a Struggle for a Democratic Base: Women." *New York Times,* September 22, 2004.

Seltzer, Richard, Jody Newman, and Melissa Voorhees Leighton. *Sex as a Political Variable: Women as Candidates and Voters in U.S. Elections.* Boulder, Colo.: Lynne Rienner, 1997.

Shafer, Byron E., and William J. M. Claggett. *The Two Majorities: The Issue Context of Modern American Politics.* Baltimore: Johns Hopkins University Press, 1995.

Shapiro, Robert Y., and Harpreet Mahajan. "Gender Differences in Policy Preferences:

A Summary of Trends from the 1960s to the 1980s." *Public Opinion Quarterly* 50 (Spring 1986): 42–61.

Sheatsley, Paul B., and Warren J. Mitofsky. *A Meeting Place: The History of the American Association for Public Opinion Research.* Ann Arbor, Mich.: AAPOR, 1992.

Shuman, Howard, and Jean M. Converse. "The Effect of Black and White Interviewers on Black Responses in 1968." *Public Opinion Quarterly* 35 (1971): 44–48.

———, Charlotte Steeh, and Larry Bobo. *Racial Attitudes in America: Trends and Interpretations.* Cambridge, Mass.: Harvard University Press, 1985.

Sigelman, Lee, and Susan Welch. "Race, Gender, and Opinion toward Black and Female Candidates." *Public Opinion Quarterly* 48 (1984): 467–75.

———, and Susan Welch. *Black Americans' Views of Racial Inequality: The Dream Deferred.* New York: Cambridge University Press, 1991.

Simmons, Wendy. "A Majority of Americans Say More Women in Political Office Would Be Positive for the Country." *Gallup Poll Monthly* (January 2001).

Simon, Rita J., and Jean M. Landis. "The Polls—A Report: Women's and Men's Attitudes About a Woman's Place and Role." *Public Opinion Quarterly* 53 (Summer 1989): 265–76.

Sinclair, Barbara Deckard. *The Women's Movement: Political, Socioeconomic, and Psychological Issues,* 3rd ed. New York: Harper and Row, 1983.

Smeal, Eleanor. *Why and How Women Will Elect the Next President.* New York: Harper and Row, 1984.

Smith, Eric R. A. N., and Richard Fox. "The Electoral Fortunes of Women Candidates for Congress." *Political Research Quarterly* 54 (2001): 205–21.

Smith, Tom W. "The Polls: Gender and Attitudes toward Violence." *Public Opinion Quarterly* 48 (Spring 1984): 384–96.

———. "A Study of Trends in the Political Role of Women, 1936–1974." (May 1975).

Sperry, Stephen L. *Are Republican Sprawlers and Democrats New Urbanists? Understanding the Spatial Analysis of the 2004 Vote.* 2005. http://gis.esri.com/library/userconf/proc05/papers/pap2184.pdf.

Stanley, Harold, and Richard G. Niemi. "The Demise of the New Deal Coalition: Partisanship and Group Support, 1952–92," in *Democracy's Feast: The U.S. Election of 1992,* edited by Herbert F. Weisberg, 220–40. Chatham, N.J.: Chatham House, 1995.

Starr, Alexandra. "'Security Moms': An Edge for Bush?" *Business Week,* December 1, 2003, 60.

Stimson, James A. *Public Opinion in America: Moods, Cycles, and Swings.* Boulder, Colo.: Westview Press, 1991.

Stoker, Laura, and M. Kent Jennings. "Life-Cycle Transitions and Political Participation: The Case of Marriage." *American Political Science Review* 89 (1995): 421–33.

Stokes, Donald. "Some Dynamic Elements of Contests for the Presidency." *American Political Science Review* 60 (March 1966): 19–28.

———, Angus Campbell, and Warren E. Miller. "Components of Electoral Decision." *American Political Science Review* 52 (June 1958): 367–87.

Stonecash, Jeffrey M., Mark D. Brewer, and Mark D. Mariani. *Diverging Parties: Social Change, Realignment, and Party Polarization.* Boulder, Colo.: Westview Press, 2003.

Stoper, Emily. "The Gender Gap Concealed and Revealed: 1936–1984." *Journal of Political Science* 17 (Spring 1989): 50–62.

Studlar, Donley T., and Ian McAllister. "Explaining the Gender Gap in Voting: A Cross-National Analysis." *Social Science Quarterly* 79, no. 4 (December 1998): 779–98.

Sweet, Lynn. "Did the Women's Vote Count? How the Vote Split in Illinois, Nation— The GOP Won Over More Women in 2004: Are the Dems Losing Their Charm?" *Chicago Sun-Times,* November 10, 2004.

Swers, Michele L. *The Difference Women Make: The Policy Impact of Women in Congress.* Chicago: University of Chicago Press, 2002.

Tate, K. *From Protest to Politics: The New Black Voters in American Elections.* New York: Russell Sage, 1993.

Tedin, Kent. "Mass Support for Competitive Elections in the Soviet Union." *Comparative Politics* 27 (April 1994): 241–71.

Thomas, Sue, and Clyde Wilcox, eds. *Women and Elective Office Past, Present, and Future,* 2nd ed. Oxford: Oxford University Press, 2005.

Traugott, Michael W., Benjamin Highton, and Henry E. Brady. *A Review of Recent Controversies Concerning the 2004 Presidential Election Exit Polls.* Social Science Research Council, 2005.

Trevor, Margaret C. "Political Socialization, Party Identification, and the Gender Gap." *Public Opinion Quarterly* 63 (1999): 62–89.

Tuch, Steven A., Lee Sigelman, and Jack K. Martin. "Fifty Years After Myrdal: Blacks' Racial Policy Attitudes in the 1990s." In *Racial Attitudes in the 1990s,* edited by Steven A. Tuch and Jack K. Martin, 226–37. Westport, Conn.: Praeger, 1997.

Tumulty, Karen and Viveca Novak. "Goodbye, Soccer Mom. Hello, Security Mom." *Time,* June 2, 2003, 26.

Uyeki, Eugene, and Lani Holland. "Diffusion of Pro-Environment Attitudes?" *American Behavioral Scientist* 43, no. 4 (2000): 646–62.

Van Liere, Kent, and Riley Dunlap. "The Social Bases of Environmental Concern: A Review of Hypotheses, Explanations, and Empirical Evidence." *Public Opinion Quarterly* 44 (Summer 1980): 181–97.

Vavrus, Mary Douglas. "From Women of the Year to 'Soccer Moms': The Case of the Incredible Shrinking Women." *Political Communication* 17 (2000): 193–213.

———. *Postfeminist News: Political Women in Media Culture.* Albany: State University of New York, 2002.

Verba, Sidney, Nancy Burns, and Kay Lehman Schlozman. "Knowing and Caring About Politics: Gender and Political Engagement." *Journal of Politics* 59 (November 1997): 1051–72.

Weisberg, Herbert F. "The Demographics of a New Voting Gap: Marital Differences in American Voting." *Public Opinion Quarterly* 55 (1987): 335–43.

Welch, Susan, and John Hibbing. "Financial Conditions, Gender, and Voting in American National Elections." *Journal of Politics* 54, no. 1 (February 1992): 197–214.

———, and Lee Sigelman. "A Gender Gap among Hispanics? A Comparison with Blacks and Anglos." *Western Political Quarterly* 45, no. 1 (March 1992): 181–99.

———, Lee Sigelman, Timothy Bledsoe, and Michael Coombs. *Race and Place: Race Relations in an American City.* New York: Cambridge University Press, 2001.

Whiteside-Mansell, Leanne, Robert H. Bradley, and Ernest Rakow. "Similarities and Differences in Parental Investment for Mothers and Fathers." *Journal of Psychology* 22 (2001): 63–83.

Whittaker, Matthew, Gary M. Segura, and Shaun Bowler. "Racial/Ethnic Group Attitudes Toward Environmental Protection in California: Is 'Environmentalism' Still a White Phenomenon?" *Political Research Quarterly* 58 (September 2005): 435–47.

Wilcox, Clyde, and Barbara Norrander. "Of Moods and Morals: The Dynamics of Opinion on Abortion and Gay Rights." In *Understanding Public Opinion,* 2nd ed., edited by Barbara Norrander and Clyde Wilcox, 121–48. Washington, D.C.: CQ Press, 2002.

———, Joseph Ferrara, and Dee Allsop. "Group Differences in Early Support for Military Action in the Gulf: The Effects of Gender, Generation, and Ethnicity." *American Politics Quarterly* 21 (July 1993): 343–59.

Winik, Lyric Wallwork. "Is It Time for a Woman President?" *Parade,* April 30, 2006, 4–5.

Wirls, Daniel. "Reinterpreting the Gender Gap." *Public Opinion Quarterly* 50 (Autumn 1986): 316–30.

Withey, Stephen B. *The 4th Survey of Public Knowledge and Attitudes Concerning Civil Defense: A Report of a National Study in March, 1954.* Ann Arbor: Survey Research Center, Institute for Social Research, University of Michigan, 1954.

Wolfe, Alan. *One Nation After All: What Middle-Class Americans Really Think about God, Country, Family, Racism, Welfare, Immigration, Homosexuality, Work, the Right, the Left, and Each Other.* New York: Penguin, 1998.

Wolfinger, Raymond E., and Steven J. Rosenstone. *Who Votes?* New Haven, Conn.: Yale University Press, 1980.

"Women and Men: Is Realignment Under Way?" Public Round-Up column, *Public Opinion* (April–May 1982): 21–32.

Young, Cathy. "Venus at the Ballot Box." *Reason* 32, no. 9 (February 2001): 17.

"The Zoology of Swing Voters." *Washington Monthly,* October 2004. http://www.findarticles.com/p/articles/mi_m1316/is_10_36/ai_n6330843/print.

Contributors

LOIS DUKE WHITAKER is a professor of political science at Georgia Southern University in Statesboro. She is the author of many pieces on women and politics and on U.S. national government, including an edited book of readings, *Women in Politics: Outsiders or Insiders?* (4th ed., Prentice-Hall, 2006), and a coedited volume with James MacGregor Burns, William Crotty, and Lawrence Longley, *The Democrats Must Lead: The Case for a Progressive Democratic Party* (Westview Press, 1992). Her research interests also include mass media and politics and state and local government. She has taught at the University of South Carolina, Columbia; the University of Alabama, Tuscaloosa; the University of San Francisco; Clemson University; and Auburn University, Montgomery. She is a past president of the Women's Caucus for Political Science: South; is a past president of the South Carolina Political Science Association and the Georgia Political Science Association; and a past program vice president for the League of Women Voters of South Carolina. She is the recipient of the Clemson University chapter of the American Association of University Professors (AAUP) Award of Merit for distinctive contributions to the academic profession (May 1992) and the Georgia Southern University College of Liberal Arts and Social Sciences (CLASS) Award of Distinction in Scholarship (2006). She presented a paper and participated in the Oxford Roundtable on Women's Rights held in the Lincoln College of the University of Oxford, Oxford, England, March 28–April 2, 2004.

SUSAN J. CARROLL is a professor of political science and women's and gender studies at Rutgers University as well as senior scholar at the Center for American Women and Politics (CAWP). She is the author of *Women as*

Candidates in American Politics (2nd ed., Indiana University Press, 1994) and the editor of *The Impact of Women in Public Office* (Indiana University Press, 2001). Carroll has also coauthored several CAWP publications that focus on the recruitment and impact of women state legislators and members of Congress, including *Reshaping the Agenda; Women in State Legislatures; Women's Routes to Elective Office: A Comparison With Men's;* and *Voices, Views, Votes: The Impact of Women in the 103rd Congress.*

ERIN CASSESE is a Ph.D. candidate in political science at the State University of New York at Stony Brook. Her research interests include public opinion, political behavior, emotion, and gender. She is currently working on her dissertation, which is titled *Culture Wars as Identity Politics.*

CAL CLARK is a professor of political science at Auburn University. He received his Ph.D. from the University of Illinois at Urbana-Champaign and previously taught at New Mexico State University and the University of Wyoming. He is the author of *Taiwan's Development* (Greenwood, 1989), coauthor of *Women in Taiwan Politics* (Lynne Rienner, 1990), *Comparing Development Patterns in Asia* (Lynne Rienner, 1997), and *The Social and Political Bases of Women's Growing Political Power in Taiwan* (Maryland Series in Contemporary Asian Studies, 2002), and coeditor of *Democracy and the Status of Women in East Asia* (Lynne Rienner, 2000).

JANET M. CLARK is a professor in and chair of the Political Science/Planning Department at the State University of West Georgia. She has a Ph.D. in political science from the University of Illinois at Urbana-Champaign. She is coauthor of *Women, Elections, and Representation* (Longman, 1987); *The Equality State: Government and Politics in Wyoming* (Eddie Bowers, 1990); *Women in Taiwan Politics* (Lynne Rienner, 1990); and *The Social and Political Bases for Women's Growing Political Power in Taiwan* (Maryland Series in Contemporary Asian Studies, 2002). She is a former editor of *Women and Politics,* a quarterly journal, and has published articles and book chapters on political participation.

M. MARGARET CONWAY is Distinguished Professor Emeritus of Political Science at the University of Florida. She is the author of *Political Participation in the United States* (3rd ed., Congressional Quarterly Press, 2000) and coauthor of *Women and Public Policy: A Revolution in Progress* (3rd ed., Congressional Quarterly Press, 2005), *The Politics of Asian Americans* (Routledge, 2004); *American Political Parties: Stability and Change* (Houghton Mifflin,

1984); *Parties and Politics in America* (Allyn and Bacon, 1976); and *Political Analysis: An Introduction* (Allyn and Bacon, 1972). She has published widely in academic journals, including the *American Political Science Review, Journal of Politics,* and *Women and Politics.*

KATHLEEN A. DOLAN received a Ph.D. in political science from the University of Maryland. She is currently an associate professor of political science at the University of Wisconsin, Milwaukee. She is the author of *Voting for Women: How the Public Evaluates Women Candidates* (Westview Press, 2004). Her primary research and teaching interests are in the areas of elections, public opinion, and gender politics.

LAUREL ELDER received her undergraduate degree at Colgate University and her Ph.D. at Ohio State University. She is currently an associate professor of political science at Hartwick College in Oneonta, New York. Her current research interests are women in elective office, the impact of gender and parenthood on public opinion, and presidential nomination politics.

KATHLEEN A. FRANKOVIC is the director of surveys and a producer for CBS News, where she has major responsibility for the design, analysis, and broadcasting of results from CBS News and CBS News/*New York Times* polls. She speaks and writes extensively about elections and public opinion, as well as the development and use of polling by newspapers and television. She is active in many research organizations and has also served on the Executive Council of the American Political Science Association. Dr. Frankovic received an A.B. from Cornell University and a Ph.D. in political science from Rutgers University. Before joining CBS News, she taught political science at the University of Vermont.

STEVEN GREENE is an associate professor of political science at North Carolina State University. He received his Ph.D. from the Ohio State University in 1999. His research interests are in psychological approaches to voting behavior, partisanship, and public opinion, especially with regard to gender differences, abortion, and the impact of parenthood. He has published many scholarly articles in outlets such as *American Political Science Review, Political Research Quarterly, Social Science Quarterly,* and *Women and Politics.*

LEONIE HUDDY is a professor of political science and director of the Center for Survey Research at the State University of New York at Stony Brook. Her general field of interest is the psychological origins and dynamics of public opinion and intergroup relations. She is the coeditor of the *Oxford Handbook of Political Psychology* (2003) and coeditor of the journal *Political Psychology*. She has written extensively on the application of psychological theories concerning intergroup relations to political beliefs and attitudes, with a special emphasis on gender, ethnic, and race relations. Her work has appeared in numerous journals, including the *American Journal of Political Science, Journal of Politics, Public Opinion Quarterly,* and *Political Psychology.*

MARY-KATE LIZOTTE is a Ph.D. student in the Department of Political Science at the State University of New York at Stony Brook, where her major field of study is political psychology. She received her undergraduate degree from Providence College. Her research interests include gender stereotypes and their impact on candidate evaluations, and the political effects of ideology, values, and emotions.

BARBARA NORRANDER is a professor of political science at the University of Arizona. Her previous works on the gender gap appear in *Public Opinion Quarterly* and various edited volumes. She also conducts research on women in elective office, voting behavior, public opinion, and party politics.

MARGIE OMERO is president of Momentum Analysis, LLC. Momentum Analysis is a Democratic polling firm, specializing in polling and focus groups for Democratic candidates and progressive causes.

Index

Gender and cultural roles, 12, 13, 33, 39, 97, 142. *See also* Women, roles in society of
Gender consciousness, 53–54, 185
Gender gap: from 1940s to 1969, 9–10, 11; definition of and issues affecting, 1–2, 10–12, 33–34, 53–57, 110–11, 141–42, 86 (*see also specific issues*); history of, 2, 9–32, 33–34, 50–51, 142, 149–51; history of scholarship on, 3–4, 170–73; importance of, 1–2, 50–52; mixed patterns in, 20–25, 52, 57–65, 72; as polling phenomenon, 33–35; predicting, 115–16
General Social Survey, 123; data from, 13–27, 94–95
Generation. *See* Age
Gilens, Martin, 66–68, 70, 71
Gilligan, Carol, 54
Goldwater, Barry, 3, 27, 38
Gore, Al: and 2000 election, 61, 64, 67, 69, 70; and partisan voting, 25; and women's vote, 75
Government: view of role of among ethnic groups, 178, 180; voters' view of role of, 15–16, 58, 71–72, 165, 171, 172, 186
Government spending: centrality to gender gap, 143, 165; views of parents, 126–28, 130, 133
Great Depression, 36, 37
Greece, ancient, 187
Greenberg, Anna, 80
Greenberg Quinlan Rosner Research, Inc., 80
Greene, Steven, 6
Gulf War, 122
Gun control, 11, 17

Harris, Lou, 38
Head Start, 143
Health care, 15–16, 39; views of among ethnic groups, 177, 180; views of parents, 127, 130, 133–34
Heldman, Caroline, 165
Hickman-Maslin Research, 46
Hill, Anita, 34
Hispanics, 171, 173–77, 181; in 2004 election, 76
Howell, Susan E., 122, 132
Huddy, Leonie, 6
Hydrogen bomb, 34

Income, 154, 156, 172; and partisanship, 148, 151–52, 153–54, 162–64, 171
Incumbency, 105, 113
Independents, 12, 147, 149, 154
International relations, 18–20
Iowa and 1932 elections, 36
Iraq war, 42, 131

Jews, 145, 160. *See also* Religion; Religiosity
Johnson, Lyndon, 16, 27
Joint Center for Political and Economic Studies, 173, 174

Kaufmann, Karen M., 1, 52
Kerry, John, 51; and 2004 gender gap, 64, 67, 68, 69, 70, 72, 75, 76, 78; and male vote, 151; and partisan voting, 25; and terrorist threat issue, 83; and voters' views on defense spending, 61
Klein, Ethel, 142
Klein, Joe, 77
Knowledge Networks, 123, 139n20
Korean War, 18
Kristof, Nicholas D., 188

Lake, Celinda, 78, 87
Lake Snell Perry and Associates, 88
Latinos. *See* Hispanics
Leadership qualities, 78, 81
Lewinsky, Monica, 42, 46
LexisNexis, 76, 77
Liberal vs. conservative viewpoints: differences among ethnic groups, 176–77; differences between the genders, 20, 54, 55, 58–59, 61, 65, 116; and married persons, 125; and parenthood, 119, 121, 122, 127, 130–31, 132, 135; and women candidates, 99–100, 112–13
Lien, Pei-te, 172–73, 178
Lin, Tse-Min, 143
Literary Digest, 37
Lizotte, Mary-Kate, 6
Lysistrata, 187–88

Macmillan English Dictionary, 86
Mahajan, Harpreet, 14, 16
Mansbridge, Jane E., 142
Manza, Jeff, 2
Marijuana, 21, 22

The University of Illinois Press
is a founding member of the
Association of American University Presses.

Composed in 10.5/13 Adobe Minion Pro
with Meta display
by Jim Proefrock
at the University of Illinois Press
Manufactured by Cushing-Malloy, Inc.

University of Illinois Press
1325 South Oak Street
Champaign, IL 61820-6903
www.press.uillinois.edu